The Writings of Frithjof Schuon
Series

World Wisdom
The Library of Perennial Philosophy

The Library of Perennial Philosophy is dedicated to the exposition of the timeless Truth underlying the diverse religions. This Truth, often referred to as the *Sophia Perennis*—or Perennial Wisdom—finds its expression in the revealed Scriptures as well as the writings of the great sages and the artistic creations of the traditional worlds.

Spiritual Perspectives and Human Facts appears as one of our selections in the Writings of Frithjof Schuon series.

The Writings of Frithjof Schuon

The Writings of Frithjof Schuon form the foundation of our library because he is the pre-eminent exponent of the Perennial Philosophy. His work illuminates this perspective in both an essential and comprehensive manner like none other.

Books by Frithjof Schuon

The Transcendent Unity of Religions
Spiritual Perspectives and Human Facts
Gnosis: Divine Wisdom
Language of the Self
Stations of Wisdom
Understanding Islam
Light on the Ancient Worlds
In the Tracks of Buddhism
Treasures of Buddhism
Logic and Transcendence
Esoterism as Principle and as Way
Castes and Races
Sufism: Veil and Quintessence
From the Divine to the Human
Christianity/Islam: Essays on Esoteric Ecumenicism
Survey of Metaphysics and Esoterism
In the Face of the Absolute
The Feathered Sun: Plains Indians in Art and Philosophy
To Have a Center
Roots of the Human Condition
Images of Primordial and Mystic Beauty: Paintings by Frithjof Schuon
Echoes of Perennial Wisdom
The Play of Masks
Road to the Heart: Poems
The Transfiguration of Man
The Eye of the Heart
Songs for a Spiritual Traveler: Selected Poems
Form and Substance in the Religions
Adastra & Stella Maris: Poems by Frithjof Schuon
Autumn Leaves & The Ring: Poems by Frithjof Schuon
Songs without Names: Volumes I-VI
Songs without Names: Volumes VII-XII
World Wheel: Volumes I-III
World Wheel: Volumes IV-VII

Edited Writings of Frithjof Schuon

The Essential Writings of Frithjof Schuon, ed. Seyyed Hossein Nasr
The Fullness of God: Frithjof Schuon on Christianity,
ed. James S. Cutsinger
Prayer Fashions Man: Frithjof Schuon on the Spiritual Life,
ed. James S. Cutsinger
Art from the Sacred to the Profane: East and West,
ed. Catherine Schuon
The Book of Keys: Advice on the Spiritual Life, ed. Joseph Patrick

Spiritual Perspectives and Human Facts

A New Translation with Selected Letters

by

Frithjof Schuon

Includes Other Previously
Unpublished Writings

Edited by
James S. Cutsinger

World Wisdom

Spiritual Perspectives and Human Facts
A New Translation with Selected Letters
© 2007 World Wisdom, Inc.

Translated by Mark Perry, Jean-Pierre Lafouge,
and James S. Cutsinger

Published in French as
Perspectives spirituelles et faits humains
L'Âge d'Homme, 2001.

Library of Congress Cataloging-in-Publication Data

Schuon, Frithjof, 1907-1998.
 [Perspectives spirituelles et faits humains. English]
 Spiritual perspectives and human facts : a new translation with selected letters /
by Frithjof Schuon ; edited by James S. Cutsinger.
    p. cm. -- (The writings of Frithjof Schuon)
 "Includes other previously unpublished writings."
 Includes bibliographical references and index.
 ISBN 978-1-933316-42-0 (pbk. : alk. paper) 1. Religion--Philosophy. 2.
Civilization--Philosophy. 3. Schuon, Frithjof, 1907-1998--Correspondence. I.
Cutsinger, James S., 1953- II. Title.
 BL51.S46553 2007
 202--dc22

                                                          2007016408

Cover Art:
"Watching the Waterfall",
hanging scroll by Xia Kui of Qiantang,
15th century, Ming dynasty

Printed on acid-free paper in Canada.

For information address World Wisdom, Inc.
P.O. Box 2682, Bloomington, Indiana 47402-2682
www.worldwisdom.com

CONTENTS

Frithjof Schuon in 1974

EDITOR'S PREFACE

We are pleased to present this new edition of Frithjof Schuon's *Spiritual Perspectives and Human Facts*.

Widely regarded as one of the greatest spiritual writers of the twentieth century, Frithjof Schuon (1907-1998) was an authority on an extraordinary range of religious and philosophical topics, and his books have been praised by scholars and spiritual teachers from many different traditions. He was also the leading representative of the perennialist school of comparative religious thought. Deeply rooted in the *sophia perennis, philosophia perennis,* or *religio perennis*—that is, the perennial wisdom, perennial philosophy, or perennial religion, as he variously called it—Schuon's perspective embodies the timeless and universal principles underlying the doctrines, symbols, sacred art, and spiritual practices of the world's religions.

Spiritual Perspectives and Human Facts, Schuon's third major work, was published in Paris in 1953 by Cahiers du Sud under the title *Perspectives spirituelles et faits humains.* Translated in 1954 by MacLeod Matheson for Faber and Faber and again in 1969 for Perennial Books by P. N. Townsend, the book has since appeared in two additional French editions: with Maisonneuve and Larose in 1989 and L'Âge d'Homme in 2001. It is upon this most recent version of the French that the present, fully revised translation is based.

Among the special features of this new edition is an appendix containing previously unpublished selections from the author's letters and other private writings. Throughout his life Schuon carried on an extensive correspondence, much of it in response to questions posed by the many inquirers and visitors, from a variety of religious backgrounds, who looked to him for advice; over a thousand of his letters have been preserved. He also composed nearly twelve hundred short spiritual texts for close friends and associates, compiled in his later years as "The Book of Keys". These and other private writings often contained the seeds of ideas that were later developed into published articles and chapters, and it is hoped that the selections included here will afford the reader a glimpse into a new and very rich dimension of this perennial philosopher's message.

The breadth of Schuon's erudition can be somewhat daunting, especially for those not accustomed to reading philosophical and religious works. The pages of his books contain numerous allusions to traditional theological doctrines, important philosophers or spiritual authorities, and the sacred Scriptures of the world's religions, but a citation or other reference is not often provided. A series of editor's notes, organized by chapter and tagged to the relevant page numbers, has therefore been added to this new edition. Dates are provided for historical figures together with brief explanations regarding the significance of their teachings for Schuon, and citations are given for his frequent quotations from the Bible, Koran, and other sacred texts. The Authorized Version of the Bible has been used throughout; since the author made his own translations from the Koran, we have chosen to render his French for these passages directly into English, though the Pickthall interpretation of the Arabic has been given a certain preference when Koranic quotations appear in our editorial notes.

It is customary for Schuon to employ a number of technical terms in his writings, drawn from a multitude of traditions and involving several languages, including Arabic, Latin, Greek, and Sanskrit. A glossary has therefore been provided as well; here one will find foreign terms and phrases appearing both in Schuon's text and in our notes, together with translations and definitions.

James S. Cutsinger

Preface

This collection of writings, written around the middle of the century—hence before most of our other books—differs from them in that instead of articles as such it consists of extracts from letters, notes from our reading, and reflections arising independently of outward circumstances and organized only later in the form of chapters. Be that as it may, *Spiritual Perspectives and Human Facts* contains issues we did not address in our later books, notably on the subject of Christianity, the *Vedānta*, spiritual psychology, and the symbolism of colors; with regard to this psychology, it goes without saying that intrinsic morality, considered in depth, constitutes a message that can never grow old and that therefore remains urgent for man as such, the man of all times. Thus even if our subsequent works contain a complete doctrine—the *sophia perennis* or, if one prefers, integral traditionalism—it seems to us that the present collection deserves to be preserved from loss for the reasons just mentioned.

Perhaps it would be worth adding that truth can never be a matter of merit, given that it belongs to no one while belonging to everyone; it is an immanent gift as well as a transcendent one. And let us also recall—from a somewhat different point of view—that according to an ancient saying from India, "There is no right superior to that of truth."

F.S. 22 March 1988

I

THOUGHT AND CIVILIZATION

1

Metaphysical knowledge is one thing and its actualization in the mind quite another. All the knowledge the brain can hold is as nothing in the light of Truth even if it is immeasurably rich from a human point of view. Metaphysical knowledge is like a divine seed in the heart; thoughts represent only faint glimmers of it. The imprint of the divine Light in human darkness, the passage from the Infinite to the finite, the contact between the Absolute and the contingent—this is the whole mystery of intellection, revelation, the *Avatāra*.

*

*   *

A proof is not convincing because it is absolute—for this it could never be—but because it actualizes something self-evident in the mind.

Proof is possible only on the basis of prior knowledge. Only the complete artificiality of a way of thinking cut off from its transcendent Principle could seek to graft a proof onto a void; it is as if one wished to search in time for the origin of eternity.

It is wrong to reject a "proof of God" just because one is ignorant of its implicit premises, which are clear to the author of the proof.

To prove the Absolute is either the easiest or the most difficult of things, depending upon the intellectual conditions of the environment.

*

*   *

Correlative to every proof is an element eluding the determinism of mere logic and consisting of either an intuition or a grace; now this element is everything. In the intellectual order logical proof is no more than a thoroughly provisional crystallization of intuition, the modes of which are incalculable because of the complexity of the real.

*

*   *

3

One can most certainly prove every truth; but not every proof is accessible to every mind. Nothing is more arbitrary than a rejection of the classical proofs of God, each of which is valid in relation to a certain need for logical satisfaction. This need increases in proportion to ignorance, not in proportion to knowledge. For the sage every star, every flower, is metaphysically a proof of the Infinite.

*

*　*

"Theological progress": this is to make explicit what earlier theologians found no need to say or to limit things to a certain level of understanding. Scholasticism—insofar as it represents a limitation—would not have been born except for a defective understanding of the Greek Fathers.

Something analogous can be said about heresy, which noisily breaks down doors that are already open in order to distract attention from its own fundamental deficiencies; but in this case there is no question of a "lesser truth" or dialectical limitation, but only quite simply of error.

*

*　*

Men of a rationalizing disposition are obsessed with "thoughts"; they see concepts, not "things", hence their abortive criticisms of inspired and traditional doctrines. They perceive neither the realities to which these doctrines refer nor the unexpressed things that are there taken for granted. They criticize in the manner of jurists whatever shocks their mental habits; unable to attain to "things" they mull over words; it is characteristic of philosophers to objectify their own limitations.

*

*　*

A metaphysical doctrine is the mental incarnation of a universal truth.

A philosophical system is a rational attempt to resolve certain questions we pose to ourselves. A concept is a "problem" only because of a particular ignorance.

*
*   *

In order to reach the truth it is necessary to awaken in oneself if possible the intellectual faculty, not to strive to "explain" realities one does not "see" with the reason; now most philosophies start from a sort of axiomatic blindness, whence their hypotheses, calculations, conclusions—all of which are more or less unknown in pure metaphysics, the dialectic of which is founded first of all on analogy and symbolism.

*
*   *

In responding to the need for logical satisfaction that wisdom normally addresses, philosophy does not limit itself to "exposition" but seeks to "explicate" things in a quasi-absolute fashion; in other words it is linked to a craving for explanation that is disproportionate, artificial, and "profane", and it regards its own extrinsic explanations as essential factors of truth; it objectifies what is only subjective and drags truth down into the depths into which it has itself fallen.

There is something of this—though with conspicuous differences in degree and quality—in all human thought owing to the disproportion between content and container and to the relativity of this container.

*
*   *

To live upon thoughts is continually to replace one set of concepts with another. In ratiocination concepts are worn threadbare without any possibility of their being replaced on this level by something better. Nothing is more harmful than this mental erosion of a truth; it is as though true ideas took their revenge on anyone who limits himself to thinking about them.

5

He whose being is too exclusively anchored in thought, who wants to realize everything in his mind but only succeeds in exhausting virtualities of knowledge, finally slips into error even if he was not in error already, just as the ascending curve of a circle changes imperceptibly to a descending curve. Despite certain fluctuations, which may be deceptive, the whole tragedy of philosophy is to be found here.

Human thought is open to every tendency and every kind of inspiration; man can "think" even disgust and nothingness.

*
*   *

Mental virtuosity, which endlessly plays with concepts without having either the ability or desire to reach a definite result, has nothing whatsoever in common with speculative genius, the formulations of which will appear "naive" to such virtuosity, which indeed is opposed to intellectual intuition as Lucifer is opposed to God.

"The wind bloweth where it listeth" (*spiritus ubi vult spirat*); this cannot mean that it must blow everywhere.

*
*   *

Modern man collects keys without knowing how to open a door; a skeptic, he flounders among concepts with no suspicion of their intrinsic value or efficacy: he "classifies" ideas at the surface level of thought but never "realizes" a single idea in depth. He treats himself to the luxury of despair, the most paradoxical form of this commodity; he believes he is experienced whereas he does nothing but avoid those experiences that are incumbent upon him and that he has not even the intellectual capacity to undergo; his experience amounts to that of a child who, having burnt itself, wants to abolish fire.

*
*   *

Contemplative thought is a "vision"; it is not "in action" like passionate thought. Its external logic is dependent on its inner vision whereas in passionate thought the logical process is as if blind; such thought does not "describe" realities that are directly perceived but "constructs" mental justifications on the basis of preconceived ideas, which may indeed be true, but are "accepted" rather than "understood".

The word "thinker" implies that an individual activity is attributed to knowledge, and this is significant. As for the "contemplative", he is able to abstain from "thinking": the act of contemplation is principial, which means that its activity is in its essence, not in its operations.

*
*　*

Reasoning can play no other part in knowledge than that of being the occasional cause of intellection, which arises suddenly—not continuously or progressively—as soon as the mental operation, conditioned in its turn by an intellectual intuition, possesses the quality that makes it a pure symbol. When the heat produced by rubbing together two pieces of wood—or by a lens catching a ray from the sun—has reached the precise degree that is its culminating point, flame suddenly bursts forth; in the same way, as soon as the mental operation is capable of supplying an adequate support, intellection instantaneously grafts itself onto this support. It is thus that human intelligence assimilates its own universal Essence thanks to a kind of reciprocity between thought and Reality. Rationalism on the contrary seeks the culminating point of the cognitive process on its own level; it seeks to "resolve" metaphysical truth as though there were a problem to be solved, or again it seeks for truth in the sphere of mental formulations and rejects *a priori* the possibility of an accessible knowledge lying beyond such formulations and therefore eluding—at least in some measure—the resources of human language; one might as well search for a word that is entirely what it designates! From this contradiction of principle flows an incapacity, first, to provide mental forms fitted to serve as vehicles for intellectual intuition and therefore truth—for poorly posed questions no more attract the light than they are derived from it—and, second, to perceive the intellectual dimensions virtually attained by a given formulation, even a defective one; rationalism proceeds like a man trying to draw the geometrical point by setting out to make it as small as possible or seeking to attain absolute perfection on the created plane while denying on the one hand the necessary imperfection of this plane and on the other the transcendence of pure Perfection.

Now a doctrinal formulation is not perfect because it exhausts infinite Truth on the level of mental logic, for this is impossible, but because it realizes a mental form capable of communicating a ray of this Truth to one who is intellectually fit to receive it; this is why traditional doctrines will always appear "naive", at least from the point of view of men who do not understand that the sufficient reason for wisdom does not lie on the plane of its formal affirmation and that there is no common measure and no continuity between thought—the developments of which have in the final analysis only a symbolic value—and pure Truth, which is identified with what "is" and thus embraces him who thinks.

2

A philosophy that sets out to be a method and nothing more, that proposes only subjective means and not objective axioms, contradicts itself *a priori*, for axioms alone can legitimize means. Faith in such means of "research" is logically no more legitimate than faith in some dogma; in both cases everything depends on intuition, and the factors that give rise to it are not discussed. The arguments of every intrinsically orthodox religion are absolutely convincing if one puts oneself in the intended setting; outside this spiritual setting everything is in question, for every argument is open to attack from the outside, there being no such thing as an absolute form.

Philosophies of knowledge assume in practice the function of religion, and yet they cannot resolve the question of their own sufficient reason nor the extent to which they are obligatory. Why must we have absolute certainty? If one knows—or believes one knows—the means of attaining it, why should one put it into practice? Only traditional metaphysics answers these questions.

*
*   *

There are no doubt contemporary philosophical problems, but there are no needs for explanation so particular to our time as to render incomprehensible those of our fathers. Even with the best—or worst—will in the world the foundations of the human mind do not alter as quickly as that. In our arguments we are addressing ourselves necessarily to certain constants of intelligence, for it is not possible to take into account all the more or less artificial postulates of an ever-changing mode of thought.

Between rationalism and existentialism there is a relationship analogous—though not identical—to that which exists between artistic naturalism and "surrealism"; without the errors of naturalism surrealism would be inconceivable, and though it represents a divergence in relation to naturalism, it is just as far removed from true symbolism as is naturalism itself. Nonetheless it is possible in principle that a surrealist work may accidentally rejoin symbolic art at some point, just as an imaginative and "experimental" philosophy may rejoin traditional wisdom as if by chance and completely unconsciously. Practically speaking such coincidences have no value in either philosophy or art; no philosophy engenders sanctity.

*
*   *

There are no metaphysical or cosmological reasons why in exceptional cases direct intellection should not occur in men who have no link at all with a revealed wisdom; but an exception, though it proves the rule, certainly cannot create it. For example, an intuition as accurate as that which forms the basis of German "phenomenology" inevitably remains fragmentary, problematical, and inoperative because of its lack of objective intellectual principles. An accident does not take the place of a principle, nor does a philosophical adventure replace real wisdom; in point of fact no one has been able to extract anything from this "phenomenology" from the point of view of effective and integral knowledge—the knowledge that works on the soul and transforms it.

A true intuition, even a fundamental one, could not assume a definitive function in a mode of thought as anarchical as modern philosophy; it must always be condemned to remain merely an ineffectual glimmer in the history of an entirely human system of thought, which for that very reason does not know that real knowledge has no history.

*
*   *

Every doctrinal error is accompanied by a psychological error regarding those unscathed by it: atheism, for instance, readily takes itself for a form of moral heroism; it cannot conceive of a theism free from all weakness, from all sentimental desire—an unjust suspicion, for anything can be accepted because of sentimentality, the nonexistence of God just as easily as the contrary.

*
*   *

That man can never rise above human subjectivity is the most gratuitous and contradictory of hypotheses: who then defines this "human subjectivity" as such? If it is human subjectivity itself that does so, there is no such thing as objective knowledge, hence no definition is possible; if something other than this subjectivity does so, it is obviously wrong to say that man cannot rise above it. Quite clearly a definition possesses value only through its objectivity, that is, through the absence of error; on the other hand one cannot seek to enclose the Universe within "human subjectivity" while at the same time allowing for a point of view beyond this subjectivity, which can therefore define it.

*

*   *

The starting point of existentialism is not existence but a certain concept of existence. Ants also exist, but they are not existentialists.

We shall be told that only existence is absolutely certain. But is not this certainty precisely something other than existence? The certainty exists, and existence is certain. If existence is a content of the certainty, the certainty has priority over existence; the matter can at least be considered in this way, and this is enough to destroy the axiom in question.

*

*   *

Existentialism always reduces cause to effect, principle to manifestation, reality to fact; existence for it is nothing but the sum of those things that exist or rather of those things that exist physically, for it is far from conceiving all the orders of existence. According to this perspective the genius of a man is nothing other than the sum of his works; from this we should in sound logic conclude that intelligence is the sum of thoughts actually thought and nothing more. Such a way of looking at things leaves no room for the concept of the possible; it is a systematic reduction of all reality and every value—especially every moral value—to bare fact: the world no longer has any homogeneity; it is merely an unintelligible discontinuity.

It is the wisdom of a child who has discovered that the vegetable kingdom is the tomato in his hand.

*

* *

Man is often just an animal, possessing as if by chance a human brain. A cow is well aware in her own fashion that she exists and grazes where she will; this is not difficult to say in human language, but before the existentialists no man dared to dignify this perception of his own existence and his freedom to choose between apples and pears as if it were a kind of wisdom.

*

* *

Is it always "man who chooses"? And who then is this "man who chooses"? Where is his limit, his center? If it is man who defines himself, what objective value can be attached to this definition? And if there is no objective value, no transcendent criterion, why think? If it is enough to be a man in order to be in the right, why seek to refute human error?

As for the "freedom of man": is man free to choose that two and two make four? "Man who chooses himself": why does man not choose something other than what he is—something other than what he has been chosen to be?

*

* *

One of the most vexatious aberrations of our era is the "historical method" with its "close criticism" of documents and its systematic contempt for all sources connected either with miraculous acts or even with exceptional coincidences. When one denies the supernatural it is unwise to hold forth on matters that have no meaning without it or to busy oneself with the psychology of those who accept it.

Critics who deny the supernatural are applying a logic that is both artificial and meticulous to things that *a priori* elude them; what is evident appears to them "naive"; they substitute for intelligence a sort of icy cunning that feeds on negation and paradox.

*

*   *

Theorists with infrahuman tendencies falsify our reality by reducing it to an artificial interplay of mechanical alternatives and by enclosing man in this way in a sort of space devoid of both air and perspective. They completely fail, for instance, to understand religious morality— the imponderables of its inner life—and they clearly allow no place for interferences from the suprahuman, for vocation or inspiration; according to such theorists, traditional morality, like their own deliberately inhuman systems, works mechanically and as it were outside God. The incorruptibility—potentially generous—of the suprahuman is replaced by the implacability of the inhuman; the world is transformed into the inexorability of arthropods.

It is not enough to believe in God; we must also believe in the devil. In our day the devil puts a false psychology in the place of logic and a false logic in the place of psychology.

When for lack of intellectual criteria one embarks on a course of systematic moral suspicion, there is no reason for stopping, for anything can be explained on the basis of moral taste; pure and simple moralism always allows man to prove that white is black or that two and two make five. This attitude is all the more incurable in that it invests facts with an apparent homogeneity, an illusion confirming man in his error; suspicion in fact never has any qualms about ascribing the same imaginary intentions to the most disparate facts; the very nature of moral psychologism excludes real explanations since these in their turn fall under the same law of suspicion, which drags everything down and which is the end of truth.

Psychological conjectures, to the very extent they are false, always betray the failings of their author.

*

*   *

Men who merely replace one sentimentality with another when laying claim to "objectivity" are all too numerous in our day; in fact their

13

so-called objectivity is merely a soft and pretentious sentimentality, which is far more illusory than a transparent "subjectivity".

True objectivity does not set up an opposition between cold and heat but transcends them both: like emptiness it stands opposed to a false plenitude, whether hot or cold, or like silence to a heavy and blind affirmation.

In too many minds "objectivity" is merely an inability to distinguish truth from error or justice from injustice. The spontaneous indignation of a good man in the face of error and injustice is taken for a lack of "objectivity"; one forgets that anger can be a criterion of veracity, hence impartiality.

Sentimental "subjectivity",[1] when it disparages what is contrary to it, betrays itself less by anger than by hatred—by eagerness for any kind of argument, then by a systematic zeal for accusation, and above all by a recourse to disparaging psychological hypotheses. Justice on the other hand is by definition disinterested: it is content with indispensable certainties; it disdains conjectures; truth, which is its very root, compels it to soberness and a generous prudence.

One of the greatest sources of error is taking what is probable to be certain and what is improbable to be impossible.

*

* *

Contemplative intelligence, traditional orthodoxy, divine inspiration: these three elements constitute doctrinal truth.

In modern philosophy there is no guaranteeing the celestial character of the inspiration, to say the least; nothing makes it probable, and even reactions against error run the risk of being caught up in error, or rather it is impossible for them not to be caught up in this way.

*

* *

---

[1] This must not be confused either with physical subjectivity, which perceives sensory phenomena in some particular way, or with intellectual subjectivity, which has some particular consciousness of the Real.

Nineteenth-century thinkers—Comte or Schopenhauer, for example—may appear old and outmoded, rather like the painters and playwrights of the same period; but those who are spokesmen of the *philosophia perennis*, even if they wrote two thousand years ago or lived at the uttermost ends of the earth, always have the freshness and perfect "timeliness" that comes from truth expressed with intelligence; real wisdom does not fade with age any more than does real art. Conceptualist relativism abolishes truth in order to set in its place a blind and heavy biological pseudo-reality.

3

Corruptio optimi pessima: traditional institutions such as royalty have never lacked "quality" so greatly as in the last several centuries—not in themselves, but in the hands of man and as human facts. For man has never been weaker and consequently has never stood in greater need of these institutions than now when they have been abolished.

*

*   *

When people speak about civilizations they are all too ready to emphasize certain fragmentary aspects, whether for good or ill: they forget that Chinese civilization is not the deforming of women's feet and that a hospital or a road is not a civilization.

A civilization is a world, that is, a totality composed of compensations. There is no complex organism without certain evils; nature is there to prove it.

*

*   *

A collectivity as such is tantamount to a principle of thickening and hardening, whence the impossibility for any collectivity to avoid abusing legitimate rights. Abuses are in human nature, especially when this nature is expressed in a collectivity; in this case certain abuses become habitual and seemingly normal. There exists no collectivity, even a sacred one, that does not commit some abuses; to renounce a traditional collectivity for the sake of suppressing abuses is to renounce the social order; it is to renounce the better for the worse, as is quite obvious. Rights that are defensive for an isolated individual become aggressive for a collectivity. It is impossible for the sacred Law to alter the constants of human nature; it can only neutralize them to the degree sufficient for safeguarding the spiritual life.

To take a collectivity as such as an intellectual norm means the progressive strangulation of intelligence.

Nevertheless a collectivity has before all else the neutrality of a natural fact and for this reason may also have the character of a relative good: it can be the passive vehicle of a divine will—*vox populi vox Dei*—on condition that it is determined *a priori* by this will, that is, by a sacred Law, but it can never be a spiritual good in a direct sense; the spirit is always struggling against it just as in man the Intellect is in conflict with the ego. The masses may be a vehicle of the spirit in a summary fashion, but of themselves they become the mouthpiece for everything subhuman in man; they are equivalent to nature, which is quantitative and blind, though fundamentally innocent.

*

*   *

In a certain outward sense the great social and political evil of the West is mechanization; it is the machine that gives rise most directly to the great evils from which the world today is suffering. The machine is characterized *grosso modo* by the use of iron, fire, and invisible forces. Nothing is more fanciful than to speak of the wise use of machines, of their serving the human spirit, for it is in the very nature of mechanization to reduce men to slavery and devour them utterly, leaving them with nothing human, nothing beyond the animal, nothing beyond the collective. The reign of the machine has succeeded that of iron, or rather it has given iron its most sinister expression: man, who created the machine, ends by becoming its creature.

There is another great evil, akin to the first: hygiene—not the hygiene that is more or less natural to man, but scientific, aggressive, and virtually unlimited hygiene. It provides machines with legions of victims and transforms humanity into a swarm of grasshoppers.

Modern man, in seeking to escape from every ill, ends by falling into every ill.

*

*   *

All civilizations are fallen, but in different ways: the fall of the East is passive; the fall of the West is active.

The fault of the fallen East is that it no longer thinks; that of the fallen West is that it thinks too much, and wrongly.

The East is sleeping over truths; the West is living in errors.[1]

*
*   *

The Westerner is superior to other men only with regard to his inventive genius; now this is itself only a deviation—conditioned by humanism and its consequences—from the creative genius that is itself common to both West and East. The West has proved its greatness by its cathedrals, not by machines or other inventions that have nothing but terrestrial ends in view.

But the only decisive criterion of human worth is the attitude of man toward the Absolute, and in this regard the least that can be said is that the European enjoys no superiority.

Furthermore, creative genius—especially inventive genius—must not be confused with pure intelligence, nor obviously with nobility. The black race has doubtless not produced a Dante or the builder of a Taj Mahal, but it has produced saints,[2] and this is what counts in the sight of God.

One must not lose sight of the fact that peoples with a very "differentiated" and "cerebral" civilization are led to underestimate certain modes of intelligence to which they are unaccustomed. There is more intelligence in African rhythms than in most psychological novels.

*
*   *

The liberty traditional civilizations guarantee is qualitative and realistic. Modernity's quantitative and idealistic conception of liberty

---

[1] By the "West" we do not mean traditional Christianity but only modernism, whether "Christian" or not; the "West" therefore includes Easterners—and other non-European peoples—contaminated by the psychosis of so-called progress.

[2] They have certainly produced great warriors and statesmen as well, but in the absence of a written literature their names have either remained mere local memories or else are wholly forgotten.

implies by definition freedom for evil, hence also freedom to abolish all liberty.

*

*   *

Charity starts from the truth that my neighbor is not other than myself since he possesses an ego, that before God he is neither more nor less "myself" than I am, that what is given to "another" is given to "me", that the neighbor is also made in the image of God, that he carries within him the potentiality of the divine presence, which must be revered in him, that the good done to the neighbor purifies us from egoistic illusion and virtually frees us from it when it is done for the sake of God.

Philosophical humanitarianism, which may or may not be atheistic, begins with the erroneous notion that man and his earthly well-being represent absolute values, that man is good by definition and hence that no one is fundamentally evil, that there are no values incompatible with earthly well-being, that what contradicts the human individual and his comforts cannot be good.

True charity may sometimes run contrary to the immediate interests of men and contrary as well to earthly well-being.

*

*   *

We often hear it said that a criticism is "sterile" because it does not involve any "constructive" proposals; this is like saying that because one is not able to show someone the proper path one has no right to tell him he is walking toward a precipice, or as if one were forbidden to notice the existence of spots on the sun on the pretext that one cannot create a sun without spots.

In fact every truth is by definition constructive; error alone is destructive. To destroy a destruction is already to construct.

II

AESTHETICS AND SYMBOLISM
IN ART AND NATURE

1

In the economy of spiritual means, beauty, which is positive and compassionate, stands in a sense at the antipodes of asceticism, which is negative and implacable; nonetheless the one always contains something of the other, for both are derived from truth and express it from different points of view.

The pursuit of the disagreeable is justified to the extent it is a form of asceticism; but it must not be carried to the point of becoming a cult of ugliness, for this would amount to a denial of one aspect of truth. In a civilization still wholly traditional, this issue could hardly arise, ugliness in this case being more or less accidental. Only in the modern world has ugliness become something like a norm or principle; in this case beauty appears as a specialty, even a luxury, whence the frequent confusion at all levels between ugliness and simplicity.

In our age the discerning of forms assumes a quite special importance: error appears in all the forms which surround us and in which we live; there is a danger of its poisoning our sensibility, even our intellectual sensibility, by introducing into it a kind of false indifference, hardness, and triviality.

*

*   *

True aesthetics[1] is nothing other than the science of forms; hence its aim is the objective, the real, not subjectivity as such. Forms, intellections: the whole of traditional art is founded upon this correspondence. Furthermore a sense of form may also play an important part in intellective speculation: the rightness—or logic—of proportions is a criterion of truth or error in every domain into which formal elements enter.

---

[1] We are using this word in its ordinary present-day meaning and not to designate theories of sensory knowledge.

23

The reflection of the supraformal in the formal is not the formless but on the contrary strict form. The supraformal is incarnated in a form that is at once "logical" and "generous", hence in beauty.[2]

*

* *

Ignorant and profane aesthetics places the beautiful—or what its sentimental idealism takes to be the beautiful—above the true, at least in practice, and thus exposes itself to errors on its own level. But if aestheticism is the unintelligent cult of the beautiful, or more precisely of aesthetic feeling, this in no way implies that a sense of beauty is mere aestheticism.

This is not to say that man is limited to a choice between aestheticism and aesthetics or in other words between an idolatry of the beautiful and a science of beauty; love of beauty is a quality that exists apart from its sentimental deviations and intellectual foundations.

Beauty is a reflection of divine beatitude; and since God is Truth, the reflection of His beatitude will be that mixture of happiness and truth found in all beauty.

*

* *

Forms allow a direct and "plastic" assimilation of the truths—or realities—of the spirit. The geometry of the symbol is steeped in beauty, which in turn and in its own way is also a symbol. The perfect form is that in which truth is incarnate in the rigor of the symbolic formulation and in the purity and intelligence of the style.

*

* *

---

[2] This is why every "descent from Heaven", every *Avatāra*, possesses perfect beauty: it is said of the Buddhas that they save not only by doctrine but also in a more direct and "plastic" way by their superhuman beauty. The name *Shūnyamūrti* ("Manifestation of the Void") applied to a Buddha is full of significance.

The man who possesses a sense of forms may or may not prefer a magnificent temple to a cottage, but he will always prefer a cottage to a palace in bad taste.

A passional and superficial aesthete always prefers the magnificent temple, and sometimes even the palace in bad taste, to the cottage.

This is the crucial difference.

*

*   *

Beauty is the mirror of happiness and truth. Without the element "happiness" there remains only the bare form—geometrical, rhythmical, or something else; and without the element "truth" there remains only an entirely subjective enjoyment—a luxury, if one prefers. Beauty stands between abstract form and blind pleasure, or rather it combines them in such a way as to imbue veridical form with pleasure and veridical pleasure with form.

Beauty is a crystallization of a certain aspect of universal joy; it is a limitlessness expressed by a limit.

Beauty is in one sense always more than it gives, but in another sense it always gives more than it is: in the first sense the essence shows itself as appearance, and in the second the appearance communicates the essence.

*

*   *

Beauty is always incomparable: no perfect beauty is more beautiful than another perfect beauty; that we may prefer a given beauty to another is a matter of personal affinity or complementary relationship, not pure aesthetics. Human beauty can be found within each of the major races, yet normally a man prefers some type of beauty in his own race rather than in another; on the other hand qualitative and universal affinities between human types sometimes show themselves to be stronger than racial affinities.

Like every other kind of beauty artistic beauty is objective, hence discernible by intelligence and not by taste; taste is legitimate to the same extent as are individual characteristics, that is, to the extent these characteristics translate positive aspects of a given human norm.

Different tastes should be derived from pure aesthetics; they should be treated as equivalent, like different visual perspectives; myopia and blindness are in no sense ways of looking but merely defects of vision.

*
*   *

In beauty what a man should "be" in an active or inward fashion he "realizes" in a passive way with regard to its perception and outwardly with regard to its production.

When a man surrounds himself with the ineptitudes of a deviated art, how can he still "see" what he should "be"? He runs the risk of "being" what he "sees", of assimilating the errors suggested by the erroneous forms among which he lives.

Modern satanism is manifested—in the most external way no doubt but also in the most immediately tangible and intrusive way—in the unintelligible ugliness of forms. "Abstract" minds, which "see" nothing, allow themselves nonetheless to be influenced in their general outlook by the forms with which they surround themselves and to which they sometimes, with astonishing superficiality, deny all importance, as if traditional civilizations did not unanimously proclaim the contrary. In this connection it is appropriate to recall the spiritual aesthetics of some of the great contemplatives, which proves that even in a world of normal forms the sense of the beautiful may acquire a special spiritual importance.

*
*   *

From an ascetical-mystical or penitential point of view beauty may appear as something worldly, for such a point of view tends to look at everything with the eye of the will; beauty is then confused with desire. But from the intellective point of view—which is that of the nature of things and not expediency—beauty is spiritual since in its own way it externalizes Truth and Beatitude. This is why the born contemplative cannot see or hear beauty without perceiving in it something of God; and this divine content allows him to detach himself all the more easily from appearances. As for the passional man,

26

he sees in beauty the world, seduction, the ego; it distances him from the "one thing needful", at least when it is a natural beauty, though not when it is the beauty of sacred art, for in this case the need for beauty is exploited by the "one thing needful" for the sake of piety, fervor, heaven.

Each of these two points of view should take account of the truth of the other: the perspective of merit cannot prevent truth from imposing itself in principle on every man, even those who are weak, and it is precisely this that gives sacred art its universal validity; for its part the perspective of the Intellect will not prevent all men from being by nature corruptible, even the strong. It is necessary to distinguish not only between contemplatives and passional men but also between man insofar as he is contemplative and man insofar as he is passional.

Slandering beauty may sometimes be useful, but it is always a kind of outrage.

*

*　*

Art should have a character that is at once human and divine: human with regard to surrounding nature, which serves as its *materia prima*, and divine with regard to the undetermined and unqualified human being, to the bare fact of our psychological existence. In the first case art detaches the human work from nature because nature—far from being merely imitated—is interpreted and transfigured according to spiritual and technical laws; in the second case the undetermined human being receives an ideal content that organizes, directs, and raises him above himself in keeping with the sufficient reason of our human state.

These two characteristics determine art and give it its reason for being.

*

*　*

Side by side with their intrinsic qualities, the forms of art serve a strictly useful purpose: in order for spiritual influences to manifest themselves without encumbrance, they require a formal setting that corresponds to them analogically; otherwise they cannot radiate even if they remain always present. It is true that they can shine forth in spite of everything in the soul of a holy man, but not everyone is a saint, and a sanctuary is constructed to facilitate resonances of the spirit, not oppose them.[3]

Sacred art is made to serve as a vehicle for spiritual presences; it is made at one and the same time for God, angels, and men; profane art on the other hand exists only for men and by that very fact betrays them.

Sacred art helps man find his own center, that kernel whose nature is to love God.

*

* *

Apart from its "conservative" and "evocative" function, which concerns the collectivity and also, more directly, certain contemplatives who draw inspiration from its symbolism and breathe its beauty, sacred art belongs to the order of "sensible consolations"; such consolations may draw a man nearer to God or may distance him from God depending on the subjective disposition of the individual and independently of the objective value of the forms.

If a contemplative "can" turn aside from art as such to the extent he seeks God in the void, he "must" on the other hand reject an individualistic art, which inevitably offers false suggestions and a false plenitude at one level or another.

*

* *

In the Middle Ages a religious man could pray in surroundings where everything testified to a homogeneous spirit as much as to an intelligence supernaturally inspired; he could also pray before a blank wall. He had a choice between the ever-truthful language of precious forms

---

[3] It will be said that angels are at ease in a stable. But this is precisely the point, for a stable is not a baroque or surrealist church.

and the silence of rough stones; and happily for him he had no other choice.

There is something in our intelligence that wants to live in repose, something in which the conscious and unconscious meet in a kind of passive activity, and it is to this element that the lofty and effortless language of art addresses itself: lofty because of the spiritual symbolism of its forms and the nobility of its style, and effortless because of the aesthetic mode of assimilation. When this function of our spirit, this intuition standing between the natural and the supernatural and producing incalculable vibrations, is systematically violated and led into error, the consequences will be extremely serious—if not for the individual, then at least for the civilization concerned.

Would a child want its mother to have a new face every day? Would a man want to rearrange his home every day? A sanctuary is like the outstretched arms of a mother and the intimacy of a home: the soul and intelligence must be able to rest in it.

Nothing is more monotonous than the illusions of originality found in men who have been inculcated from childhood with a bias for "creative genius".

*
*   *

The multiform beauty of a sanctuary is like the crystallization of a spiritual flux or of a stream of blessings: it is as though this invisible and celestial power had fallen into matter—which hardens, divides, and scatters—and transformed it into a shower of precious forms, into a sort of planetary system of symbols surrounding us and penetrating us from every side. The shock, if one may so call it, is similar to that of the blessings themselves: it is direct and existential; it goes beyond thought and seizes our being in its very substance.

There are blessings that are like snow, others like wine; all can be crystallized in sacred art. What is given outward expression in such art is at once doctrine and blessing, geometry and the music of Heaven.

*
*   *

The reproach of "naturalism" does not concern the simple fact of knowing how to observe nature but rather the prejudice that would reduce art solely to the imitation of nature. A more or less exact observation of nature may coincide with a traditional—hence symbolic and sacred—art, as is proven by the art of Pharaonic Egypt or the Far East; it is then the result of a fundamentally intellectual objectivity and not of a passional and empty naturalism. The spiritualized realism of Chinese landscape painters has nothing in common with worldly aestheticism.

Disproportions do not of course make art sacred any more than correctness of proportions leads *ipso facto* to the defects of naturalism. Christian art has had an undue contempt for nature, hence also no doubt for a certain aspect of intelligence; the naturalism of late Gothic statuary, and particularly that of the Renaissance, was therefore able to appear superior in the eyes of men who no longer understood the spiritual value of such art as that of Autun, Vezelay, Moissac. In principle Christian art could have combined a deeper observation of nature with its wholly symbolistic spirituality, and indeed in certain works it has succeeded in doing so, at least partially and insofar as the symbolism did not require particular proportions;[4] but in fact it was difficult for this art to reconcile perfection of observation with perfection of the symbol, given the contempt for the bodily—and the natural in general—that the Christian perspective involves.

*

*　　*

"Truth" in art can by no means be reduced to the subjective veracity of the artist but resides first and foremost in the objective truth of forms, colors, materials: an ignorant and profane art will therefore be far more "false" than a faithful copy of an ancient work, for the copy will at least transmit the spiritual truth of the original whereas the profane work will transmit only the psychological "truth"—hence the error—of its author.

---

[4] We are not speaking of disproportions motivated simply by a regard for perspective in Byzantine cupolas or the facades of certain cathedrals.

Subjectivism, whether artistic or philosophical, repudiates itself once it objectifies itself, for to lay claim to truth—or any other value—is to acknowledge objective criteria.

*
*   *

Few prejudices are so contradictory and futile as the mania for absolute originality, the ambition of an artistic creation seeking to start from zero, as if man could also create *ex nihilo*; if the attempt is made, what it ends in is the subhuman aberrations of surrealism: it is Lucifer, who while falling sees his splendor transformed into horror. Artists want to inflict on us modes of originality that are utterly improbable, as if they had the right—they who are like ourselves and are our contemporaries—to such excessive singularities. Had they been ancient Atlanteans or beings from another planet we might in principle believe them, but since they are men of modern culture we know them for what they are; their originality can only be an affectation and a false philosophy.

It is by reestablishing links with ancient truth that one comes to understand it and to find a new and spiritually legitimate originality. An art that "seeks" is always false; ancient art never sought for anything; if sometimes it changed, it was because of inspiration, not an effort that could have no motive.

*
*   *

The "sincerity" to which certain artists lay claim is far too empty of content and too arbitrary to be able to reconnect with any truth, unless we are to call "truth" a state of psychological fact having no horizons, which—it must be acknowledged—is a common enough abuse of language. The pretentious pseudo-sincerity of the "creators", far from starting from primordial innocence—or from the healthy spontaneity of a barbarian—is merely a reaction against complications and stresses unknown to the primitive; it is as it were a perverted veracity, for it is contrary not only to objective truth but also to the natural modesty and good sense of a virtuous man. What is normal is that a human being should seek his center of inspiration beyond himself, beyond his sterility as a poor sinner: this will obligate him to ceaseless corrections, to a continual adjustment before an outward norm—in short, to modifications that will compensate for his ignorance and lack of universality; a normal artist does not touch his work up because he is dishonest but because he takes account of his own imperfection; a good man corrects himself wherever he can.

The work of an artist is not a training in spontaneity, for talent is not acquired but a humble and well-informed search—whether assiduous or joyously carefree—for a perfection of form and expression that is in keeping with sacred prototypes having an inspiration at once heavenly and collective; this inspiration in no way excludes that of the individual but assigns it its range of action and at the same time guarantees its spiritual value. The artist effaces and forgets himself; so much the better if genius gives him wings. But before all else his work retraces that of the soul, which is transformed in conformity with a divine model.

Few things are so falsely dramatic and so ridiculously out of proportion in their principles and results as the strange moralism of those who make artistic "research" into a sort of religion that is at once icy and passionate.

*

* *

We must never lose sight of the fact that as soon as art is freed from being a pure and simple ideography—which is perfectly within its rights, for how should the decorative element of art be banned when it is everywhere in nature?—it has a mission from which nothing can make it deviate: to transmit spiritual values, whether salvific truths or cosmic qualities, including human virtues.

Art that is deliberately individualistic and founded on the prejudice of genius does not exteriorize either transcendent ideas or profound virtues: it objectifies the individual fact alone; this fact may be accidentally qualitative, but in the absence of prototypes and traditional principles there is every likelihood it will not be so.

Art in the most general sense is a vocational activity conformed to an essentially normal and therefore normative function.

*

*   *

Poetry should express a beauty of the soul with sincerity; one might also say: with beauty, a sincerity. It would serve no purpose to make so obvious a point if in our day definitions of art had not become increasingly falsified, whether because the characteristics of one art are improperly attributed to another or because completely arbitrary elements are introduced into the definition of a given art, or all art—for example, a preoccupation with its "timeliness", as if the value or lack of value of a work of art could depend on knowing whether it is recent or ancient or on one's believing it to be ancient if it is recent, or conversely.

In contemporary poetry beauty and sincerity are generally lacking: beauty for the simple reason that the souls of poets—or rather of those who fabricate what takes the place of poetry—are devoid of it and sincerity because a contrived and churlish quest to find unusual expressions excludes all spontaneity. It is no longer a question of poetry, but of a sort of cold and lifeless work of jewelry composed of fake gems, a meticulous elaboration at the very antipodes of what is beautiful and true. And since the muse no longer gives anything, having been slain *a priori*—for the last thing an "up-to-date" man would accept is to appear naive—vibrations are provoked in the soul, and it is cut into fragments.[5]

Whatever the caprice of "the moment", it is illogical to cultivate a nonpoetical poetry and to define poetry in terms of its own absence.

*

*   *

Metaphysical or mystical poets such as Dante and some of the troubadours, as well as Sufi poets, expressed spiritual realities with the help of the beauty of their souls. It is a question of endowment far more

---

[5] The same remarks are valid in relation to contemporary music; it is no longer music but something else. At the opposite extreme from the "vibratory" or "acoustic" arts, we have come across tendencies that seem to be opposite but are in reality complementary, namely, attempts at "dynamic", even "vegetative", architecture.

than of method, for not every man has the gift of sincerely expressing truths that go beyond ordinary humanity; even if the concern is only to introduce symbolic terminology into a poem, it would still be necessary to be a true poet in order to succeed without betrayal. Whatever one may think of the symbolic intention of the *Vita Nuova* or the *Khamriyah* (the "Ode of Wine" by Omar ibn al-Farid) or the quatrains of Omar Khayyam, it is not possible knowingly to deny the poetical quality of such works, and it is this quality that justifies the intention in question from an artistic point of view; moreover the same symbiosis of poetry and symbolism is to be found in prototypes of divine inspiration, such as the Song of Songs.

It is sometimes said that the Eastern civilizations are dead, that they have no more poetry. To the extent this is true they are in the right: it is better to confess being dead than to feign life.

*

*   *

Architecture, painting, and sculpture are objective and static: these arts above all express forms; their universality is in the objective symbolism of these forms.

Poetry, music, and dance are subjective and dynamic: these arts *a priori* express essences; their universality is in the subjective reality of these essences.

Music distinguishes essences as such but unlike poetry does not distinguish their degrees of manifestation: it can express the quality of "fire", but since it is not "objective" it is not able to specify whether it is visible fire, passion, fervor, or the flame of mystical love, or the universal fire—that is, the angelic essence—from which all these expressions are derived. Music expresses all this at one and the same time when it gives voice to the spirit of fire; and it is for this reason that some hear the voice of passion and others the corresponding spiritual function, whether angelic or divine. Music is capable of presenting countless combinations and modes of these essences with the help of the secondary differentiations and characteristics of melody and rhythm; rhythm, it should be added, is more essential than melody: it is the principial or masculine determination of musical language whereas melody is its expansive and feminine substance.

The angelic essences have been compared to streams of pure water, of wine, of milk, of honey, of fire; they correspond to so many melodies, so many musical categories.

*

*   *

A building, whether a temple, palace, or house, represents the universe—or a given world or microcosm—seen in conformity with a given traditional perspective; hence it also represents the "mystical body", caste, or family, according to the particular case.

Dress gives outward expression to either the spiritual or social function of the soul, and these two aspects may be combined. Clothing is opposed to nakedness as the soul is opposed to the body or as the spiritual function—that of priest, for example—is opposed to animal nature. When clothing is combined with nakedness—among Hindus, for example—nakedness appears in its qualitative and sacred aspect.

*

*   *

Byzantine, Romanesque, and primitive Gothic arts are theologies: they proclaim God, or rather "realize" Him on a certain level.

The pseudo-Christian art inaugurated by the neopaganism of the Renaissance seeks and realizes only man; the mysteries it should suggest are suffocated in a hubbub of superficiality and impotence, inevitable features of individualism; in any case it inflicts tremendous harm on the collectivity, above all by its ignorant hypocrisy. How could it be otherwise, seeing that this art is merely a disguised paganism and takes no account in its formal language of the contemplative chastity and immaterial beauty of the Gospel spirit? How can one unreservedly describe an art as "sacred" that offers to the veneration of the faithful carnal and showy copies of nature, even portraits of concubines painted by libertines, forgetful as it is of the quasi-sacramental character of holy images and forgetful too of the traditional rules of the craft? In the ancient Church and in the Eastern Churches even down to our own times, iconographers prepared themselves for their work by fasting, prayer, and sacraments, adding their own humble and pious inspirations to the inspiration that had fixed the immutable type of the image; they scrupulously respected the symbolism—always susceptible to an endless series of precious nuances—of forms and colors. They drew their creative joy not from inventing pretentious novelties but from a loving re-creation of revealed prototypes, whence a spiritual and artistic perfection that no individual genius could ever attain.

*
*   *

The Renaissance still retained certain qualities of intelligence and grandeur whereas the Baroque style could hardly express anything but the spiritual penury and the hollow and miserable turgidity of its period.

Late Gothic statuary has all the characteristics of a dense and unintelligent bourgeois art; it was all too easy for the Renaissance to set against it the noble and intelligent art of a Donatello or Cellini. Nonetheless, taken as a whole, the ravages of Gothic art are a small matter beside those of the Renaissance, an art profane, passional, and pompous.

No doubt incompetence and bad taste are to be encountered everywhere, but tradition neutralizes them and reduces them to an always tolerable minimum.

*
*   *

The first thing that strikes one in a masterpiece of traditional art is its intelligence, an intelligence that surprises whether by its complexity or its power of synthesis, an intelligence that envelops, penetrates, and uplifts.

Humanly speaking, certain artists of the Renaissance are great but with a greatness that becomes small when compared to the greatness of the sacred. In sacred art genius is hidden, as it were; what is dominant is an impersonal, vast, and mysterious intelligence. A work of sacred art has a fragrance of infinity, an imprint of the absolute. In it individual talent is disciplined; it blends with the creative function of the tradition as a whole; this cannot be replaced, far less surpassed, by human resources.

The Sainte Chapelle: a shimmer of rubies and sapphires set in gold. No individual genius could invent its splendors.[6] One would think they had sprung from the lily and the gentian.

*
* *

Latin Christianity has never been able to eradicate completely the paganism of antiquity. After having smoldered for centuries beneath the spiritual and artistic marvels of medieval civilization, it burst forth, appearing in a heavier and more brutal form; it took its revenge by destroying the normal expressions of the Christian genius on the intellectual level as well as on the artistic[7] and other levels.

The Renaissance, a Caesarism of the bourgeois and bankers, was an intrinsic heresy on the level of forms.

*
* *

Hindu art has something of the heavy motion of the sea and at the same time the exuberance of a virgin forest; it is sumptuous, sensual, and rhythmic; intimately linked with dancing, it seems to originate in the cosmic dance of the Gods. In certain respects the Tamil style is heavier and more static than that of the Aryan Hindus of the North. Muslim art is abstract, but also poetic and gracious; it is woven of sobriety and splendor; the style of the Maghreb is perhaps more virile than the Turkish and Persian styles, but these—especially the Persian—are by way of compensation more varied. Within the framework of Chinese art, which is rich, powerful, and full of the unexpected and mysterious, the Japanese style represents a tendency toward sobriety, elegance, and—in a certain sense—the inspired; the Tibetan style, which developed between the Chinese and Hindu styles, is heavy and

---

[6] Pierre de Montereau drew these splendors from tradition; he gave it an interpretation that was extraordinarily serene, joyful, and transparent.

[7] We are speaking of the full development of the Renaissance as found in a Michelangelo, Titian, or Correggio and not of the often virginal and tender, and in any case still Christian, painting of the Quattrocento.

somber, at times rough, often fiery; the Burmese and Siamese style is delicate, cheerful, and refined.

*
* *

The art of Islam unites the joyous profusion of vegetation with the pure and abstract rigor of crystals: a prayer niche adorned with arabesques owes something to a garden and to flakes of snow. This mixture of qualities is already found in the Koran, where the geometry of ideas is as if hidden under the blaze of forms.

Islam, being possessed by the idea of Unity, if one may so express it, also has an aspect of desert simplicity, of whiteness and austerity, which alternates in its art with the crystalline joy of ornamentation. The cradle of the Arabs is a landscape of deserts and oases.

Muslim art shows in a quite transparent way how art should repeat nature—in the widest sense—in its creative modes but without copying it in its results.

*
* *

When the arts are enumerated the art of dress is too often forgotten even though it has an importance as great, or almost as great, as architecture. Doubtless no civilization has ever produced summits in every field; thus the Arab genius, made of virility and resignation, has produced masculine garments of unsurpassed nobility and sobriety, whereas it has neglected feminine dress, which is not destined to express the "eternal feminine" in Islam as Hindu dress does, but to hide the seductive charms of woman; the Hindu genius, which in a certain sense divinizes the "wife-mother", has on the other hand created a feminine dress unsurpassable in its beauty, dignity, and femininity. One of the most expressive—and least known—forms of dress is that of the American Indians, with its rippling fringes and its ornaments of a wholly primordial symbolism: here man appears in the solar glory of the hero and woman in the proud modesty of her impersonal function.

The art of dress of every civilization, and even of every people, embraces multiple forms in time and space, but the genius always remains the same, though it does not always reach the same heights of direct expression and immediate intelligibility.

*
*   *

There are two aspects to every symbol: the first reflects the divine function in an adequate manner and thus constitutes the sufficient reason for the symbolism whereas the other is simply the reflection as such and hence contingent; the first of these aspects is the content, the second the mode of its manifestation. When we say "femininity" we have no need to consider the possible modes of expression of the feminine principle; it is not the species or race or individual that matters, only the feminine quality; it is the same with every symbolism: thus the sun on the one hand displays a content, which is its luminosity, heat, central position, and immutability in relation to the planets, and on the other hand it displays a mode of manifestation, which is its matter, density, and spatial limitation; now it is clearly the qualities of the sun and not its limitations that manifest something of God.

This manifestation is adequate since a symbol is fundamentally nothing other than the Reality it symbolizes to the extent this Reality is limited by the particular existential level in which it "incarnates". This is necessarily so, for nothing is absolutely outside God; if it were otherwise there would be things that were absolutely limited, absolutely imperfect, absolutely "other than God", a supposition that is metaphysically absurd. To say that the sun is God is false to the extent it implies that "God is the sun"; but it is equally false to pretend that the sun is only an incandescent mass and absolutely nothing else, for this would be to cut it off from its divine Cause; it would be to deny that the effect is always something of the Cause. Even though they pay tribute to the absolute transcendence of the divine Principle, it is unnecessary to introduce into the definition of symbolism reservations that are nonetheless foreign to a purely intellectual contemplation of things.

In addition there exist simple metaphors: these are pseudo-symbols, that is, images that are basically ill chosen. An image that does not touch the essence of what it seeks to express is not a symbol but an allegory.

*

*   *

When we speak of forms in the widest sense we include colors as well, which also belong to the "formal" order while being independent qualities in relation to tangible forms. Religions are divergent forms that are nonetheless analogous, there being no analogy without divergence, but they also contain secondary forms, which may be described—following the same visual symbolism—as so many "colors of the spirit". Affective and combative spiritual positions are "red"; contemplation and quietude are "blue"; joy is "yellow"; pure truth, "white"; the inexpressible, "black". Of course colors also have many other meanings according to the degree of reality or category of things considered.

Let us now consider colors in their own nature and in their immediate language: red has something of intensity, of violence, blue of depth and goodness.[8] Our gaze is able to move, to lose itself, in blue, but not in red, which rises before us like a wall of fire. Yellow partakes at once of intensity and depth, but in a "light" mode; it has a certain "transcendence" compared to the two "heavy" colors; it is like an emergence toward whiteness. When mixed with blue it gives to the contemplativity of this color a quality of "hope", of saving joy, a liberation from the enveloping quietude of contemplation. Red excites, awakens, and "exteriorizes"; blue gathers and "interiorizes"; yellow rejoices and "delivers". Red is aggressive and moves outward; the radiance of blue is deep, welcoming, and leads inward; the radiance of yellow is "liberating" and spreads in all directions. The combination of inward withdrawal (blue) with joy (yellow) is hope (green); hope is opposed to passion (red) because unlike passion it does not live in the present, but in the future; it is also opposed to passion in its two aspects of introspection and joy.

Purple is excessively "heavy" since it is composed of two heavy colors, one hot and the other cold; orange on the other hand is exces-

---

[8] The sky is blue and so is the mantle of the Virgin, *Mater misericordiae*. Christ is clad in white and red: sanctity and life, purity and love. Certain Vishnuite schools distinguish between a love that is "red" and a love that is "blue", the first no doubt corresponding to an activity and the second to a passivity.

sively "hot" because it is composed of two hot colors, one heavy and the other light. Green is neither excessively heavy nor excessively hot, for it is composed of a heavy color and a light color, one cold and the other hot; it is the only happy mixture. In purple the mingled elements are too different; in orange they are too much alike; green on the contrary unites opposites that are situated on different planes and cannot be in conflict; it therefore manifests equilibrium. Purple on the other hand expresses excessive weight, fatigue, and languor, and orange expresses "overheating", the joyous excitement of desire, not a transparent joy like yellow. Or again: if orange is seduction, purple is regret and green pardon. In the ternary of secondary colors it is green that is at the summit and liberates; in the ternary of primary colors it is yellow.

Because it combines two colors that are opposed in two different respects, green possesses an ambiguity—"by definition" in a certain way—that gives it a character of "surprise" and "strangeness"; it has two dimensions—whence its mystery—whereas its opposite color, red, is simple, indivisible, instantaneous. Green is hope, promise, happy expectation, good news; it has an aspect of unexpectedness, gaiety, and mischievousness; it possesses neither the violent action of red nor the inscrutable—and inwardly unlimited—contemplativity of blue; nor is it the open, simple, and radiant joy of yellow.

Red is the present moment. Green, its opposite, is duration with its two dimensions, past and future, the future being represented by yellow and the past by blue. Seen spatially blue is space and yellow the flashing center, a center that reveals itself and liberates, displaying a new dimension of infinity. It is the sky transpierced by the sun.

The opposition between red and green marks a direct antinomy; between blue and yellow, on the other hand, the opposition is harmonious, their relationship being complementary. In the same way blue and red on the one hand and red and yellow on the other are harmoniously opposed, in the first case because one is cold and the other hot and in the second case because one is heavy and the other light; the opposition between blue and red expresses royal dignity made of rigor and generosity, the opposition between red and yellow joyous intensity made of sensuality and happiness. The pair red and green expresses divergent opposition; but on the spiritual level these colors also symbolize love and knowledge, which are in fact divergent as attitudes, their transcendent synthesis being symbolized by white.

Similarly blue and yellow symbolize contemplation and grace, which are the two necessary poles of knowledge; but whereas white is like a transcendent synthesis of the opposition between red and green, the synthesis of blue and yellow is direct: it is green, which is a mixture not an integration. As for white and black, these are supracolor and noncolor; they are opposed like light and darkness or Being and nothingness. On the other hand red is opposed to white as passion is to purity, and it is opposed to black as life is to death. Red and green are also earthly life and resurrection.

Green and red can have a malefic meaning to the extent they are opposed to white by their violence: red in a passionate manner and green in a perfidious or venomous manner. Yellow and black are also susceptible to such a meaning—yellow to the extent it contradicts blue, as the seduction of false paradises[9] contradicts the contemplation of piety, and black to the extent it denies white, as ignorance denies wisdom or as guilt excludes innocence.

Blue and white cannot have a malefic significance strictly speaking: blue because its radiation is in a certain sense spherical or circular and in this way contemplative and white because it is absolutely neutral, transcendent, and primordial. On the other hand they may have a more or less negative meaning: white in this case is emptiness, outwardness, which is opposed to the qualitative plenitude of colors as well as to the secrecy of black, to spiritual inwardness; in this last case it is the profane aspect of day, which is opposed to the sacred aspect of night. Blue is cold, which is opposed to heat, or water-quantity, which is opposed to fire-quality, hence to blood, which is also hot and qualitative.

The benefic aspect of colors—and the elements—is always essential, direct, unconditional; the malefic aspect is accidental, indirect, conditional, for it exists only by opposition and negation.

---

[9] This is the malefic aspect of gold.

2

The Gospel tells us that when Jesus prayed he lifted his eyes toward heaven; the Scriptures also describe how Christ was taken up into heaven and finally hidden by a cloud. These facts are strictly necessary: from the earthly point of view God is indeed "on high" even though in reality He is nowhere in the spatial world. If Christ had to "ascend", this is because he still belonged to the visible domain; once he was no longer visible he no longer "ascended"; he had passed out of space. This is indicated by the cloud that finally hid him from the sight of men; this cloud, this "veil", marks symbolically—and the symbolism resides in the very nature of things—the passage from formal to supra-formal manifestation and then the passage from manifestation as such to the Principle or from the created to the Uncreated.

*

*   *

When we read trustworthy hagiographies we are struck by the frequency—we would almost say by the ease—of miracles in the Middle Ages and antiquity. If the saints of later times—and especially those of our own—live in a less miraculous setting, one could say this is because the cosmic environment is too remote from celestial realities and too emptied of grace for there to be any frequent occurrence of great miracles. If a saint of our period had lived in the Middle Ages, he might well have walked on water; if in spite of everything he were to walk on water now—a contradictory supposition—he would risk holding up the inevitable unfolding of events: he would make the end of the world and the completion of the divine plan impossible.

*

*   *

The posthumous states—for the simple reason that they embrace what is neither terrestrial nor spatial—are of a complexity beyond description in human language: revelations can give only diagrams, which contradict one another to the extent that their perspectives diverge. Moreover the posthumous conditions may themselves differ

43

greatly in keeping with different religions, for these can determine the modalities of the posthumous states by their respective structures: by this we mean that the temporary heavens and hells of Hinduism do not correspond to the perpetual heaven and hell of Monotheism, which is doubtless connected with the fact that Monotheists bury their dead whereas Hindus burn them.[1]

On the other hand the various revelations contain nothing that prevents the symbolic definitions or descriptions from being taken literally: the Semitic religions do not even state precisely that heaven and hell are not to be found in space; analogous remarks can be made about the *Mānava Dharma Shāstra*.

But these objections are of importance only from a specific point of view, which plays no part in dogmatic formulation, for what alone matters in regard to our final ends is that we should have a qualitative—and symbolically sufficient—notion of cosmic causality insofar as it governs our posthumous destinies.

Biblical facts or sacred facts in general cannot help but corroborate symbolism since it is in the very nature of things: holy persons have risen visibly to the sky; blasphemers have been swallowed up by the earth. Symbolism is a concrete reality founded on real analogies.

*

*   *

If one told a Tibetan that Kailasa is merely a pile of earth and rock having a certain height and circumference, he would reply: this heap we can measure is not Kailasa.

The sacred mountain, seat of the Gods, is not to be found in space even though it is visible and tangible.

It is the same with regard to Benares, the Ganges, the Kaaba,[2] Sinai, the Holy of Holies, the Holy Sepulcher, and other places in this category: it is as if the one who is present there had passed beyond

---

[1] Monotheists extend the posthumous conditions that are of concern to them to all men, and their doctrine then becomes purely symbolic, as we explained in our book *L'œil du cœur.*

[2] Let us recall here that the sanctuary of Mecca is far more ancient than Islam, Christianity, or the teaching of Moses.

space; he finds himself virtually reintegrated in the nonformal Prototype of the sacred place; in touching holy ground the pilgrim actually "walks" within the supraformal and is purified, whence the effacement of sins in these locations.

Certain geographical accidents, such as lofty mountains, are connected through their natural symbolism with the great primordial sanctuaries, and it is for this reason that the most diverse peoples—especially those whose tradition takes a "mythical" or "primordial" form—avoid climbing to the very summit of mountains for fear of provoking "the anger of the Gods".

*
*   *

For the man of the golden age to climb a mountain was in truth to approach the Principle; to watch a stream was to see universal Possibility at the same time as the flow of forms.

In our day to climb a mountain—and there is no longer a mountain that is the "center of the world"—is to "conquer" its summit; the ascent is no longer a spiritual act but a profanation. Man, in his aspect of human animal, makes himself God. The gates of Heaven, mysteriously present in nature, close before him.

*
*   *

Untouched nature has in itself the character of a sanctuary, and it is thus regarded by most nomadic and seminomadic peoples, particularly the American Indians; among the ancient Germans, a primitive sedentary people who rejected architecture in the strict sense, sanctuaries had specific locations, but always in virgin nature. The forest of Broceliande and the grove of Dodona are examples of a similar traditional outlook among the Celts and Greeks respectively, in spite of the fact that these peoples possessed a sacred architecture and an urban civilization; for Hindus the forest is the natural dwelling place of sages. A particular spiritual "exploitation" of the sacred aspect of nature is found in all traditions that possess—even indirectly—a primordial and therefore mythological character.

The struggle of the American Indians against a white and urban invasion has a profoundly symbolical character: it is a holy war in defense of a sanctuary, and this sanctuary is nature in all its virginity and grandeur. Urban civilization, with its inevitable mixture of refinement and corruption, is like a sickness that consumes the earth and pushes the frontiers of untouched nature back further and further; the Indian of the plains and forests of North America was a child of this nature and a priest of this primordial sanctuary. And this is why the heroism of a Pontiac, a Tecumseh, a Tashunka Witko (Crazy Horse), and a Tatanka Iyotanka (Sitting Bull) has in it something that touches us closely.

On one side concrete Nature, which places man at her center; on the other side abstract civilization, which makes him its periphery.

*

* *

The American Indians address their worship not only to "our Father the Sky" but also to "our Mother the Earth", these two being aspects of the "Great Spirit".

The Earth is always God, but God understood in a particular relationship that authorizes the use of feminine symbolism: it is not God in His uncreated reality but in His beneficent, "preserving", and "maternal" action in relation to creation. Likewise when a Christian prays: "Give us this day our daily bread", his thought does not imply any immanentist pantheism; he knows very well that fruits do not grow by virtue of a direct and miraculous divine intervention. But since God is the cause of all good, it is He whom we must thank for daily bread even though it is only given us through the intermediary of nature and not like the manna that fell from heaven. This habitual—or natural—divine activity finds its immediate expression in Mother Earth, who nourishes us and to whom we shall return. All true symbolism resides in the very nature of things; the earth from which we live is truly a reflection in the material order of divine generosity.

*

* *

Animals that reflect the quality of "goodness" (*sattva* in Sanskrit) are static and peaceful: the Indian ox, with its uneven back and its horns forming a semicircle, calls to mind snowy ridges above which rises the solar disc; the beauty of its eyes adds a sort of contemplative sweetness to this picture. The sheep, the dove, and the swan are quasi-paradisiacal animals because of their innocent and peaceful nature; the white color adds a quality of celestial purity.

The bison and camel incarnate the mountain but more especially its "earthly" aspect: the bison its massive, fearsome, hostile aspect, and the camel its patient, contemplative, priestly aspect. The bear also manifests an aspect of "earth" in its heaviness and unpredictability.

Animals having a dynamic symbolism (*rajas*) incarnate a celestial aspect that is awe-inspiring but also at a lower level a passional aspect: the tiger is cosmic fire in all its rage and splendor; like fire it is terrible and pure. The lion is solar: the passional aspect is here neutralized by a kind of royal serenity; like the eagle—which in its own order manifests the principle of lightning, revelation—the lion in its fashion expresses the force of the spirit.

The lowest animal species, those that repel us, manifest most directly the quality of ignorance (*tamas*); they are repugnant to us because they are like "living or conscious matter" whereas the law of matter is precisely unconsciousness. Monkeys shock us for the opposite reason, that is, because they are like men who have been deprived of the central consciousness that characterizes mankind; they are not "conscious matter" but consciousness decentralized, dissipated.[3] On the other hand there exist higher animals that possess an inferior "spiritual" form, and conversely: man does not like either swine or hyenas but feels no antipathy toward such insects as bees, butterflies, or ladybirds.

*
* *

---

[3] To the objection that there are sacred monkeys, in India for example, we would reply that a distinction must be made between an intrinsic symbolism and a partial symbolism, the first residing in the fundamental nature of the being in question and the second in an attribute. For instance, the extreme agility of monkeys can, like the fidelity and vigilance of dogs or the sagacity of snakes, have a positive symbolism.

The psychological economy of a traditional civilization needs extrinsic errors in order to be a vehicle for the intrinsic truths of which the tradition is the depository. If this is true with regard to its dogmatic propositions in their literal and exclusive aspect—the attribution of absolute uniqueness to facts, the faulty interpretation or denial of facts or truths relating to other dogmatic systems—it is still more obviously true in the case of information pertaining to the conjectural knowledge of men; a number of ancient and medieval books contain in fact many fables it would be foolish to take literally. Man is limited, and everything in his life consists of compensations; fables are the inevitable price that must be paid for transcendent and salvific truths.[4]

---

[4] It is hardly necessary to state that many things modern science takes for fantasies are—or were—realities. It is curious to observe that certain procedures of a science that seeks to be "exact" are fundamentally illogical: for example, taking an improbability for an impossibility or concluding that a thing of which one has no positive proofs does not exist.

III

CONTOURS OF THE SPIRIT

1

Anthropomorphism, though unavoidable in religions, is a two-edged sword: inevitably it brings with it contradictions, which cannot be neutralized indefinitely by calling them "mysteries".

What has to be understood is that the divine nature implies manifestation, creation, objectification, the "other-than-Self", and that this projection implies imperfection, hence evil; the "other-than-God" cannot be perfect, God alone being good.

God projects this goodness into His manifestation, which implies imperfection because of remotion. God never directly wills evil, but He accepts it to the extent that it manifests the world by metaphysical necessity: the "projection" of Himself willed by His infinity; the mystery is not in evil but in infinity. The divine Person directly wills evil only by way of justice, for reestablishing equilibrium; the possibility of evil does not come from the Person of God but from the infinity of His nature. The Vedantists express this mystery of infinity by saying that *Māyā* is without origin.

The Infinite is what it is; a man may understand it or not.[1] Metaphysics cannot be taught to everyone but if it could be there would be no atheists.

*
*   *

Anthropomorphism cannot avoid indirectly attributing absurdities to God; but it is impossible to speak of God to the majority of men without using an anthropomorphic symbolism, especially since God really does include a personal aspect, of which the human person is a reflection precisely.

When we say that God wills only what is good, this is completely true only if God is considered from a definite, hence restricted, viewpoint, and only if one specifies that evil is to be regarded as such, that is, as it appears to creatures. It is important to add that good has the

---

[1] The word "understand" has in this case an altogether relative and provisional meaning.

upper hand over evil even in the world, despite the sometimes contrary appearances presented by a given fragment of the cosmos in a given existential situation.

Mercy is the first word of God; it must therefore also be His last word. Mercy is more real than the whole world.

*

*   *

There are men who are indignant at the idea of having to "earn heaven" while others lose it; this is to forget the real basis of the problem, which lies beyond the alternative egoism-altruism: in fact the only question to be asked is whether in our heart of hearts we want to love or hate truth and virtue. In other words love of truth and the good is an ontological axiom, which must be faced directly; the posthumous states, whether celestial or infernal, cannot but illustrate the incommensurability of the difference between the real and the unreal. It is clearly impossible to hate truth and its beauty out of pity for those who hate them or to lie out of love for those who lie; one accepts the true and the good without conditions, as their nature requires and as our nature requires. What heaven accomplishes is truth and virtue; he who knows their worth also knows why their absence is hell. The fact that a fundamental rejection of truth—and of what it implies for man—is a possibility is one of the mysteries of the Infinite, which we must accept as we accept our own existence and which we may either understand or not.

We do not love truth and the good just because we want to gain something; if in loving them we do gain something, this shows we were right to love them. We may be of the opinion, humanly speaking, that we deserve nothing, whether good or bad, but we cannot doubt that truth is infinitely real and precious and that its absence must therefore imply a sort of inverted infinity.

*

*   *

The whole drama played out between the Infinite and Existence is symbolized in the story of the earthly Paradise. Adam's desire—the cause of sins but not itself sin, according to Islam—is like the shadow of the principle of contradiction or nothingness implicit in the divine infinity; this principle is not itself evil, but it is the distant metaphysical source of evil since it is the cause of the world insofar as it is a "splitting into two" of the Real, separation, remotion.

The whole problem lies in the fact that the serpent was in Paradise. If it had not been there, Paradise would have been God, or rather it would not have had any separate existence. To exist is not to be God, hence to be "bad".

*

*   *

The very fact that existence has been called esoterically "a fault to which no other fault can be compared" shows that the fall of Adam is nothing other than the actualization of the separative principle of existence on the plane of existence. In Hindu terms one would say that Eve represents the expansive and passional cosmic quality (*rajas*) and that the serpent—which is necessarily found in Paradise since Paradise is created—is the subversive and dark quality (*tamas*).

In the story of the earthly Paradise there are four degrees of causality or responsibility, which are represented by God, Adam, Eve, the serpent. Judaism and Christianity include Eve and Adam in the sin, though in different degrees; Islam attributes the sin to Satan; metaphysically, if one went beyond the level where the notion of "sin" has a meaning, one could attribute the negative cause to God Himself, for evil cannot come about by chance.

If Islam denies the sin of Adam—not in the sense of an "error committed" but in the sense of an intentional transgression—and denies at the same time the culpability of prophets in general, this is for the metaphysical reason that God, of whom Adam and the prophets are direct representatives (*khulafā*, from *khalīfah*), is without imperfection while nonetheless being the first, and indirect, Cause of imperfections; if the Bible by contrast affirms the sin of Adam, this is for the cosmological reason that he was the first human manifestation of evil, without which there would have been no sins in the world.

*

*   *

According to Christian doctrine Adam sinned; the fall was the first sin.

For Islam Adam could not sin; he was the first of the prophets, and they are beyond sin. On the other hand Adam was a man, and human nature implies limitations, hence the possibility of faults, without which nothing would distinguish it from God. It is a fault (*dhanb*),[2] that is, a sort of inadvertence or confusion and not an intentional transgression (*ithm, zulm*), which caused the loss of Eden. The first pair was pardoned for this fault after suffering its consequences on this earth; it is a peculiarity of the faults of prophets that they carry with them sanctions in this life and not in the next: David and Solomon had to suffer here below, not in the beyond. According to this way of seeing things it is only through Cain that sin came into the world.

Christianity does not concede the impeccability of prophets in general or of Adam in particular; but since it could not allow the prophets to suffer the pains of fire—even before the coming of Christ—it placed them in limbo; now this conception of limbo, a "non-heaven" that is not hell, takes on a theological function similar to the Islamic conception of a fault, a "demerit" that is not a sin.

Christianity, with its "historical" mode of thinking, attributes to original sin what Islam attributes to earthly nature as such. In a sense the Christian perspective is situated in "time" and that of Islam in "space".

*
*   *

The Christian perspective is founded on the fall of Adam, which requires as its complement the Messianic redemption; the Islamic perspective for its part considers humanity just as it is, in its collective state so to speak, and it rests on the idea of "message" (*risālah*), of "messengers" (*rusul*), that is, on the necessarily multiple manifesta-

---

[2] In itself this Arabic word designates a "fault" considered as an "excrescence"; this makes it possible to understand why existence (*ex-stare*) is a "fault to which no other can be compared", according to a *hadīth*. A desire is an "excrescence" but cannot be considered a "sin"; on the other hand every sin has by definition an aspect of *dhanb*, and this justifies the designation of every transgression by this word.

tions of the eternal Word; since it has a beginning, this line of messengers requires a final synthesis: the Prophet, who is the "seal" (*khātam*) of the prophetic cycle. The "mythologies" intersect without inner contradiction; mutual misinterpretations arise from ignorance of their respective points of departure, from the error of attributing one's own postulates to others.

The Hindu perspective begins with Reality, not with man; the fall is one cosmic accident among thousands of others.

The Buddhist perspective, like the Christian, begins with man: it is founded on the distinction between suffering and Deliverance, but it speaks of man only to reduce him to nothingness. This apparent nothingness is the sole Reality, infinite Plenitude.

*

* *

There is a certain complementary relationship between the Buddhist and Shankarian reactions: Buddhism reacted against a Brahmanism that had become somewhat sophisticated and Pharisaical, and Shankara reacted against the doctrinal simplifications of Buddhism—simplifications that were certainly not erroneous in themselves but contrary to the traditional metaphysics of India. If Brahmanic spirituality had not suffered a measure of obscuration, the peaceful expansion of Buddhism would not have been possible; in the same way, if the Buddhist point of view had not been centered on man and his final ends, Shankara would not have had to reject it in the name of a doctrine centered on the Self.

Therein lies the great difference: the Buddha delivers by eliminating what is human after first defining it as suffering; Shankara delivers solely by the knowledge of what is real, what is pure Subject, pure Self. But to eliminate everything human is not possible without metaphysics, and to know the Self is not possible without eliminating what is human: Buddhism is a spiritual therapy, which as such requires metaphysics,[3] whereas Hinduism is a metaphysics, which by the same token requires a spiritual therapy.

---

[3] "According to the teaching of the Buddha there are two orders of truth: supreme truth and the truth of appearances. Those who have not yet discovered the difference

*

* *

In Shankarian terms ignorance appears as the superimposition of an "I" on the "Self" and then, secondarily and by way of consequence, as desire.

Hinduism sees primarily ignorance; Buddhism sees desire.

*

* *

Buddhism does not begin with the notion of the ego as do the religions of Semitic origin but with the wholly empirical reality of suffering; its spiritual springboard is not the container we are but the content we live: the "I" is an ephemeral assemblage of sensations, hence the apparent denial of the "soul", which results from the same perspective as the apparent denial of "God". Buddhism is merely being logically consistent in denying the continuity of the sensory soul.

Only when the abstract container that is the ego becomes in turn an empirical content does the metaphysical outlook intervene, which for its part excludes *a fortiori* all egocentricity. Buddhism becomes metaphysical when the "I" is concretely perceived as "desire", and thus as "suffering", in the process of extinction.

*

* *

Buddhism sees the world only as a chaos of irreducible substances (*dharmas*), of which the numberless combinations produce subjective and objective appearances; like Christianity it does not have a cosmology, strictly speaking, which means that both of these two great perspectives regard the world not in its reality or unreality but solely with reference to the means of leaving it. For the Buddhist even more than for the Christian, to seek to know the nature of the world is a distraction; for the Hindu, however, knowledge of the cosmos is

between these two truths have not understood the deepest meaning of the doctrine" (Nagarjuna in the *Mādhyamika Shāstra*).

an aspect of knowledge of the Absolute since it is nothing other than *Ātmā* as *Māyā* or the "universal Soul" as "creative Illusion". This perspective, which begins with the Absolute, is truly metaphysical whereas the Buddhist and Christian perspectives, which begin with man, are initiatic, that is, centered above all on spiritual realization; since they are intrinsically true, however, they also contain the Hindu perspective, and conversely.

The Shankarian refutation of Buddhism does not show why Buddhism is false but why Hinduism cannot admit it without nullifying itself.[4]

*
*   *

Christianity begins with the fall of Adam and presupposes that man is the fall; Islam begins with the illumination of Adam after the fall— "And Adam received words from his Lord, and the Lord turned Himself toward him" (*Sūrah* "The Cow" [2]:35)—that is, with the first revelation; or again, and more directly, it begins with the illumination of Abraham, which for its part is nothing other than monotheistic revelation.

In other words Christianity is founded on the primordial fall of the unique man, Islam on the nature of collective man or man as such, Buddhism on the suffering of man, and Hinduism on the illusion of existence, whether human or otherwise. Judaism—the Mosaic law—sees in man a permanent revolt against the Law, hence the moral consequence of the fall of Adam rather than the fact of this fall; it might be said that it neutralizes this consequence, whereas Christianity eliminates its cause.

*
*   *

---

[4] In a similar way the Ramanujian refutation of Shankarian advaitism is far less an attack than a defense: Ramanuja defended a possible mode of spirituality; he made himself the spokesman of *bhakti*, hence also of its limitations.

A traditional perspective or "mythology" is to total Truth what a geometrical form is to space. Each fundamental geometrical form—such as the point,[5] the circle, the cross, the square—is an adequate image of the whole of space, but each excludes the others.

In empty space every point is the center and thus the starting point of a symbolically valid measurement, but no "measurement" of space is absolutely adequate or it would be space itself. The various starting points of the traditional mythologies—the creation of the world, the fall of Adam, the Abrahamic revelation, the sufferings of ignorance—are as it were so many reference points in metaphysical space.

*

* *

The Christian perspective distinguishes between the flesh and the spirit; it rejects the flesh in favor of the spirit.

The Islamic perspective distinguishes between what is carnal and base and what is carnal and noble, the former being symbolized by food,[6] hence the excellence of fasting, and the latter by sexuality, hence the excellence of marriage; but this second point is far more relative than the first.[7]

In his heart the Christian prefers a chaste polytheist to a polygamous monotheist.

*

* *

Western people tend to look at everything in relation to human fact; Orientals—especially Hindus—consider things primarily in relation to

---

[5] The objection that the geometrical point is not a "form" is here invalid, for we are speaking of the empirical point taken as the limit of visibility.

[6] Or rather by its quantitative aspect, for in itself food is looked on as a blessing.

[7] It would be completely false to believe that sexuality constitutes a necessary element of Muslim spirituality. Many Muslim saints have undergone long periods of abstinence or ended their lives in chastity. The Koran goes as far as to say: "You have an enemy in your wives and your children."

divine principle. Earthly love, for example, has the double aspect of human fact and of manifestation or symbol of a divine principle: the tale of Krishna and the Gopis does not shock a Hindu since for him the fact is transfigured by the principle. No one could dispute that this perspective is in the nature of things; the ambiguity lies only in the inadequacy of the human receptacle, of his contemplative capacity or spiritual plasticity.

Purity is in Krishna himself, not in his abstentions; what he touches becomes pure because he is Krishna; now he touches only what is pure by virtue of a divine prototype even though the corresponding human fact may have an aspect of impurity, and indeed must have such an aspect on the physical level.

*

*   *

Morals can vary, for they are founded on social requirements; but virtues do not vary, for they are enshrined in the very nature of man; and they are in his primordial nature because they correspond to cosmic perfections and *a fortiori* to divine qualities.

For the moralist the good lies in action; for the contemplative it lies in being, of which action is only a possible and at times necessary expression.

*

*   *

Hindus and peoples of the Far East obviously do not have the notion of "sin" in the Semitic sense of the word: they do not distinguish actions based on their intrinsic value but on their appropriateness in relation to cosmic or spiritual reactions as well as to their social utility; they do not distinguish between the "moral" and the "immoral" but between the advantageous and the harmful, the agreeable and the disagreeable, or the normal and the abnormal, leaving themselves free to sacrifice the first—but outside every ethical classification—for a spiritual reason. They are capable of pushing renunciation, abnegation, and mortification to the very limit of what is humanly possible but without being "moralists"; the Asian sage renounces the moral just as

59

much as the immoral insofar as these words designate not virtues or vices but categories of action.

The Semitic perspective gives actions an absolute character while attaching extrinsic conditions to them. For an Asian everything is a question of economy, equilibrium, finality; he does not think there is any need for a man to guard himself against certain dangers with a preconception, hence an illusion.

*
*   *

The Gospel—with its exclusively spiritual, hence in a sense extra-social, morality—says not one word about war; the Koran on the contrary regulates it;[8] be that as it may, the Christian conquerors of the Moors were far more pitiless and intolerant[9] than the Moors who conquered the Christians.[10] Muslims see a mark of "hypocrisy" in such disproportions whereas Christians reproach Muslims for the "down-to-earth" quality of their morality; Muslims will say that morality should be socially effective, to which Christians will reply that it should be a spiritual ideal, and so on. If we mention these things, it is not with the intention of depicting an irresolvable polemic but in order to show the inevitable interplay of compensations that regulates the entire human order, just as it does the entire cosmic order. No truth is ever responsible for human frailties; no truth can neutralize them completely in collective life. In order to forestall certain objections let us add that those modern Europeans who dominate—or have dominated—Muslim peoples are clearly no longer representatives of Christianity; they represent a civilization that necessarily involves a certain humanitarianism by virtue of its religious indifference, its over-

---

[8] The *Mānava Dharma Shāstra* likewise regulates it, and in a somewhat "idyllic" manner since it forbids the molesting of spectators. The *Bhagavad Gītā* treats the subjective, or rather the spiritual, aspect of the problem.

[9] This trait is without doubt an unconscious heritage of Judaism as well, the situation of which was quite different, however.

[10] It is necessary, however, to take into account the fact that Muslims could only be regarded as "pagans" by Christians of the Middle Ages, whereas Islamic dogma establishes a legal distinction between Monotheists (the "people of the Book", *ahl al-Kitāb*) and idolatrous polytheists.

estimation of earthly comfort, and its idolatrous worship of the human animal; but the only legitimate humanitarianism is that which takes account—to the extent this is possible, that is, in conformity with the nature of things—of human welfare in its entirety, hence above all man's spiritual well-being; when this is neglected or even rejected, all the treasures of the earth cease to have any value. Unfortunately it is impossible for man—especially collective man—to concentrate his efforts simultaneously on all the dimensions of what is true and good.

If Buddhism, which also possesses a morality designed for contemplatives, has to a certain extent been able to pacify peoples who were formerly bellicose, this may be connected to the fact that the law of "karmic" causality and the successive advents of the Buddhas appear in this case as the sole expressions of divine will; man must therefore take upon himself—from the point of view of "concordant actions and reactions"—all the risks involved in such equivocal acts as the elimination of a life or the destruction or theft of someone else's property.

*
*   *

Confucianism divides men into rulers and ruled; it requires a sense of duty from the first and filial piety from the second. Here we see that the social law is not at all detached from the spiritual meaning of the whole revelation: it necessarily possesses concomitant spiritual elements that concern man as such, that is, man considered independently of society. Indeed every man rules or determines something that is placed in some way in his keeping, even if it is only his own soul, which is made up of images and desires; on the other hand every man is governed or determined by something that in some way surpasses him, even if it is only his Intellect. Thus each man bears in himself the double obligation of duty in relation to the inferior and piety in relation to the superior, and this double principle lends itself to incalculable applications: it includes even inanimate nature in the sense that anything may serve—with regard to us and according to circumstances—as a celestial principle or terrestrial substance.

Chinese wisdom foresees an application of the universal pair "Heaven-Earth" (*Tien-Ti*) that is first of all social and then personal, and thereby a conformation to the "Ineffable" (*Wu-Ming*) from which this pair proceeds. The point of connection between Confucianism and Taoism is in the virtues: Confucianism considers their social and human value and Taoism their intrinsic and spiritual quality. Man is the place where Earth and Heaven meet.

Egoism must be extinguished between devotion and duty.

*

* *

The abrogation (*naskh*) of certain Koranic verses is explained by differing degrees of universality: thus the verse that teaches that the "Face of God" is everywhere, "in whatever direction ye may turn", finds itself abrogated (*mansūkh*) by the verse that orders turning for prayer in the direction (*qiblah*) of the sacred mosque (of Mecca).

The principle of this abrogation is encountered in all sacred Scripture in one form or another: for example, when the Gospel enjoins a man to "hate" his father and mother in order to follow Christ after first commanding him to love his neighbor as himself, there is a difference of level and meaning, not a contradiction.

Shankaracharya explained the apparent contradictions of the *Veda* in the same way: by distinguishing the provisional concept (*anuvāda*) from the fundamental idea (*apavāda*), which serves to correct and abrogate the preceding concept in a manner that is consistent with different spiritual requirements and levels of understanding.

*

* *

The Bible says that God promised Abraham descendants as numerous as the sands of the desert and the stars of the firmament; according to the commentary of Saint Augustine the sand here symbolizes the descendants of Abraham after the flesh, the Jewish people, and the stars his spiritual posterity, Christianity. In our day it seems the fashion to dismiss this as a "contrived interpretation" or even "poetry", as if the very form of the divine promise did not possess a meaning and God had busied Himself with literature. If every word of Scripture has a meaning—as the traditions attest—it must be possible for this

62

meaning to be discovered with the help of the Holy Spirit, as in fact it has been by a number of inspired men.

There is no "contrived" interpretation among the inspired commentators; a hermeneutical meaning is always true; if the interpretation is false, there is no reason to call it "contrived".[11]

*

* *

Liturgy is a symbolism that envelops rites in order to make their meaning outwardly explicit and in such a way as to mark the real discontinuity between the sacred and the profane or the divine and the human, above all the collective human.

[11] "The Holy Spirit teaches all truth: it is true there is a literal meaning the author had in view, but since God is the author of holy Scripture, every true meaning is at the same time the literal meaning; for all that is true comes from the Truth itself, is contained in it, is derived from it, and is willed by it" (Meister Eckhart). Again, according to Meister Eckhart, the Apostles respectively symbolize the twelve powers of the soul, namely, five inner senses, five outer senses, the reason, and the will; when, for example, it is said in Scripture that the Apostles Peter and John "ran together to the tomb" (of Christ) this means that reason and will (or doctrine and method) penetrate one another reciprocally in the spiritual soul in order to attain to the essence of things. We may also recall this passage of Dante: "The Scriptures can be understood and must be explained according to four meanings (the literal, the allegorical, the moral, and the anagogic). The fourth is called the anagogic, which refers to what surpasses the meaning. . . . This is what comes about when one gives a spiritual interpretation to a Scripture which, while true in its literal meaning, further signifies the higher things of eternal Glory, even as can be seen in the Psalm of the Prophet where it is said that when the people of Israel came out of the land of Egypt, Judea was made holy and free. While it is manifestly true according to the letter, what is to be spiritually understood is no less true, namely, that when the soul comes out of sin it is rendered holy and free in its power" (*Convivio*, 2,1). According to Maimonides, it is the very obscurity of numerous scriptural passages that indicates in a providential manner the plurality of meanings in Scripture. The *Zohar* says, "Woe to the man who pretends that Scripture teaches us only simple stories. . . . If it were thus we also could make a Scripture that would be even better than Holy Scripture, since profane books can include transcendent ideas." "This also is a form of silence," says Saint Basil, "that the obscurity of which Scripture avails itself in making doctrines difficult to understand is for the benefit of its readers."

In Christianity the liturgical element is more developed[12] than in Judaism or Islam; the reason for this lies in the fact that Christianity, being esoteric in origin and structure, has a greater need to underline the separation between the sacred and the profane;[13] this need does not arise from esoterism as such but from its religious, hence social, application, that is, from its exoteric extension.

The liturgical element is found in one degree or another in every ritual system—especially in Buddhism—and always for the same fundamental reasons.

*

*   *

To speak of tradition is to speak of continuity: in this continuity there is something absolute, as in tradition itself. In order to grasp the character of a tradition there is no need to seek out inaccessible or unverifiable criteria; the essential elements—the constants—of the tradition suffice.[14] To understand a given symbol it is enough to consider its nature or form, then its doctrinal—hence traditional—definition, and finally the metaphysical and spiritual realities of which the symbol is the expression.

*

*   *

To speak of tradition is to speak of plenitude: if certain religions have no sacred language, this does not prove that they are in this respect

---

[12] We are not thinking here of the more or less late additions to the Christian liturgies but of their essential forms, which go back to the Fathers of the Church.

[13] A distinction that exists wherever there are traditional collectivities.

[14] When Voltaire wrote, "We shall take good care not to seek to pierce the impenetrable obscurity covering the cradle of the Church at its birth" (*Essai sur les moeurs et l'esprit des nations*), he was unwilling to recognize first of all that the same remark might be made in relation to every historical event—everything in the relatively distant past inevitably has obscure aspects—and second that the Church transmits, and transmits by definition since it is a tradition, all the clarifications its traditional character requires. In such a setting only those things are obscure that do not need to be clear.

defective but that they have no need of one; they compensate for this apparent lack by elements proper to themselves.[15] The meaning expressed by speech is independent of language itself; this independence must therefore be manifested somewhere, even if the contrary aspect—the connection between language and its content—appears as a relative norm:[16] there must be revelations that determine only the content of the divine word and not its linguistic dress, "replacing" as it were the sacred language with other immutable supports.

Principles are not fully developed forms: they must be applied in conformity with the nature of things as presented in each particular case and without seeking to transfer the constituent elements of one organism to another that excludes them.

*
* *

Similar things could be said about the role played by cosmology: highly developed among Semites, Hindus, and others, it has far less importance for Christians and Buddhists; this difference is necessary because, from a certain point of view, the science of the created is useless for deliverance whereas from another point of view it contributes to it indirectly. In Hinduism itself *Yoga* and *Vedānta*, which converge directly upon spiritual realization, by no means presuppose a study of the *Vaisheshika*, the *Nyāya*, or the *Sānkhya*, which are cosmological doctrines, and this is without even mentioning *bhaktas*, who sometimes have no science at all; in the same way Sufism includes branches that are in no way concerned with cosmology, either directly or by implication, and that replace it with a spiritual "psychology"

---

[15] Buddhism and Christianity each possess several liturgical languages, but these are not the very "flesh" of the revelation. If someone wishes to regard this as a lack, he ought to be just as astonished by the fact that Islam, unlike Christianity and Judaism, requires no rite of membership; circumcision is not an indispensable condition for this purpose.

[16] In a similar way castes, though naturally inherent in every complete collectivity, cannot determine individuals in an absolute manner; hence there must be traditional societies that adopt another point of view, even an opposite point of view—that of the equality of men before God—and that because of this ignore social classifications.

or—one might say—a "microcosmology", and this is precisely what Christianity and Buddhism do. "Why have I taught you nothing about the world? Because this would be in no way useful to you for deliverance." This saying of the Buddha not only shows the reason for the relative lack of a science of this order[17] but also how this apparent lack results from the nature of things and is compensated by the tendency of the whole doctrine toward "the one thing needful".

*
*   *

In the theory of *Avatāra*s the historical point of view is of capital importance not only with regard to the existence of the God-Man but also regarding his spiritual level: when a tradition proposes or requires the cult of a particular mediator, it guarantees his sanctity by this very fact. Since the *Avatāra*s correspond to a possibility, there is no reason for maintaining that the avataric person has the value of a symbol alone; on the contrary it must be admitted not only that he is truly the heavenly mediator but even that he must be so, for otherwise the tradition would have no effective meaning. We do not see why Heaven would deceive those who are faithful to it, still less why it would be obliged to deceive them—why it would be so wretched, illogical, and devious.

The function of symbol proper to the *Avatāra* depends strictly on the superhuman scope of his person; it is this that gives the cult its efficacy and legitimacy. The sacramental image of the Buddha is at the same time a metaphysical symbol and a real presence. It is necessary to distinguish between a symbol as such and a symbol vivified by a celestial presence.

*
*   *

---

[17] This lack concerns primarily the general form of the doctrine and the function incumbent on cosmology in the tradition as a whole, for in fact every religion includes a theory of the world: Christianity inherited that of the *Torah*, to which is linked that of the Apocalypse, whereas Buddhism holds *grosso modo* to the Brahmanic cosmos, subject to certain differences resulting from its own perspective.

Christianity puts the main accent on Christ, whose personality absorbs the message: the great argument of Christianity is Christ, the God-Man. One could almost say that it is he who justifies or guarantees the truth; the difficulty of Trinitarian dogma disappears before the immense radiance of the incarnate Word.

Islam puts the main accent on the message, which absorbs the messenger, Muhammad: the great argument of Islam is Unity, which becomes *ipso facto* the argument of the Prophet; it is the blinding and incontrovertible truth that justifies and guarantees its herald.

What cannot be questioned "from outside" in Christianity is the spiritual perfection and celestial character of Christ; and what *a priori* cannot be contested in Islam is the unity of God, hence the truth of the message.

*

*   *

What is characteristic of Christianity—as also of Hindu and Buddhist "avatarism"—is that revelation assumes a human form, whereas it appears elsewhere in the form of a book.

The *Logos* in itself is neither "Word" nor "Son" nor "Book" nor "Buddha", but it appears respectively as such according to its mode of earthly manifestation. In a certain sense the "Trinity" is a defining of God in relation to Jesus; before Jesus there was no Trinitarian dogma, though we are speaking here of words and not the deeper meaning of the dogma. In any case the Trinitarian conception—as a dogma—carries with it the danger of an attitude that attributes in practice a relative character to God and an absolute character to the world.

Islam, since it sees the *Logos* as "divine Word" and "revealed Book", considers only the prophetic or revealing mission as such from the human side, without distinguishing any modes; it sees everything in relation to Unity: there are no "incarnations" since these imply a "splitting into two", as the Christian doctrine[18] proves precisely.

[18] Islam acknowledges, however, that Jesus was born of a virgin by the Holy Spirit (*Rūh al-Quddūs*), though without deducing theological consequences that for it are not required; for Unity, as conceived by Islam, "absorbs" every possible "divine characteristic".

In Hinduism the *Logos* is the Principle of "divine reverberation", if one may use this expression to translate the term *Māyā*. Hinduism has the power to combine all the perspectives, which elsewhere are mutually exclusive.

*

*   *

Christianity has a certain dramatic quality that involves a danger of individualism and deviation; Islam for its part "sought to avoid" this risk by tending toward equilibrium, whence the opposite danger, that of platitude; to speak of form is to speak of limit and at the same time of the possibility of error.

Christianity aims to teach a unique and incomparable fact; its foundation is miracle. Islam on the other hand aims to teach only what every religion essentially teaches; it is like a diagram of every possible religion; its foundation is the self-evident. In Islam the idea is everything; a Muslim would not dream of dissociating the truth of the idea from its salvific effectiveness; but in Christianity it is the mediator, the miracle, the unique fact that takes precedence over everything else; the mediator is here the criterion of truth, as we said above: the miracle, which proves his superhuman quality, serves as evidence by opening the heart to grace.

By its form Christianity is a predestined support of the way of love; Islam for its part is allied by its form to *gnosis*, for its pivot is universal truth (the *Shahādah*), and it conceives the love of God in relation to the knowledge of Unity. The Muslim saint is essentially a "knower by God" (*ʿārif biʾ Llāh*), and love appears above all as the half-human, half-heavenly savor of knowledge.

Essentially all religions include decisive truths, mediators, and miracles, but the disposition of these elements, the play of proportions, can vary according to the conditions of the revelation and its human receptacles.

*

*   *

In the Latin Church misfortune did not come from the Moors in Spain but from a poorly neutralized pagan antiquity, then from the Roman

68

mentality, and later—as a reaction against it—from the Germanic mentality. The pagan mind was too naturalistic and rationalistic, the Roman mind too juridical and political, and the Germanic mind too imaginative and prone to simplification.[19]

In the Eastern Church misfortune did not come from the Turks, who invaded the Balkans, or the Mongols, who invaded Russia, but from the autochthonous lay powers, which—with their nationalistic and worldly tendencies—oppressed the Church even in its organic life. If Asian domination was a misfortune for the laity, it was nonetheless a protection for the inner life of the Churches, which for centuries were embedded as it were in the timeless stability of Asia.

Christianity was born under a foreign yoke, and it could be said that a legacy of this is almost a need to be oppressed in order to be protected from its own laity. One understands why Islam has neutralized the lay element—or the element that might have been such—by enclosing it in a sacerdotal system that knows no fissure. Islam, at least in some respects, is a "democratic theocracy" of married monks.

*

*   *

Paganism, when not reduced to a cult of spirits—a cult that is atheistic for all practical purposes, though without excluding the theoretical idea of God[20]—is properly speaking an "angelotheism"; the fact that worship is addressed to God in His "diversity", if one may put it this way, is not enough to prevent the reduction of the Divine—in the thoughts of men—to the level of created powers. Divine unity has precedence over the divine character of this diversity: it is more

---

[19] These defects express in an inverse manner intellectual qualities that are manifested in figures like Pythagoras, Thomas Aquinas, and Meister Eckhart; for example, what amounts to imaginativeness and simplification in the Germanic race appears among the spiritual men of this race as an intelligence that is somehow concrete and symbolic and as a realism that seeks the nature of things without deviation; this Germanic genius can in fact do nothing, however, without the concurrence of the Mediterranean genius.

[20] There are fetishist negroes who are not ignorant of God but are astonished that Monotheists should address Him since he dwells in "inaccessible heights".

important to believe in God—hence in the One—than to believe in the divinity of some universal principle.

Hinduism does not lose sight of Unity; it has a tendency to see Unity within diversity and within each element of this diversity. It would therefore be a serious error to compare Hindus with the pagans of antiquity, for whom the divine diversity was practically quantitative.

The polytheistic—or angelotheistic—world that was the West of antiquity could be regenerated only by a laying bare of the mysteries: this is the historical significance of Christianity. We should add that the first Christians could have had no notion that such a function belonged to the Christic mysteries, for they had no idea of a "West" that was liable to "founder", especially since they believed the end of the world to be near and were awaiting the *Parousia*; they aimed to save souls, not a continent.

*
*   *

In one respect pagan antiquity was less decadent than our own period, but in another it was more so. Paganism consists in the reduction of religion to a sort of utilitarianism, which leads to syncretism and heresy: syncretism because all sorts of divinities and forms of worship are added to the original cult without any assimilation or integration and heresy because divine qualities are confused with angelic powers, which are in their turn brought down to the level of human passions; the very way in which the ancients represented the gods proves clearly that they no longer understood them. Esoterism for its part had no hold on the common run of men; it could not impose on them a spiritual idealism whose foundations were accessible only to an elite. Neoplatonism could do nothing against the general ignorance or the unleashing of passions, although indirectly and mysteriously its presence must have been a factor leading to a relative equilibrium.

The modern West suffers under the double disadvantage of being ignorant of all metaphysical contemplation[21] and of possessing a

---

[21] Scholasticism answers to the human need to think but is not a contemplative method.

rationalist pseudo-wisdom, which drags man down into abysses that are strictly subhuman; but in the midst of its chaos it benefits from the presence of a way of love, which is as such open to all, namely Christianity.[22] What results from this is the paradox of a civilization far more decadent than that of ancient Rome but sheltering, in spite of everything, relatively fewer "pagans", or this at least is the case in certain countries and insofar as it is possible to evaluate matters as complex as this; on the other hand those who are directly involved in the creation of modern civilization and who determine its course are far more "pagan" than were the decadent Romans, not to speak of the general decline of the human level characteristic of our times. Here as in all domains one must take into account the interplay of compensations.

Had Greco-Roman religion not been degenerate and "pagan", it would have been a sort of Hinduism; the same can be said of the Celtic and Germanic religions.

*

* *

At times religions reject truths that are outward—as well as peripheral from the point of view that concerns them—in order to express inward and essential truths, for what counts in the case of the Absolute and our final ends is essential and salvific truth, which is in no way at the mercy of facts.

God gives more than He promises, never less; sometimes He gives heavenly truth in exchange for some earthly truth but never the opposite, unlike modern science; an earthly truth—a fact—may be the pivot of a given religious "mythology", but it may be irrelevant or even embarrassing for another such perspective. What matters in a religion is its central affirmation, its qualitative content, which is indispensable for man and of which the peripheral arguments are like a protective enclosure.

---

[22] In some Balkan countries Islam also assumes this compensatory role, with the difference of perspective required in this case.

*

*   *

The formal homogeneity of a religion requires not only truth but also errors—though these are only in the form—just as the world requires evil and just as Divinity implies the mystery of creation by virtue of its infinity.

Absolute truth exists only in depth, not on the surface.

Religions are "mythologies", which as such are based on real aspects of the Divine and on sacred facts—hence on realities but on aspects alone; this limitation is at once inevitable and completely effective.

*

*   *

A man may begin with what is intellectually evident, with a direct participation in the all-consciousness of the Self, and in this case arguments coming from outside and resting on an objective certainty—presumed to invalidate the inward certitude—will count for nothing. But a man may also begin with an outward certainty, a divine fact, a miracle, and if this is the solid ground beneath his feet, arguments claiming to represent inward evidence—not in such a way as to invalidate the miracle but so as to contest the absolute character attributed to it—will no longer carry any weight.

Intellective meditation and passional prayer—an extreme opposition, which in no way means all prayer is passional or all meditation intellective.

When an individual falsifies these two positions by usurping "God-Subject" or "God-Object", he falls into rationalism in the one case and into fetichism in the other.

2

The great question is to know what gives our whole being its impetus, what fundamentally convinces us and draws us out of ourselves: it may be a "religious mythology", if such an expression is permissible—that is, a combination of fundamental elements and images that confer upon us the grace of sensing the truth and being willing to do "this" in order to reach "that"—but it may also be an essence hidden in our nature, a profoundly evident truth or thirst for the Infinite; in this case grace will not reach us on a more outward level; it cannot be conveyed to us through an "imagery" that fails to touch the center of our soul.

*
*   *

Metaphysical doctrines, where they are not expressed directly in the sacred Scriptures themselves, as in the *Upanishads*, the *Brahma Sūtra*, and the *Tao Te Ching*, constitute more or less late fixations of intellectual perspectives;[1] if from the beginning there was an oral and secret teaching—because of the very nature of things[2]—it must nonetheless have been much more concise than later developments and commentaries, and *mutatis mutandis* this is precisely the case with the Hindu and Chinese Books we have named. In the beginning *gnosis* had nothing "systematic" about it: no doubt it was actualized in keeping with the "intellectual style" of the revelation concerned, but according to diverse and original intellections; its supports were for-

---

[1] In this order of things evaluations are inevitably quite approximate; situations may differ from one milieu to another.

[2] For it is senseless to explain delicate truths to someone who does not have either the capacity or desire to understand them. "The things we are going to say seem to some of the multitude to be different from the Scriptures of our Lord; but let them know that it is by the Scriptures themselves that these things live and breathe; from them they draw their whole grounding, but from them they take only the spirit and not the language" (*Stromata* of Clement of Alexandria). It is true that later on *gnosis* had to abandon an independent terminology in order to avoid any appearance of conflict with scriptural language and dogmatic formulas.

mulas and symbols, including the phenomena of nature[3] and the soul. Later on, for a variety of reasons—the collective tendency toward a kind of coarsening and forgetfulness, then the growing number of disciples who were more and more widely scattered and less and less capable of spontaneous intellection, and finally the polemics provoked as much by official lack of understanding as by heresies—explicit syntheses became necessary, re-adaptations formulated in writing and inevitably taking on some of the characteristics of a system. Furthermore, it is not impossible in metaphysics for one doctrine to borrow dialectical keys from a given foreign doctrine, though one must not exaggerate the importance of these adaptations, which are purely a matter of form; but since they are possible, there is no reason for not admitting they have taken place. There is no doubt that Neoplatonism played such a role in relation to esoterisms of Semitic origin;[4] there is also the well-known role played by Aristotelianism in Latin theology, a role that is questionable in several respects.

*
*   *

If we begin with the idea that Truth is in the depths of our being as a nonformal light, of which we have only to become aware, doctrinal formulations will appear above all as barriers against error; it is the purifying of the heart, its liberation from the obstacles eclipsing it, that will be all essential.[5] The nonformal and unlimited Truth may give rise

---

[3] The Koran often says that the phenomena of nature are "signs" (*āyāt*) for those "endowed with understanding"; nothing could be clearer.

[4] If this is certain for the Greek Fathers, we do not see why it would not be probable for Muslims as soon as they came to know the Platonic writings; the fundamental arguments are identical in both cases. The same can be said of the Cabalistic elements one encounters in Christian *gnosis*: far from proving that this *gnosis* had a non-Christian source, their presence is explained by the Jewish origin of Christianity; the Cabala can only incidentally play the part of a formal support, for Christ must be the source of every doctrine and for all the more reason of *gnosis*, the scriptural foundations of which are to be found above all in Saint John.

[5] In his *Treatise on Metaphysics* Omar Khayyam says that Sufis are "those who seek knowledge, not by reflection and speculation [like theologians and philosophers], but by purifying their soul [the passive and static ego], correcting their character [the active and dynamic ego], and freeing the intellect from the obstacles that arise from

to widely diverse doctrinal formulations, not just between one school and another, but even within the teachings of a single sage.[6]

When the virtues are realized to their very limit—even as far as their universal and divine prototypes—they coincide with metaphysical truths: to be humble, charitable, and truthful in a quasi-absolute manner—which is impossible outside of truth—is to "know"; it is certainly impossible to know in an absolute manner without being humble, charitable, and truthful. Truth is necessary for the perfection of virtue just as virtue is necessary for the perfection of truth.

*

*　*

The Asian sage incarnates a perspective; insofar as he thinks and acts he identifies himself with it and abides in the nonformal truth beyond all thought. On the other hand he does not concern himself with the psychology of perspectives other than his own; their truth is generally a matter of indifference to him, though he may be aware of it incidentally; he does not linger over a science of mental forms, and he has no reason for doing so.

In the conditions of humanity today, however, such a science has become more and more useful and is even indispensable: whoever

bodily nature. When this purified substance is presented before the divine Glory, the [intellectual, principial] models of the [mental, manifested] knowledge will surely be revealed in this other world [of transcendent Reality]." Many Sufi books, notably the celebrated Epistle of al-Qushayri, which has been called the gateway or key to Sufism, concern themselves with essential morality, and this is full of meaning. The Vedantic renunciation of action denotes another intellectual and methodic perspective: omitting action for the sake of contemplation is in the final analysis the same thing as omitting sin because of its obscuring effect on the heart-intellect. "Works do not serve for perceiving the Real," says Shankara, "but for purifying the mind." For Chaitanya the chief thoughts of the *bhakta* should be concerned not only with the divine Name and the symbolical play of the *Avatāra* Krishna, but also with the perfections, the virtues.

[6] The works of Ibn Arabi offer examples of this; this diversity proves not only the relativity of doctrinal expressions but also their spontaneity and independence within traditional orthodoxy. The same Ibn Arabi acknowledges moreover that perfect asceticism can open the heart to the loftiest of intellectual intuitions without any metaphysical science and simply on the basis of the *Shahādah*.

does not know how to discern the truth in every mental form containing it runs the risk of losing, with a given form, the whole of the
truth.

*
*   *

Doctrine is one thing and sanctity another. To subordinate doctrine to
sanctity—that is, to the personal realization of doctrine—is to refrain
in advance from making use of doctrine since no one can canonize
himself; it is also to ruin doctrine, which ceases to be something absolute in its own order. "Objective" doctrine is a different thing from
knowledge actualized in a particular "subject".

It is illogical to reject a particular doctrine in the name of sanctity
or a particular sanctity in the name of doctrine.

*
*   *

There are certainly truths and spiritual attitudes that are not accessible
to every intelligence while they are nonetheless excellent and even
necessary for some men; whether we wish to call them "esoteric" or
something else, their existence is in the nature of things.[7]

To deny esoterism—and it is the thing, not the word, that matters—is to deny that there are spiritual values that not every man can
understand; to say that this incomprehension is a criterion of their
uselessness is to sacrifice truth to expediency.

Far from being a luxury esoteric doctrines are on the contrary the
response to imperious logical needs; the spiritual finality they envisage

---

[7] In his treatise on humility Saint Bernard speaks of the soul that "falls asleep in truth":
"but its heart watches, and it seeks during this time to penetrate the greatest secrets
of truth in order that it may be able to subsist in the remembrance of these mysteries,
having come again to itself. It is there that it sees things that cannot be seen and hears
things that cannot be explained, which man is not permitted to speak about because
they surpass all the knowledge one night can give to another night. It is nonetheless
true that one day explains itself to another day and that it is permitted to speak of
wisdom among the wise and to communicate spiritual things to the spiritual."

76

corresponds to man's deepest aspiration: it is God within us who wills to be delivered.

*
*   *

Gnosis is for those whose intelligence is naturally turned toward the universal essences; to them the world of forms will be as if transparent; its intelligibility comes from the essences, not the forms.

Ordinary intelligence lives in forms; it surpasses them only artificially and with effort. For the average man the "solid earth", the "concrete", is the formal plane; the essences are for him only "abstractions".

*
*   *

The words of Christ to Nicodemus, the Samaritan woman, and the rich young man express various aspects of the distinction between esoterism and exoterism taken in the widest sense, for it is not exclusively a question of *gnosis* but above all of love; in its own way love also pierces and consumes forms, "riches", the "world". Love burns up the world and leaves only God remaining; it goes far beyond simple obedience to the religious Law. Mystical asceticism, like *gnosis*, is esoteric, at least in principle.

In Islam esoterism appears as the quasi-ineffable and purely qualitative essence of dogma (*īmān*) and law (*islām*), an essence actualized by "spiritual virtue" (*ihsān*). One may also say that Sufism is believing sincerely that God is One; here everything depends on sincerity (*sidq*), which is the spiritual quality of faith: to believe sincerely is to believe as though one saw; it is to assent with all our being; it is therefore to be detached from multiplicity, from diversity, from all that is not the One; it is the entire path, all the way to union. Unitary faith is the first participation in divine Unity; depending on its different aspects it is a *gnosis*, a love, a being. The poverty (*faqr*) of the contemplative (*faqīr*, "poor one") is the necessary consequence of a unitary faith that is pure, that is, sincere, total, integral, negating multiplicity and therefore "riches"—just as the rejection of the "world" in Christianity is the necessary consequence of the perfect love of God.

77

*

*   *

Exoterism never goes beyond the "letter"; it puts the accent on the Law—not on a realization of one kind or another—hence also on action and merit. It is essentially a "belief" in a "letter"—a dogma considered in its formal exclusiveness—and an obedience to a ritual and moral Law. Moreover exoterism never goes beyond the individual; it is centered on heaven rather than God, which amounts to saying that this difference has no meaning for it; the Absolute is conceived only with respect to the relative.

*

*   *

Exoterism does not come from esoterism but directly from God.[8] This truth reminds us of Dante's thesis that the empire comes from God and not from the papacy. "Render unto Caesar the things that are Caesar's, and unto God the things that are God's."[9]

*

*   *

Intellectual qualification lies far less in the capacity to understand certain metaphysical concepts—a capacity that is always relative and often illusory—than it does in the purely contemplative quality of the intelligence; this quality implies the absence of passional elements, not in man but in his spirit. Purity of intelligence is infinitely more important than its actual capacity: "Blessed are the pure in heart," said Christ, and not "Blessed are the intelligent."

---

[8] Even in Christianity and Buddhism, which strictly speaking have no "outward law", the exoteric application was divinely foreseen, as is proven by their "letter" itself.

[9] This saying of the Gospel confirms what Dante says in the *De Monarchia*: "So it is clear that the temporal authority of the monarch descends on him without any intermediary from the universal Source of authority; this Source, in itself one and simple, pours out in a multitude of streams by the overflowing of its goodness."

The "heart" means the Intellect and by extension the individual essence, the fundamental tendency, of man; in both senses it is the center of the human being.

*

* *

Intellectual qualification must be accompanied by moral qualification; otherwise it is spiritually inoperative, that is, it will not permit one to pass beyond certain limits.

The relationship between "intellectuality" and "spirituality" is like the relationship between center and circumference in the sense that intellectuality transcends us whereas spirituality enfolds us. Intellectuality becomes spirituality when the whole man, and not only his intelligence, lives in the truth.

It is false to reduce the meaning of the word "morality" to actions alone; it concerns the virtues just as much. A certain Arab saint was a "noble brigand" before his conversion; now nobility is a moral qualification. Actions may be accidental; virtues are essential. Virtue is to action what essence is to form.

The moral point of view does not coincide with the social point of view except insofar as it is limited to actions, which by definition cannot be absolute since they are forms and not essences. And this explains why sin is not only a way of acting but also a way of being or again why action is sinful not only when it transgresses a law, hence a form, but also—and above all—when it manifests a vice, hence a kind of essence; in the latter case the sin is in no way relative to some legal form. The law comes from without, but the human norm is within; it is a law written in our human substance, hence a permanent revelation of the heart.

*

* *

There are men who can understand gradually, through symbolical expressions, what they would be incapable of understanding through complex theories; this does not indicate the relativity of truth, which is immutable—whether "doctrinal" or not—but the relativity of the practical role played by formulations.

Again there are others who have the capacity for understanding theories, but whose understanding is merely conceptual and fixed as it were in one dimension: they savor the formal homogeneity of the doctrine, whence the paradox of a formal understanding accompanied by an essential incomprehension.

Esoteric truth is a two-edged sword: there are men who lose God because they are ignorant of this truth, which alone would save them, and there are others who think they understand it and forge for themselves an illusory and arrogant faith, which they put into practice in place of God.

*

* *

Esoterism is hidden by its nature, not by its form. The average Muslim does not grasp the essential nature of Sufism, and yet he is not unaware of its existence; if he is not a heretic he knows very well that *tasawwuf* is the way of those who seek God and who possess a mysterious science that is subtle, sometimes paradoxical, and difficult to approach. In religious esoterism the qualitative content has a right to secrecy but not the framework; the framework is always visible, but the majority of men do not know its significance and ask nothing better than to remain in ignorance of it.

It is evident that many of the elite have never concerned themselves with esoterism and that many who have concerned themselves with it are by no means of the elite.

*

* *

Orthodoxy is the conformity of an idea—or a form in general—to a particular revealed perspective or a particular aspect of truth.

God sometimes intervenes independently of orthodoxy, but orthodoxy cannot make up for the absence of God.[10] Sometimes truth

---

[10] God is infinite. If certain theologians identify God with Being, this is not because they deny the infinity of God—far from it—but because they identify Being with the Infinite, which is quite another matter; to see only the ontological aspect of

comes into collision with logic in transcending it—or with a certain logic, one of concepts or things—but logic never transcends truth. There may arise unforeseen and paradoxical interferences of the Cause in the effect, but the effect can never exclude the Cause. Orthodoxy is the channel and criterion of inspiration; it is not its prime mover. It is a guarantee of nonformal truth only on the level of forms.

The Pharisees replaced God with a quasi-mechanical orthodoxy calculated to exclude all divine inspiration; they reduced religion to a formalism, which is something it could never be; otherwise the reproaches of Christ would have had no object.

Pharisaic formalism suppresses both the transcendent freedom of God and the intelligent and immortal personality of man.

*

*   *

There are two elements in tradition: orthodoxy and grace. Without ever contradicting orthodoxy, grace gives it new forms of expression as circumstances may dictate, but these expressions in no way depend on our own will; quite the opposite is true.

In these two elements dwells a third, which in reality comes first: the divine will, whose dimensions man can never grasp all at once.

*

*   *

God binds himself in His promises because He is absolute; but He remains free in His grace because he is infinite.

the Infinite is not to deny the Infinite as such. To acknowledge the infinity of God is thus implicitly to acknowledge "Beyond-Being", of which Being is as it were the "determinative affirmation". A similar remark ought to be made regarding the scope of the word "salvation": because of the very fact that it is scriptural, this term cannot allow for any principial restriction; it necessarily designates all liberation from suffering and death, whether or not this liberation implies a transcending of individuality. The sacred terminology is wholly to be found in Scripture, the truth of which cannot be partial.

Man is bound by the law because he is multiple and inconsistent; but he is free in virtue because he has something unique and irreplaceable in his immortal person.

Virtue is something that must come from man himself in the sense that it cannot be added to him from without, and in this sense alone.

*

* *

Truth involves antinomies that are always reducible; but virtue involves real conflicts because truth transcends what is human. Sometimes it is less difficult to be virtuous when one finds oneself enclosed in a limited truth, hence in a simplistic homogeneity, than when one finds oneself in a sense at the point of intersection between antinomic truths. Truth can contradict certain manifestations of charity, if not charity in the deepest sense, though the hierarchy of values will not allow a decisive discrimination. It will then be for grace, for God, to tip the scale in favor of the right solution; without grace man can do nothing even if nourished with wisdom and filled with virtue.

*

* *

The Pharisees possessed orthodoxy and regularity, but they did not possess either grace or the virtues. They did not possess grace because in practice they put their orthodoxy and regularity in place of the living God; and they did not possess the virtues because they replaced human values—moral qualifications—with outward observances, which being thus isolated lost their efficacy.

Christ did not deny their authority—"they sit in Moses' seat"—but in spite of this he condemned them.

3

According to the teaching of the Sufis, Christ brought only an esoterism (a *haqīqah*); this results not only from the doctrine of the Gospel[1] but also from the particular character of the rites;[2] without

---

[1] It is in this sense that one can say, for example: *Moysis doctrina velat quod Christi doctrina revelat.* Sufis call Jesus the "Seal of Sanctity" (*Khātam al-wilāyah*), and Muhyi al-Din Ibn Arabi comments on this in his *Lights* (*Anwār*): "The Seal of universal sanctity, above whom there is no other saint, is Jesus (Sayyidna Isa). We have met several contemplatives of the heart of Jesus. . . . I myself was several times united with him in my ecstasies (*ahwāl*), and through his ministry I returned to God in my conversion (*tawbah*) . . . and he gave me the name of friend and prescribed for me austerity and spiritual destitution." "My kingdom is not of this world," Christ said; sometimes Muslims set against this formulation this *hadīth* of the Prophet: "I bring you not only the good things of the other world but also the good things of this world," namely, a legislation that concretely regulates all the circumstances of life and is not exclusively a spiritual law; in its own way this *hadīth* confirms the opinion that Christ brought only a *haqīqah*.

[2] According to Nicholas Cabasilas, a Byzantine theologian of the fourteenth century and a follower of Saint Gregory Palamas, Baptism confers supernatural being or "principle of operation", Confirmation sets this principle in motion, and the Eucharist feeds its life; the three books of Solomon correspond respectively to these three degrees, Proverbs relating to conversion, Ecclesiastes to illumination, and the Song of Songs to union. This doctrine is founded on Saint Paul's *in ipso vivimus et movemur et sumus.* According to Saint Simeon the New Theologian, Baptism is the foundation of all spirituality; it is "virtual deification", "regeneration of the whole man"; it confers "spiritual light" and makes us "heavenly men" and "gods"; in case of loss, not of the baptismal gift, which is ineffaceable, but of the actual state of grace it confers, this state—the source of which always remains essentially and exclusively Baptism—must be gained anew by ascetic practices, tears, doctrinal instructions, and charismatic blessings conferred by holy men (laying on of hands, holy oils, holy water). It may be recalled that in the East Confirmation immediately follows Baptism and is virtually incorporated in it. "Here we see something that will henceforth remain a characteristic of the sacramental theology of the Eastern Church, and this is *a parallelism between the sacraments and mysticism.* This characteristic appears in Origen, is developed by Gregory of Nyssa, and finds its latest and most perfect expression in Nicholas Cabasilas. . . . *Baptism is the sacrament of initiation, Chrismation that of progress, and Eucharist that of union*" (Jean Daniélou, *Origène*). "At the same time the whole spiritual life is represented as plunged in the sacramental life that feeds it. We have already remarked on the parallelism between the three ways ('illumination', 'cloud', and 'darkness') and the three chief sacraments; Baptism corresponds to the first way in its double aspect of purification and illumination, Confirmation corresponds to the second in its double

this specific character, this laying bare of spiritual realities until then hidden, the coming of Christianity would be unintelligible. On the other hand Christianity assumed from the very start the function of a "universal message" (a *risālah*, as Muslims call it); it cannot display the character of *gnosis* in its actual form, and so it presents itself as a way of love,[3] accessible in principle to every man, though fully realized only by those who are "chosen".

An exoterism can prescribe obedience to God and justice toward the neighbor; it cannot prescribe love of God and neighbor, for these attitudes are essentially qualitative; they belong, as the Sufis would say, to the domain of "spiritual virtue" (*ihsān*).

When one speaks of "Christian esoterism", this can have only three senses: one is referring to a way of love that has its point of departure in the general form of Christianity and emphasizes the mysteries of redemption and the sacraments,[4] or to a *gnosis* that is *a priori*

---

aspect of obscuration of the visible world and elevation toward the invisible world, and finally the Eucharist is related to the mystical life both as union and as a going out of the world and the self. The sacramental life is truly conceived as a 'mystagogy', a progressive initiation leading the soul to the very summits of the mystical life, all the way to 'sober intoxication'. . . . Thus, in the commentary on the Twenty-Third Psalm (XLV, 692 A-B), 'the shadow of death' represents Baptism, the 'staff' and the 'oil' represent Confirmation, and the 'table prepared' and the 'cup that runneth over' represent the Eucharist. The full meaning is given this Psalm if we recall that it was chanted during the procession that led the newly baptized from the baptismal font to the communion table" (Jean Daniélou, *Platonisme et Théologie Mystique*). Baptism is said to confer the virtuality of the Edenic state by abolishing "original sin" whereas Confirmation is described as conferring the potential for "deification" by transmitting the fullness of the Holy Spirit, the Eucharist actualizing "deification" in conjunction with the spiritual virtues of man. Let us recall in this connection the "keys of the kingdom of Heaven" symbolized by the two keys—gold and silver—of the *Pontifex Maximus*, guardian of the "greater" and "lesser" mysteries.

[3] "But covet earnestly the best gifts: and yet shew I unto you a more excellent way. . . . Though I speak with the tongues of men and of angels and have not charity, I am become as sounding brass or a tinkling cymbal" (Saint Paul, 1 Corinthians 12:31-13:1).

[4] "Unto you it is given to know the mysteries of the kingdom of God: but to others in parables; that seeing they might not see, and hearing they might not understand" (Luke 8:10). In his *Treatise on the Holy Spirit* Saint Basil says, "For a doctrine is one thing and a definition another: one keeps silence concerning a doctrine; definitions on the contrary are proclaimed." In speaking of doctrine and the sacraments, the Fathers readily made use of the terminology of the Greek mysteries, and this could not have been pure coincidence.

doctrinal and metaphysical and transcends forms by its very nature,[5] or to forms of esoterism that were non-Christian in origin but became Christianized, such as Hermeticism and the craft initiations.

*

*   *

The sufficient reason for the craft initiations lies above all in the need man has to find a meaning in the art to which he devotes himself by vocation; for since the exercise of a craft is necessary to man, it could not legitimately be regarded as a loss of time for the immortal soul, nor could it be situated outside the life of the spirit. This obvious truth was already in the divine Truth before becoming apparent to the human mind: hence it appeared in facts before it could proceed from reasoning. All this amounts to saying that there must be modes of spirituality attached to the crafts, whatever the form of the dominant religion; and since the arts are more ancient than the historical religions, the spiritual modes they comprise had to survive within these

---

[5] According to Clement of Alexandria, it is knowledge, *gnosis*, that the Apostle is alluding to when he says to the Corinthians: "I hope that your faith may grow so that I may be able to tell you the things that are beyond you." And Clement adds, "By this he teaches us that *gnosis*, which is the perfection of faith, extends beyond ordinary instruction." Again Saint Clement—as one called this Father of the Church before Benedict XIV (eighteenth century) struck him from the Roman martyrology—speaks in his *Stromata* of "those happy men I had the good fortune to hear who had preserved the true tradition of the blessed doctrine they had directly received from the holy apostles, Peter, James, John, and Paul"; and he also says, "*Gnosis*, having been left by the apostles to a small number of the faithful, has come down to us without writing." Similarly Saint Irenaeus—who is as little suspect of "Gnosticism" as possible—refers like Clement, Origen, and others to an oral and secret tradition emanating from Christ and transmitted by the apostles; Saint Dionysius likewise speaks of "two theologies, one common and the other mystical", the mystical having its "secret traditions" and the common its "public tradition". According to Evagrius Ponticus, justice requires that one speak enigmatically of the secrets of the mystical life "in order not to cast pearls before swine"; for him as for his predecessors the mysteries concern the Intellect, though this does not mean he presents the difference between *gnosis* and the mysteries of the way of love in a systematic manner; as in Sufism, the two perspectives are most often combined. Meister Eckhart seems to have been the most explicit representative of *gnosis* in the Middle Ages; another example, later but still sufficiently representative, is without doubt Angelus Silesius.

religions; the vocation of building sanctuaries therefore coincided with the vocation of the corresponding craft initiation.

The strictly "objective" character of the material arts implies a mathematical basis and not an emotional mysticism; because of this aspect they are indirectly connected to *gnosis*. But the arts also have another aspect, that of "work"—not of "contemplation" or "combat"—and by virtue of this characteristic they are linked with the possibilities of "craftsmen", not those of "priests" or "warriors".

In the Middle Ages the major inspiration for work certainly came from religion, but the execution—the work itself, the creative pro-cess—depended on the specific wisdom of the builders, a wisdom that was "gnostic" in nature but limited as to its level. It should be added that the craftsman's way can be integrated perfectly well into a way of love (a *bhakti*), and this for two reasons: first because its intellective or "gnostic" character—deriving from *jnāna*—is limited to cosmology and second because action (*karma*) is just as much a normal vehicle for love as it is for cosmological knowledge.

In any case the presence in a civilization of craft initiations is suf-ficiently explained by the very existence of traditional arts; now arts are vocations, like other functions and methods.

*

* *

The alchemist transforms lead into gold: from base and heavy nature he extracts the noble and dazzling essence, the pure Intellect, which *a priori* is found buried beneath the lowly weight of fallen nature.

The stonecutter removes the formless element from rough stone, making of it a geometrical truth, a norm, a beauty ordered according to a universal prototype: it is thus that he hammers his soul to elimi-nate what is chaotic, arbitrary, coarse.

The mason coordinates scattered substances and makes them into the habitation of God: from being an indeterminate chaos, his soul becomes the temple of the divine presence, the temple of which the Universe is the model.

Here one sees several forms of inward asceticism founded on physical operations; the contemplative intelligence gives meaning to analogies that are in the nature of things.[6]

*

* *

From the point of view of religion the craftsman's wisdom is a normal fact; since it is in the category of "philosophy", it is useful for man and suited for the realization of human perfection; the secret character of this wisdom coincides with that of the craft. But religion would contradict itself if it supposed that such a "philosophy", having lost its connections with the craft itself, could in turn serve as a "religion" in fact if not in principle.

In a general way one could say as much of Hermeticism: its survival among Muslims, Christians, and Jews does not show us that it had a vital importance for these different environments, but that from the religious side nothing was opposed to the particular vocation it implies.

*

* *

In Islam spiritual possibilities appear as superimposed levels; in Christianity, however, there is basically only one spiritual possibility—leaving aside its modes—and man participates in it in a more or less direct or indirect way. A Muslim may be either an exoterist or an esoterist, and in the latter case he may be a saint; but a Christian can only be a child of his time or a saint, whatever may be conveyed—according to the case—by this word. In Islam there is as it were no sanctity outside of esoterism; in Christianity there is no esoterism outside of sanctity.[7] In relation to the human chaos Islam is an equilibrium

---

[6] This parallelism between art in action and spiritual development appears very strikingly in Zen Buddhism, where archery for instance gives rise to a whole initiatic science. *Zen* is derived from the original *Dhyāna*.

[7] These formulations have nothing absolute about them and mark in each case a kind of predominance rather than an exclusivity of mode; nonetheless they shine a clear

that takes account of all possibilities and includes a way of spiritual realization; Christianity for its part is identified almost entirely with such a way; it has no social application, strictly speaking, since it has no legislation outside spiritual laws. For Islam man is distinct from his sin, and it suffices that he should abstain from it; for Christianity, which is centered on "deification", man is necessarily a "sinner" and must therefore change himself;[8] Islam realizes this perspective in its "inward dimension", Sufism, for which existence itself is already a "fault" or "imperfection" (*dhanb*): the individual, whether "good" or "bad", is then an "associate" (*sharīk*), that is, a "false god", and must be extinguished—without loss of the Personality—in the "unicity of Reality" (*wahdat al-Wujūd*).

*

*   *

To say that Sufism is identified with a particular doctrinal formulation would be quite false, for metaphysics is not a necessary criterion of spirituality, at least in its speculative manifestation; if metaphysical doctrine is an absolute necessity for the intellectual contexts in which it is actualized—as well as for the whole tradition insofar as it has moved away from its origins and needs intellectual lights and guarantees—such a doctrine may nonetheless not be indispensable for a particular form of spirituality.

*

*   *

The life of Ibn Arabi, spokesman of the strictest metaphysics, is interwoven with marvels, visions, miracles; he speaks of the shame of sin and tears, of examination of conscience, of contrition, penitence, and other elements that seem at first sight to have no connection with knowledge. He accepted visions without becoming attached to them—an attitude we find again in Saint Teresa of Avila or, closer to

light on certain fundamental differences between the two traditions in question.

[8] It goes without saying that this difference is only in the manner of looking at these things *a priori*.

our times, in Sri Ramakrishna—and this proved all the easier for him because he possessed all the criteria necessary for a rigorous discernment of appearances.

Saint John of the Cross presents an outlook that is the very opposite of this: without explicitly formulating a metaphysics, he ruthlessly rejected every vision and sensory satisfaction.

There is a science infused with knowledge or love, which is independent of all effort of intellection; it is connected on the contrary—though not in a way that can be outwardly calculated—with purity of heart and therefore with ascetic purification; the unsentimental and nonimaginative rigor of such purification guarantees, together with other factors, the integrity of the states of contemplation. In a popularized mysticism these guarantees inevitably fall to the ground because of the practical impossibility of an integral asceticism.

*

* *

From a certain point of view the word "esoterism" has a relative meaning depending on the level to which it is applied: thus *gnosis* is esoteric in relation to love, and both are esoteric—though to different degrees—in relation to simple religious obedience.

Unlike *gnosis* the way of love is in principle open to all: it is preached publicly, and the qualifications it requires are moral rather than intellectual. "Many are called, but few are chosen,"[9] says the Gospel.

*

* *

The recognition of foreign religions depends on various psychological, or even simply geographical, contingencies, and it does not in itself

---

[9] A text in the *Philokalia* expressly declares that Hesychasm is addressed to all. In India the preaching of *bhakti* by Chaitanya is a particularly convincing example of this universal radiation of love and its capacity for combining "inwardness" and "outwardness" in one and the same contemplative reality.

possess any element of spiritual necessity:[10] no revelation directly suggests it, to say the least; sages like Plotinus and Porphyry, despite their Pythagorean esoterism and metaphysical knowledge, did not understand Christianity. In a similar way the reciprocal exclusiveness of Hindu schools—Shankara is in no way an exception—clearly proves that in normal conditions[11] an understanding of alien forms is not a necessary manifestation of the transcending of forms; we may even say that if an effort at comprehension is not made, this is consistent with the "faith"—not "belief" but "fervor", *shraddhā* in Sanskrit—which excludes all weakness and hesitation and without which no way is possible.

On the other hand the principial recognition of a supraformal truth that must be found also in alien forms is a necessary result of *gnosis*.

*

* *

The passivity of the true mystic[12] is the qualitative complement of celestial activity: when God is active, the creature is passive; the

---

[10] Nothing obliges an orthodox Hindu to accept the validity of foreign religions, though in fact many Hindus look on the religions of the "barbarians" (*mlecchas*) as devotional ways (*bhakti-mārgas*).

[11] Conditions are abnormal in the present world because everything is called into question. In large part it is precisely the formal divergences of the one truth that give the semblance of reason to skepticism: modern man flounders among antinomies that were unknown to men of old.

[12] The word "mystical" denotes something connected in one way or another to a suprarational communication with the Divinity; since this word is European, it must necessarily coincide with the mode of spirituality known in the West, which is a way of love. As for the word "mysticism"—given the "diminishment" it involves in relation to the substantive "mystic"—it can be used to designate a path that is lacking any method properly so called and that is characterized by the predominance of a moralistic and sentimental individualism; in fact, however, the difference in question is not always so clear. We may add that in German the word *Mystik* has the sense of "spirituality" whereas *Mystizismus* means only a play of fantasies. The theological definition of "mystical states" is doubtless too extrinsic; this is explained by the fact that the way of love is nurtured on faith and asceticism, not intellection, and is centered on grace, not knowledge.

participating activity of the Intellect does not enter into this mode of spirituality, and the activity of the will plays only an exceedingly indirect role in relation to grace. On the other hand the true mystic is active in his ascetical discrimination among appetites and sensations of every kind—unless these involve a form of certitude that is intrinsic and divine, as in the case of prophecy. As for the false mystic, he is passive toward all phenomena since he seeks sensations, not divine Reality—an aim that is precisely contrary to the ascetic principle.

This question of mystical "passivity" brings us to that of spiritual "consolations":[13] far from being reducible to sentimentalities, as the word itself might lead one to suppose,[14] such consolations are to be explained in relation to the natural separation of the soul from God, and even more in terms of the "desolation", the "trials", the "nights of the soul", the "dryness" that result from the inevitable experience the soul has of its own nothingness. When the soul is dying between this nothingness and divine darkness—when it suffers from the discontinuity between the ego and the Infinite—it is in need of graces reestablishing or facilitating its equilibrium.

In Sufi terms it could be said that such inspirations are connected with the "enlarging" (*inshirāh*)[15] or "expansion" (*bast*) that alternates

---

[13] There is a scriptural foundation for these consolations in the opening of 2 Corinthians.

[14] "Spiritual consolations are gifts more precious than all the riches and honors of this world. And if the sensibility is itself moved, this completes our devotion, for then our whole being is united to God and tastes God. Sensibility is to be dreaded when it takes us away from God, but it is very well regulated when it unites us to God" (Saint Alphonsus Liguori, *Love for Jesus Christ*). A Hindu *bhakta* would speak no differently. The sentimental nuance of the term "consolation" comes from the perspective of love and from nothing else; but it is impossible to deny that the notions of "consolation", "aridity", and "trial" give rise to sentimental abuses in the field of popularized—in practice individualistic—spirituality, which we might call "mysticism" or a "tendency toward the mystical".

[15] The Koran says: "Have We (God) not enlarged thy breast and lifted the load which weighed on thy back? . . . Verily after hardship cometh ease" (*Sūrah* "Have We Not Enlarged?"). "In consolation," says Saint Ignatius Loyola, "God shows all things to us as easy"; now intuition of the easy aspect of a thing is independent of the feeling the intuition may produce; "substantial consolation" is *a priori* a "perception" or, as the Sufis would say, an "unveiling". "My yoke is easy, and my burden is light," says Christ: this "ease" or "mildness" corresponds to a reality of which the contemplative has only to become aware, but this is often not possible without grace because of the

with "contraction" (*qabd*);[16] natural equilibrium must be broken in order that supernatural equilibrium might be found.

Every man needs grace just as every man needs faith, and this is apart from any question of *gnosis*; the opposite opinion is either a question of words or the worst of illusions.

*

*   *

Grace has impersonal and apparently illogical aspects that cannot be grasped by a moralizing anthropomorphism; nonetheless to say that grace is absolutely "gratuitous" is to express its impersonal character in moral terms even though this idea of gratuitousness refers in the first place to divine freedom.

Grace surrounds us infinitely, and it is only our hardness that makes us impervious to its radiation, which is in itself omnipresent; it is the soul that is absent, not grace. In normal conditions this hardness yields to the efforts of the soul joined with spiritual means,[17] but accidental fissures—or what appear to be so because of our ignorance of the causes—may also occur in such a way that a man suddenly finds himself enraptured by the irradiations of pre-existing grace. Now the man in question may not have the strength, virtues, and intelligence needed for adapting himself, and in this case he will be what is called—rightly or wrongly—a false mystic. This amounts to saying that a false mystic may be a "true mystic in disequilibrium", the word "mystical" referring only to the passive states of rapture and not to the active resources of the man; it is in no way necessary to assume that these states are false in themselves, that their causes must be pathological or diabolical or both at once;[18] in other words the criteria of

---

"heaviness" of his state.

[16] According to Ibn Arabi and others, *al-Rahmānu tanaffasa* means: God the infinitely Good enlarged, deployed, and "consoled" the cosmos (*al-kawn*) after the constriction or "distress" (*karb*) in which it found itself before its manifestation, hence in its state of potentiality. The divine Exhalation is what gives the world—and the human microcosm—its existence at every "moment".

[17] Obviously grace is always the initial cause or motive force of these conditions.

[18] This was the case with Nietzsche when writing his *Zarathustra*, but here precisely

falsity are not necessarily in the objective nature of the states in question, but they are always in the disequilibrium of the subject, in his lack of spiritual virtue, his incapacity for integrating these states into his ordinary consciousness and active life.[19]

Only the false mystic is completely passive; the true mystic cannot be so on the level of his will since sanctity requires equilibrium, hence strength. There are men who become saints because nature—or Providence—has placed them over an abyss; not wishing to be swallowed up, they have no choice but sanctity.

From another angle one must never lose sight of this: every quality—in relation to its essential reality, not its degree of existence—really "is" what it represents; it is never entirely separated from the universal "genius" from which it is derived; every beatitude "is" in some manner Beatitude as such even if the individual particularities happen to be morbid. Diabolical illusion could not reside in the positive nature of the facts; it is by detaching symbols from God—that is, by turning them aside not from their nature or content but from their positive function in relation to us—that the devil makes them illusory and satanic. Everything is true in its qualitative content and false in its existential limitation; the devil seduces with this content and kills with this limitation.

In the mystical life the subjective fact is relative; it may be a support but it is not a guarantee. Its value lies in its analogical quality and its danger in its character of opposition in relation to God, a character that pertains in principle to every existential relativity. In certain cases—depending on individual perspectives, methods, states of grace, and dispositions—it is the analogy that predominates in the inner life and removes from the simple fact its deadly limitation; in other cases

---

no confusion is possible with true inspiration.

[19] Orientals feel no awkwardness in recognizing grace in its accidental connections with disequilibrium; such is the case with the *majādhib* (*majdhūb*, "attracted") Muslims, for example; the Orthodox Church knows similar cases. In the East the criterion of the "false mystic"—taking this word in keeping with the idea usually attached to it—is not the morbid state, provided real graces are joined to it, but the satanic inspiration that may become grafted onto such a state; it goes without saying that the unbalanced man who benefits from graces is nonetheless deemed abnormal and "irregular", so that a strict distinction between the saint and the illumined psychopath is always maintained.

the opposite occurs: the limitation, the bare fact, will remove from the analogy its power of grace. Sublime states border on abysses.

*

* *

The "activity" of the initiate—that is, the man who possesses a metaphysical doctrine and a corresponding method in addition to initiation—cannot be taken to mean that the individual oversees or controls divine action, for the individual, which is precisely what must be transcended, cannot judge what surpasses him. What judges is the impersonal intelligence illuminated by the Intellect, not fluctuating and self-interested thought; and what is judged is the totality of the human repercussions of grace, not grace itself.

*

* *

When *bhakti* becomes exoteric intellection becomes more and more excluded and is replaced by a moral individualism, which tends to be sufficient in itself. The technical element of spirituality, concentration, finds itself replaced by sentimentality; in place of symbolism there is literalism and anthropomorphism.

In an integral spirituality there are two active positions and one that is passive: the spirit is active in its participation in metaphysical truths not because it is engaged in work but because intellectual contemplation is active by its very nature, which means that its activity is essential or principial; on the other hand the will is active in concentration and in everything connected with it—in short, in the elimination of "distractions" in the widest and deepest sense. But man always remains passive in relation to grace just as reason is passive in relation to intellectual intuition; nonetheless God is not arbitrary and does not refuse His grace to the soul that has put itself in the required state of readiness just as nature does not refuse fire to wood that is dry and sufficiently heated by rubbing.

Grace intervenes to the extent that obstacles are eliminated but without losing its divine freedom; for it may give itself gratuitously, hence without any apparent merit on the part of man and for reasons God alone knows. Conversely it may come about that regular methodical activity does not attract grace, but then its regularity is only apparent and altogether outward, and it suffers from a fundamental flaw in its intention: in such a case activity is not directed toward truth and the glory of God but toward man's secret vanity. It is for this reason that the intention must be ceaselessly purified, which is possible only with divine aid.

*

* *

In a spirituality that is exteriorized and popularized the intelligence is entirely passive, whereas the will is active only on the strictly individual level and not in direct connection with contemplation. Passivity in relation to grace extends in this case to all the planes of intelligence.

There remains also this difference: in an integral spirituality virtue is passive in the sense that it is a conformity to a pre-existent inner reality, whereas in exoterism it is active in the sense that it is an individual affirmation, *creatio ex nihilo*, merit; its character is not contemplative but practical.

Contemplation is like resting in space, and the will is like a battle against time; space contains what "is" and time what "may be". Virtue possesses two aspects: it reflects the nature of things, but from another point of view it also reflects what "should be".

IV

VEDĀNTA

1

The *Vedānta* stands out among explicit doctrines as one of the most direct formulations possible of what constitutes the very essence of our spiritual reality; this directness is offset by its requirement of renunciation or, more precisely, total detachment (*vairagya*).

The Vedantic perspective finds its equivalents in the great religions that regulate humanity, for truth is one; the formulations, however, may be dependent on dogmatic perspectives that restrict their immediate intelligibility or that make it difficult to express them in a straightforward way. In fact, whereas Hinduism is composed of what might be called autonomous fractions, the monotheistic religions are organisms in which the parts are formally bound up with the whole.

Hinduism, while it is organically linked with the *Upanishads*, is nonetheless not reducible to Shivaite and Shankarian Vedantism, although this must be regarded as the essence of the *Vedānta* and thus of Hindu tradition.

*

* *

Shankarian *Vedānta*, which is what we are thinking of especially here—and which is divine and immemorial in its origin and in no sense the creation of Shankara, who was only its great and providential spokesman—is concerned above all with the mental virtues, those which converge upon perfect and permanent concentration, whereas moral systems, whether Hindu or monotheistic, extend the same principles to the domain of action, which is nearly suppressed in the case of the wandering monk (*sannyāsin*). In the case of the Muslim, for example, calmness of mind (*shama*) thus becomes contentment (*ridhā*) or confidence in God (*tawakkul*), which in fact produces calmness of mind. *Vedānta* retains the alchemical essence of the virtues.[1]

---

[1] This is what Ibn al-Arif also does when he seems to reject the religious virtues one by one; in reality he detaches them from both the self-interested ego and the anthropomorphic aspect of the Divinity in order to keep only their essences. Let us note that Hinduism also knows contentment (*santosha*) and confidence in God (*prapatti*), but

*

*   *

According to *Vedānta* the contemplative must become absolutely "Himself"; according to other perspectives, such as those of the Semitic religions, man must become absolutely "Other" than himself—or "myself"—which amounts to exactly the same thing from the point of view of pure truth.

*

*   *

In Sufism the term *Huwa,* "He", in no way signifies that the divine Aseity is conceived in an objectified mode, but only that it is beyond the subject-object distinction, which is designated by the terms *anā-anta*, "I-thou".

The "divine Subject", in "descending" to the plane of cosmic objectification, illuminates it by virtue of the mystery of "Spirit", *al-Rūh*; and it "sustains" as well as "absorbs" this plane by virtue of the mystery of "Light", *al-Nūr*.[2]

*

*   *

The demiurgic tendency is conceived in *Vedānta* as an objectification and in Sufism as an individuation, hence in fact as a subjectification: God in this case is not pure "Subject" as in the Hindu perspective but pure "Object", "He" (*Huwa*), That which no subjective vision limits; this divergence is present only in the form, for it goes without saying that the Vedantic "Subject" is anything but an individual determination and that the Sufi "Object" is anything but the effect of "ignorance"; the "Self" (*Ātmā*) is "He", for it is "purely objective" inasmuch as it excludes all individuation, and the "He" (*Huwa*) is "Self", hence "purely subjective", in the sense that it excludes all objectification.

the *sannyāsin* goes beyond them.

[2] On this subject see the chapter *Al-Nūr* in our book *L'œil du cœur*.

The Sufi formula *Lā anā wa lā Anta: Huwa* ("Neither I nor Thou: He") is thus equivalent to the Upanishadic formula *Tat tvam asi* ("That art thou").

*
* *

Where the Vedantist speaks of the "unicity of the Subject"—or more precisely of its "nonduality", *advaita*—a Sufi speaks of the "unicity of Existence", that is, of "Reality", *wahdat al-Wujūd*; the difference in Hindu terms is that the Vedantist emphasizes the aspect *Chit* ("Consciousness") and the Sufi the aspect *Sat* ("Being").[3]

What surpasses individuality and all separateness in man is not only pure "Consciousness" but also pure "Existence". Asceticism purifies the existential side of man and thus indirectly the intellectual side.

If a man confined himself to "being", he would be holy; this is what Quietism believed it had understood.

*
* *

Ātmā is pure Light and Bliss, pure "Consciousness", pure "Subject".[4] There is nothing unrelated to this Reality; even the "object" least in

---

[3] At least in the school of *Wujūdiyah* (from *Wujūd*, "Existence", *Wujūd mutlaq* being "absolute Existence", God), though not in the school of *Shuhūdiyah* (from *shuhūd*, "unmediated vision", the word *Shāhid* meaning "Witness", exactly like the Sanskrit word *Sākshin*); the perspective of *Shuhūdiyah* is very similar to that of *Vedānta*. The two perspectives necessarily have a Koranic foundation, but the first is doubtless more in conformity with the most apparent meaning of the Book; the second has been falsely accused of immanentism because of its thesis concerning the "Sole Witness" and the indefinitely diversified "mirrors".

[4] Far from being merely psychological, the notion of the "subject" is primarily logical and principial and therefore cannot be restricted to any particular domain; the obvious subjectivity of the faculties of sensation already proves that the pair "subject-object" does not belong solely to the realm of psychology. All the more is it true that metaphysical notions such as the "Witness" (*Sākshin*) in the *Vedānta* or the "Knower" in Sufism (*al-ʿĀqil*, with its complement *al-Maʿqūl*, the "Known"), or again the "divine Subjectivity" (*Anniyah*, with its complement *Huwiyah*, the "divine Objectivity"), have nothing whatsoever to do with psychology.

conformity with it is still it, but "objectified" by *Māyā*, the power of illusion resulting from the infinity of the Self.

This is the very definition of universal objectification. But it is necessary to distinguish further between two fundamental modes within it—one "subjective" and the other "objective"—of which the first is the following: between the object as such and the pure and infinite Subject there stands in a certain way the objectified Subject, that is, the cognitive act, which by means of analysis and synthesis brings the bare object back to the Subject: this function—objectifying in relation to the Subject, which then projects itself as it were onto the objective plane, or subjectifying in relation to the object, which is integrated within the subjective and thus returned to the divine Subject—is the knowing and discerning spirit, the manifested intelligence, the relative consciousness: relative and therefore liable in its turn to become an object of knowledge.

The other fundamental mode of objectification may be described as follows: in order to realize the Subject, which is *Sat* (Being), *Chit* (Knowledge or Consciousness), and *Ānanda* (Bliss), it is necessary to know that objects are superimposed upon the Subject and to concentrate one's mind on the Subject alone. Between the objective world, which is then identified with "ignorance" (*avidyā*), and the Subject, the Self (*Ātmā*), there is interposed an objectification of the Subject; this objectification is direct and central: it is revelation, truth, grace, hence also the *Avatāra*, the *guru*, the doctrine, the method, the *mantra*.

Thus the sacred formula, the *mantra*, symbolizes and incarnates the Subject by objectifying it; and by "covering", or rather putting itself "in place of", the objective world—this dark cavern of ignorance—the *mantra* leads the spirit lost in the labyrinth of objectification back to the pure Subject.

This is why the *mantra* and its practice, *japa*, are referred to as "recollection" in the most diverse traditions: with the aid of the symbol, the divine Name, the distracted and separated spirit "remembers" that it is pure "Consciousness", pure "Subject", pure "Self".

*

*   *

That the Real and unreal are "not different" does not in any way imply either the unreality of the Self or the reality of the world; the Real is not "nondifferent" with respect to the unreal, but the unreal is "nondifferent" with respect to the Real—not insofar as it is unreality but insofar as it is a "lesser Reality", which is nonetheless "extrinsically unreal" in relation to absolute Reality.

*

* *

Māyā—the illusion or "divine art"[5] which expresses *Ātmā* according to indefinitely varied modes and of which *avidyā*, the ignorance concealing *Ātmā*, is the purely negative aspect—proceeds mysteriously from *Ātmā* itself in the sense that *Māyā* is a necessary consequence of the infinity of *Ātmā*; Shankaracharya expresses this by saying that *Māyā* is without beginning.

Ātmā is beyond the opposition subject-object; one may call it the "pure Subject", however, when one begins with a consideration of "objects", which are so many "superimpositions" in relation to *Ātmā*.

Māyā is the objectifying or manifesting tendency. The principal degrees of objectification or manifestation are the "feet" (*pādas*) of *Ātmā* or, from the viewpoint of the microcosmic sequence, its "envelopes" (*koshas*). Each degree of objectification is equivalent to a more or less indirect image of *Ātmā* and reflects it inversely; at the same time each degree brings about an inversion in relation to the one which is above it and by which it is contained, and this is because the relationship Subject-objectification or Principle-manifestation is repeated from one *pāda* or *kosha* to another; thus animic or subtle objectification is principal in relation to corporeal or gross objectification, and likewise nonformal objectification is principal in relation to formal objectification, which itself contains both the animic and corporeal planes. But the universal and fundamental inversion between the Subject and objectification is never done away with as a result of the inversions contained within the objectification itself, for

[5] Ananda K. Coomaraswamy suggested the word "art" as a translation of *Māyā* to show its positive function.

these are never produced under the same relationship nor under any relationship capable of nullifying the first inversion: inversion within an inversion is therefore never an inversion of the inversion, that is, a re-establishment of the "normal" relationship. In other words the subordinate inversion—which, within the great inversion represented by the cosmos in relation to the Self, appears as if it ought to overcome it since it inverts it symbolically—is in its turn inverted in relation to the divine Norm: thus an opaque body does not become transparent when painted white to compensate for its opacity even though the color white represents light or transparency, hence the negation of opacity; and the fact that a body is black adds nothing to its opacity.[6] Therefore, even though formal manifestation, both subtle and gross, is inverse in relation to nonformal manifestation, this inversion does not do away with the inversion realized by nonformal manifestation in relation to that nonmanifestation—or nonobjectification—which is the Self, the Subject.

*

*   *

It is very easy to label as "vague" and "contradictory" something one cannot understand because of a failure of "intellectual vision". In general, rationalist thinkers refuse to accept a truth that presents contradictory aspects and is situated, seemingly beyond grasping, between two extrinsic and negative statements. But there are some realities that can be expressed in no other way. The ray that proceeds from a light is itself light inasmuch as it illuminates, but it is not the light from which it proceeded; therefore it is neither this light nor something other than this light; in fact it is nothing but light, though growing ever weaker in proportion to its distance from its source. A faint glow is light for the

---

[6] When Sufism teaches that the trees of Paradise have their roots above, it would be wrong to try to grasp this idea by means of the imagination, for the relation in question, once it is translated into terrestrial forms, is expressed precisely by the terrestrial position of trees; in other words, if one were to behold the trees of Paradise, a spirit endowed with the appropriate faculty of vision would accept them as "normal", exactly in the same way as the mind accepts the trees on this earth. In this regard it is instructive to note that the retina of the eye receives only inverted images; it is the mind that reestablishes the normal and objective relationship.

darkness it illuminates but darkness for the light whence it emanates. Similarly *Māyā* is at once light and darkness: as "divine art" it is light[7] inasmuch as it reveals the secrets of *Ātmā;* it is darkness inasmuch as it hides *Ātmā*. As darkness it is "ignorance", *avidyā*.[8]

*
*   *

In spiritual realization the cosmic tendency of objectification is captured by the symbol: in the natural course of its drawing away from *Ātmā*, the soul meets the objectification—no longer indirect but direct—of the pure "Subject"; the indirect objectification is the world with its endless diversity, and the direct objectification is the symbol, which replaces the pure "Subject" on the objectified plane. *Ātmā* is in the center of man as "Subject", pure and infinite, and around man as the indefinitely differentiated objectification of this "Subject". The *yogin* or *mukta*, the "delivered one", perceives *Ātmā* in everything, but the man who is undelivered must superimpose on the world the synthetic and direct image of *Ātmā* in order to eliminate the superimposition represented by the world itself in relation to *Ātmā*. A symbol is anything that serves as a direct support for spiritual realization, for example a *mantra* or a divine Name, or in a secondary way a written, pictorial, or sculptural symbol such as a sacred image (*pratīka*).

*
*   *

The revelation of Sinai, the Messianic redemption, and the descent of the Koran are so many examples of the "subjectivizing objectification"

---

[7] "*Māyā*, precisely because she is the divine 'art' inherent in the Principle, is also identified with 'Wisdom', *Sophia*, understood in exactly the same sense as is given it in the Judeo-Christian tradition; and as such she is the mother of the *Avatāra*" (René Guénon, "*Māyā*", in *Études Traditionnelles*, July-August 1947). This is what Islamic esoterism designates by the terms "Science" (*'Ilm*) and "Light" (*Nūr*).

[8] In Islamic terminology "association" (*shirk*) corresponds to this "ignorance", that is, the fact of associating a "superimposition" with Unity.

effected by the symbol, in which *Ātmā* is "incarnated" in *Māyā* and *Māyā* "expresses" *Ātmā*.

*
*   *

To say, as do the Vedantists, that *Māyā* is an attribute of *Īshvara* and that *Māyā* expresses *Īshvara* while at the same time veiling Him signifies clearly that the world is derived from the infinity of *Ātmā*; one could also say that the world is a consequence of the absolute necessity of Being.

*
*   *

If *Māyā* is presented as a postulate, this must not be understood in a philosophical or psychological sense as if it were a question of a "hypothesis", for this postulate is necessary and therefore corresponds to an objective reality. Insofar as *Māyā* is a purely negative factor of objectification, it cannot be known positively; it therefore imprints itself on the intelligence as an "unextended" and "ungraspable" element.

*
*   *

Māyā in a certain sense is the possibility for Being of not being. All-Possibility must by definition and on pain of contradiction include its own impossibility.

It is in order not to be that Being incarnates in the multitude of souls; it is in order not to be that the ocean squanders itself in a myriad of flecks of foam.

If the soul obtains deliverance, this is because Being is.

*
*   *

Nothing is outside absolute Reality; the world is therefore a kind of inward dimension of *Brahma*. But *Brahma* is without relativity; and yet the world is a necessary aspect of the absolute necessity of *Brahma;* expressed another way, relativity is an aspect of the Absolute.

Relativity, *Māyā,* is the *Shakti* of the Absolute, *Brahma.*

If the relative did not exist, the Absolute would not be the Absolute.

*

* *

The essence of the world, which is diversity, is *Brahma;* it might be objected that *Brahma* cannot be the essence of a diversity since it is nonduality. Certainly *Brahma* is not the essence of the world, for in relation to the Absolute the world does not exist; but one can say that the world, to the extent it does exist, has *Brahma* for its essence, for otherwise it would have no reality whatsoever. Diversity itself is simply the inverse reflection of the infinity—or all-possibility—of *Brahma.*

*

* *

Natural things are the indirect objectifications of the Self; the supernatural is its direct and lightning-like objectification.

The cosmos is the total objectification, "made in the image of God", which includes all other cosmic objectifications.

The cosmic objectification of the Self presupposes the divine objectification, Being: *Īshvara* or *Apara-Brahma.* Sufism expresses it by this formula: "I was a hidden treasure, and I wished to be known."

*

* *

"Union" (*yoga*): the Subject (*Ātmā*) becomes object (the *Veda,* the *Dharma*) that the object (the objectified subject, man) might become the (absolute) Subject.

"Deification": God became man that man might become God. "Man" pre-exists in God—this is the "Son"—and "God" pre-exists in man: this is the Intellect. The point of contact between God and man is objectively Christ and subjectively the purified heart, intelligence-love.

"Unification" (*tawhīd*): the One (*illā 'Llāh*) became "nothingness" (*lā ilāha*) that "nothingness" might become the One; the One became separate and multiple (the Koran) that the separate and multiple (the soul) might become the One. The "multiple" pre-exists in the One—this is the uncreated Koran, the eternal Word—and the "One" pre-exists in the multiple: this is the heart-intellect and, in the macrocosm, the universal Spirit.

2

The conceptions of Ramanuja are contained in those of Shankara and transcended by them. When Shankara sees a direct and tangible manifestation of the unreality of sensory objects in their localization and duration, he does not say that they do not exist insofar as they are objects, as Ramanuja seems to have believed, but he says that insofar as they are existing objects they are unreal. Ramanuja maintains truths against Shankaracharya that Shankaracharya never denied on their own level.

Ramanuja has a tendency to "concretize" everything in relation to the created world, a tendency that corresponds very well with both the Vishnuite point of view and the Western outlook, which shares the same perspective.

*

*　　*

The antagonism between Shankara and Nagarjuna is of the same order as that between Ramanuja and Shankara, with this difference, however: when Shankara rejects the Nagarjunian doctrine, it is because its form corresponds—independently of its real content and spiritual potential—to a more restricted perspective than that of *Vedānta*. When on the other hand Ramanuja rejects the Shankarian doctrine, it is for the opposite reason: the perspective of Shankara surpasses that of Ramanuja not merely by its form but in its very foundation.

In order truly to understand Nagarjuna or the *Mahāyāna* in general, it is necessary to take account of two facts before everything else: first that Buddhism presents itself essentially as a spiritual method and therefore subordinates everything to the methodic point of view and second that this method is essentially one of negation; from this it follows that metaphysical reality is considered in relation to method, that is, as "state" and not as "principle", and that it is conceived in negative terms: *Nirvāna*, "Extinction", or *Shūnyā*, "Emptiness". In Buddhist wisdom "affirmation" has the same meaning and function as ignorance in Hindu wisdom; to describe *Nirvāna* or *Shūnyā* in positive terms would amount—in Vedantic language—to wishing to know the pure

Subject, "divine Consciousness", *Ātmā*, on the plane of objectification itself, hence on the plane of ignorance.

*
* *

When Westerners refer to something as "positive" they almost always think of manifestation, the created, whence their preference for the Ramanujian perspective and their mistake in attributing "abstractions" to Shankara—or Plato.

God is "abstraction" for the world because the world is "abstraction" in relation to God;[1] now it is God who is real, not the world.

*
* *

People all too readily believe that the content of a statement is false to the extent it can be attacked dialectically; now every statement whose content is not a fact that can be tested physically or rationally, hence every transcendent truth, can be contradicted by arguments drawn from experience. Shankara never said that the inevitably human formulation of a truth—concerning absolute "Consciousness", for example—could not be attacked; he said that such formulations were intrinsically true, something reason alone could not verify. When Advaitists assert that "Consciousness" has a particular nature and that the example of deep sleep shows it, this does not at all mean that they themselves need this example or can be discomfited by a demonstration of the fissures it necessarily contains; obviously one makes use of an example not because of an opposing aspect but for the sake of analogy; opposing aspects do exist, but they need not be taken into account. If we say that any light is like the sun compared to an opaque body, the fact that this light has neither the form nor the dimensions

---

[1] It should be noted here that the word "God" does not and cannot admit of any restriction, and this is for the simple reason that God is "all that is purely principial", hence also—and *a fortiori*—"Beyond-Being"; one may not know this or may deny it, but it cannot be denied that God is "That which is supreme", hence That which nothing can surpass.

110

nor the matter of the sun is absolutely without significance in this connection; if an example differed in no way from the thing to be demonstrated, it would not be an example but the thing itself.

*
*   *

Intellectual intuition conveys *a priori* the reality of the Absolute.

Reasoning thought infers the Absolute by starting from the relative; thus it does not proceed by intellectual intuition, though it does not inevitably exclude it.[2]

---

[2] "In our philosophy God is essentially and before all else the first Cause and prime Mover. Our reason for admitting His existence, our motive in recognizing in Him certain attributes, is that the existence and attributes in question are inferred, whether in a mediate or an immediate manner, from the existence of our starting point, the Cosmos. *Ducitur tamen ex sensibilibus intellectus noster in divinam cognitionem ut cognoscat de Deo quia est, et alia hujus modi quae oportet attribui primo Principio* (Saint Thomas, 1 *Contra Gent.*, 3). For the Vedantist the question presents itself in a completely different way. For him the point of departure is the Absolute, the Supreme *Brahma*. He first determines what the Absolute is, the infinite Being, the *ens a se et per se*; when he has established its attributes, he then tries to explain the world in relation to Him—or to That—who is without restrictive qualifications, without dependence, and who is therefore the Unconditioned. This difference in starting points leads to important consequences. We Scholastics never feel tempted to deny the existence of the sensible world. It is the very basis of our doctrine. To suppress it would be tantamount to cutting the ground from beneath our feet. We will give up anything rather than give up the world of experience, for to renounce this would be to give up everything. It is possible that certain fragments of the real do not fit very well into our philosophical monument; so be it: we shall carve and adapt them, or better still we shall admit our insufficiencies. But to abandon the reality of the world—this we cannot do, for it is the cornerstone, and if we remove it the whole edifice will come crashing down. Our theodicy may therefore collide with apparent antinomies; but one thing at least is certain: a creator is required in order to make our world intelligible, and so a creator we shall have, even if it is difficult to reconcile the creation with the infinite immutability of an absolute that is a subsisting perfection and plenitude. The attitude of the Vedantist is and must be quite different. He begins with the Supreme and its attributes. Now the Supreme—whether one calls it God in Himself or *Para-Brahma*, which for the moment is of no importance—is Being itself, and more than that it is infinite. It is Intelligence in the pure state, saturation of Bliss, Being that is immense, necessary, and sufficient. It is in everything, and nothing else is outside it. This is the thesis, the starting point, of the doctrine; and the rest, if it is explainable, must be explained in relation to this primary truth. We say: let all else perish, but the reality of the Cosmos must remain! The Vedantist says: let the rest perish, but the Supreme

Arguments have an absolute value for philosophy; for intellectual intuition their value is symbolical and provisional.

Shankara did not "construct a system";[3] he did not "seek a solution" for a given "problem"; he did not suffer from what he himself calls the disease of doubt.

Shankara is like a colorless glass through which the rays of light are allowed to pass intact whereas Ramanuja is comparable to a colored glass, which in transmitting light imparts to it a certain tint; this means that Ramanuja's doctrine is also inspired and not invented. Sages are instruments for the crystallization of pure Light; they are anything but inventors of systems. It is intellection that determines everything, the mode of expression being dictated by the requirements of the respective traditional form. With philosophers in the ordinary sense of the word, the initiative comes from the human side—from mental rest-

---

must remain what it is: the absolute of Being, implying eternity, independence, and aseity!" (G. Dandoy, *L'ontologie du Vedānta*). No better definition could be given of the differences between pure metaphysics, which proceeds directly from the Intellect, and philosophy, which proceeds from reason; it is fair to add, however, that the passage quoted does not entirely do justice to Scholasticism and that the distinction is too systematic; nonetheless it has the merit of contrasting the viewpoints with perfect clarity. According to the same author, "The theory of the self in *Advaita* is established almost entirely on the basis of a gratuitous hypothesis, which is that the self is purely actual. Only one thing truly pertains to the self, namely, that the self always manifests *in actu*—that is, according to *Advaita*, as pure consciousness or intellectual light. Now this hypothesis does not rest on any proof." If there is a gratuitous hypothesis, it is certainly the assertion that there are hypotheses in metaphysics; moreover, nothing in metaphysics rests upon "proofs"; examples figure in it only as illustrations and play a part only in a clearly defined respect; it is useless to set out to attack their inevitable flaws, which are of no interest to the metaphysician and which in no way weaken his thesis. Furthermore Vedantists have never affirmed, as the author we have quoted seems to believe, that consciousness cannot in any way "turn back on itself", for otherwise it would be impossible to have the least notion of it; what they have stated is that it cannot in itself become its own object, which is something quite different. *Advaita* does not "suppose" that the Self is *actus purus*, and it does not "conclude" that all potentiality is but illusion; since it is not a philosophy, it is founded upon neither suppositions nor conclusions, nor any other mental crutches.

[3] We mean by this an assemblage of concordant reasonings hierarchically arranged. It is true that one can always describe an orthodox doctrine as a "system" when comparing it to some system in nature, such as the solar system; in fact a doctrine is naturally an assemblage of ideas arranged harmoniously around a central idea, from which they are derived according to various "dimensions".

lessness, doubt, the absence of a contemplative quality; their attitude is not "prophetic" but "Promethean".

*

* *

God cannot change; hence He cannot be the cause of a change as such. He is the cause of all things, and He is therefore the cause of what appears to us as change; but He is its cause not insofar as it is a change but insofar as this apparent change—which for us is real—affirms an aspect of the Immutable. Or again, to consider simply change as such: God is its cause only insofar as the change, or all change, expresses the divine infinity or all-possibility in the language of diversity.

The world cannot have God for its cause insofar as it is subject to change; from the standpoint of its negative character, the world is not. On the other hand, insofar as it expresses infinity—not insofar as it negates immutability—change must have God for its cause, and in this respect the world exists even though in the final analysis it is reducible to this cause itself. To the extent it is ontologically positive the effect is not really distinct from its cause.

*

* *

It has sometimes been argued that the delivered sage, the *vidvān*, having attained the state from which there is no return into the "karmic" chain of "samsaric" existences, has passed beyond our knowledge and can therefore no longer speak or teach. Now Advaitists have never denied the double nature of the *vidvān*. If Christianity were not the religion of the West and if the twofold nature of Christ were not a dogma, no doubt the same philosophers who look for contradictions in the *Vedānta* would declare the two natures of Christ to be "incompatible" and would describe this dogma as a "failure"; they would do the same with regard to the Trinity.

*

* *

It is contradictory to maintain—in order to deny the reality of the absolute Subject—that the intellective light is real only in relation to its projection on an external object and that it therefore has a merely relative and extrinsic reality. A contrast can reveal the nature of something or bring out its value, but it cannot create this nature; it cannot reveal a nature that does not exist. God is Light in Himself, not because He illuminates our darkness; on the contrary He illuminates the darkness because He is Light in itself; He is not Love because He loves but He loves because He is Love.

*
*   *

Between the soul and *Brahma* there is at once continuity and discontinuity, depending on how the relationship is viewed: continuity from the point of view of essential nature, which is "consciousness", and discontinuity from the point of view of "actual" nature, which is pure "Consciousness" on the divine side and objectified consciousness on the human side—objectified in its very cosmic root and consequently darkened, limited, and divided by *avidyā*, ignorance. It follows that the individual substance, even when empirically emptied of its "objective" contents, is by no means thereby rid of the fundamental vice of objectification, which can be eliminated only by Knowledge.

A given being as such—to the extent, in other words, that it is a mode of objectification—necessarily regards the one and only "Consciousness", from which in reality it is not distinct, as "external"; parallel to their state of "identity" and on another plane, the *Avatāra*s worshiped God as "outside" themselves.

The great defect of the soul—the "original sin"—is not the accidental objectification that causes a being to be distracted by one or another given thing but rather the fundamental objectification that makes this possible; now the fundamental objectification is collective and hereditary and belongs to the species, not to the will of the individual.

Pseudo-Vedantist "subjectivism"—which in reality is solipsism—is unable to explain the objective homogeneity of the cosmic environment.

*

* *

When objectified as *jivātmā* or *ahankāra, Ātmā* is the subject of mental objectification; it is thus a subject already objectified, secondary, and relative.

When the individual empties his mind of every object, he approaches *Ātmā* in a certain symbolical way; but the objectification represented by the individual as such is not thereby abolished—far from it. Spiritual realization is neither solipsism nor autosuggestion.

*

* *

Christ could say: "Why callest thou me good? There is none good but one, that is God." This signifies that everything necessarily participates in the essential attributes of relativity.

Shankaracharya used such expressions as this: "I prostrate myself before *Govinda*, whose nature is supreme Bliss." And Ramakrishna said: "In the Absolute I am not and you are not and God—to the extent He is personal—is not, for the Absolute is beyond all speech and thought. But as long as there still exists something outside myself, I must worship *Brahma* within the limits of my mind as something outside me."

*

* *

Direct analogy and inverse analogy: as for the first, a tree reflected in water will never be anything but a tree; as for the second, the reflected tree will always be upside down.

Between God and the world, the Principle and manifestation, the Uncreated and the created, there is always—though in different respects—both direct analogy and inverse analogy. Thus the ego is not only a reflection but also a negation of the Self; therefore God can be called the "divine I" by analogy with what is positive, conscious, and immortal in the human "I", but He can also be called "He" in opposition to the negative, ignorant, and unreal aspects of the human "I". The word "Self" expresses the analogy as opposition.

*

*   *

To say that Reality can never be attained by one who maintains the "objective illusion" is to forget that "union" does not at all depend on some particular terminology but on the fusion of two distinct elements, whether one calls them "subject" and "object" or something else; it amounts in any case to replacing the objective illusion, which is normal since it is general, with a subjective illusion, which is an abnormal and therefore far more dangerous error. In order to be united to something it is by no means necessary to begin by pretending that one is not separate from it in any way or in any respect—in short, that one does not exist; one must not replace intellection with a facile and blind conviction.

*

*   *

It is useless to seek to realize that "I am *Brahma*" before understanding that "I am not *Brahma*"; it is useless to seek to realize that "*Brahma* is my true Self" before understanding that "*Brahma* is outside me"; it is useless to seek to realize that "*Brahma* is pure Consciousness" before understanding that "*Brahma* is the almighty Creator".[4]

*

*   *

It is not possible to understand that the statement "I am not *Brahma*" is false before having understood that it is true. Likewise it is not possible to understand that the statement "*Brahma* is outside me" is not precise before having understood that it is; and likewise again it is not possible to understand that the statement "*Brahma* is the almighty Creator" contains an error before having understood that it expresses a truth.

---

[4] "No man cometh unto the Father, but by me." The following *hadīth* has the same meaning: "He who desires to meet God must first meet His Prophet."

*

*   *

If it were necessary to have realized the Self in order to be able to speak of it, how could a person who had not realized it know that it is necessary to have realized it in order to be able to speak of it? If some sage could alone know that it is the Self because he had realized it, how could his disciples know he had realized it and alone knew what the Self is?

Under these conditions there would remain only absolute ignorance face to face with absolute knowledge: there would be no possible contact with the Self, no spiritual realization, no difference between the intelligent man and the fool or between truth and error. To attribute to knowledge a purely subjective and empirical background that is at the same time absolute amounts to the very negation of the Intellect and thus of intellection; it is also a negation of inspiration and revelation—in other words a denial first of intelligence, then of its illumination by the Self, and finally of the Prophetic and Law-giving manifestation of the Self in a given world. It is thus the destruction of tradition, for the unicity and permanence of the *Veda* would remain inexplicable in these conditions; every "realized being" would write a new *Veda* and found a new religion; the *Sanātana Dharma* would be devoid of meaning.

*

*   *

Intellection, inspiration, revelation: these three realities are essential for man and the human collectivity; they are distinct from one another, but none can be reduced purely and simply to a question of "realization". The "realized" man can have inspirations that are distinct from his state of knowledge as far as their production is concerned,[5] but he cannot add one syllable to the *Veda*; and in any case inspirations may

---

[5] There are numerous examples of this: thus Sri Ramana Maharshi said that his stanzas (*Ulladu Narpadu* or *Sad-Vidya*) came to him as if "from outside", and he even described how they became fixed in his mind without the collaboration of his will.

depend on a spiritual function, for instance that of a pontiff,[6] just as they may also result from a mystical degree; as for revelation, it is very clear that the most perfect spiritual realization cannot bring it about, although conversely such a realization is its *conditio sine qua non*.

Intellection for its part is an essential condition of the realization in question, for it alone can give the human initiative its sufficient reason and efficacy. This fundamental role of pure intelligence is an aspect of "becoming what one is".

In a certain sense revelation is the intellection of the collectivity, or rather it takes its place; it is the only way of knowing for the collectivity as such, and this is why the *Avatāra* through whom the revelation is brought about must—in his normative perfection—incarnate the humanity he at once represents and illumines.

This is why the prayer of a saint is always a prayer of all and for all.

*

*   *

To believe with certain "neoyogists" that "evolution" will produce a superman "who will differ from man as much as man differs from the animal or the animal from the vegetable" is not to know what man is: it is one more example of a pseudo-wisdom that deems itself vastly superior to the "separatist" religions but in fact shows itself more ignorant than the most elementary catechism. For the most elementary catechism does know what man is: it knows that by his qualities, and as an autonomous world, he stands opposed to the other kingdoms of nature taken together; that in one particular respect—that of spiritual possibilities and not of animal nature—the difference between a monkey and a man is "infinitely" greater than that between a fly and a monkey. For man alone is able to leave the world; man alone is able to return to God; and this is the reason he cannot be surpassed by a new earthly being in any way. Man is central among the beings of the earth; this is an absolute position; there cannot be a center more central than the center if definitions have any meaning.

---

[6] This is directly connected with "grace of state", "authority", "infallibility", and the "aid of the Holy Spirit".

This neoyogism, like other similar movements, pretends that it can add an essential value to the wisdom of our ancestors; it believes the religions are partial truths that it is called upon to paste together after centuries or millennia of waiting and then to crown with its own naive little system.

*

* *

It is far better to believe the earth is a disk supported by a tortoise and flanked by four elephants than to believe—in the name of "evolution"—in the coming of some "superhuman" monster.

A literal interpretation of cosmological symbols is harmless if not positively useful whereas a scientific error such as evolutionism is neither literally nor symbolically true; the repercussions of its falsity are incalculable.

*

* *

The intellectual poverty of neoyogist movements provides an incontestable proof that there is no spirituality without orthodoxy. It is certainly not by chance that all these movements are in league as it were against the intelligence; intelligence is replaced by a form of thinking that is feeble and vague instead of logical, "dynamic" instead of contemplative. All these movements are characterized by an affectation of detachment with regard to pure doctrine, the incorruptibility of which they hate; for in their eyes this purity is "dogmatism"; they fail to understand that Truth does not deny forms from the outside but transcends them from within.

Orthodoxy includes and guarantees infinitely precious values, which man could not possibly draw from himself.

3

By virtue of his unalterable individual substance Sri Ramakrishna was a *bhakta*; now a *bhakta* is not a man who "thinks", that is, a man whose individuality actively participates in supra-individual knowledge and who is therefore able "himself" to apply his transcendent knowledge to cosmic and human contingencies; on the contrary the *bhakta* attains and possesses knowledge not in an intellectual but in an ontological manner. On the individual level the thinking of a *bhakta* is reduced to a sort of "planetary system" of his personal realization; otherwise it is the whole tradition, that from which the *bhakta* sprang, that "thinks" for him; it is the tradition that settles all problems situated outside the "system" in question. The objection that Ramakrishna was also a *jnānin* has no validity here, for quite apart from the fact that the distinction between *jnāna* and *bhakti* is before all else a principial one and in no way excludes an indefinite number of combinations between these two attitudes, the human substance of the *Paramahamsa* was plainly "bhaktic"; *jnāna* was able to deepen this human substance but not to change it. A sage is not a diagram but a "living" man; otherwise there would be no diversity among *muktas*; in other words the most perfect knowledge never does away with diversity; the individual substance always remains qualitatively what it is.

And this is very typical of Ramakrishna: he does not "think"[1] but endeavors to provoke oracles; it is Heaven that must think for him; for example it was Heaven that had to resolve the question of how the scriptural affirmation "gold is clay and clay is gold" was to be understood—a question the *jnānin* Shankaracharya would have settled in an instant as regards realization and with a stroke of the pen as regards dialectic. Nonetheless the procedure of Ramakrishna is entirely legitimate within the framework of *bhakti* since, as we have said, it is not *a priori* "intellectual"; *bhakti* plumbs mysteries through

---

[1] We have put this word in quotation marks to indicate that it has different shades of meaning and should not be taken in too restrictive a sense. Human language cannot do justice to all possible shades of the real. To the easy retort that Ramakrishna did "think"—which we have never doubted—we answer that it is not possible for us to write volumes about words.

"being" not "intelligence", and this ontological plasticity allows it to achieve a point of view from which it appears superior to "intellectuality" conceived in its mental and external aspect.

To say that Ramakrishna took up a standpoint where doctrinal truth no longer counted would be senseless; and yet it must be said that he was quick to look upon opinions—as far as their positive content is concerned—as "forms" expressing an element of truth; in other words he was fond of discovering one single and self-same essence at the root of opinions; he did not therefore place himself *a priori* at the intellectual point of view of orthodoxy but at the ontological point of view of reality.

*
*   *

Ramakrishna represented "realization" more especially insofar as it relativizes or even eliminates "theory"; unlike Shankara he did not represent the "Self" insofar as it objectifies itself through doctrine. From this it follows that "argumentation" could not be intellectual with Ramakrishna as it was with Shankara but had to be existential or ontological, if one may put it this way; this explains why he did not reply to the doubts of his disciple Narendra by means of a doctrinal demonstration but by an experience of "realization", a state of consciousness, hence of "being" not "thinking". But this also explains a certain lack of intellectual instinct in Ramakrishna: he took the mental dynamism of Narendra as marking an aptitude for *jnāna*, the kind of dynamism he himself lacked. And there lay his error: he wanted to place this unfamiliar "intelligence" at the service of "realization" without first taking account of the fact that intelligence is a different thing from mental power and that such power, when not determined by the pure Intellect, is prejudicial to the very "realization" that was precisely "everything" in Ramakrishnian spirituality. In this there was a kind of temptation or seduction: instead of keeping strictly to what was in conformity with his nature and his spiritual genius, the master encroached indirectly upon ground that was no longer his own, that of doctrinal intellectuality; he no doubt believed he must give his message of "realization" an "intellectual" dimension, which he himself did not need and which in fact betrayed him.

His strength lay in "realization" not "theory", as we have said; it is precisely for this reason that he was able—and obliged—to "incarnate" what is found at the heart of every revelation and is beyond all theoretical expression. Nonetheless, however paradoxical this may seem, his strength was also his weakness: he abhorred study and underestimated the scope of mental formulations; and yet mental formulations for their part did not leave him alone but surrounded him on every side. Seeing as he did only the divine "Mother" at the root of all things, he was little inclined to take false opinions seriously; he himself could abstain from "thinking", but this was not the case for other men—even less so insofar as the invading proximity of a spirit of criticism and debate made thinking a kind of obligation, even if only for purely defensive reasons.

*

* *

There is something in Ramakrishna that seems to defy every category: he was like the living symbol of the inward unity of religions; he was in fact the first saint to wish to enter into foreign spiritual forms, and in this consisted his exceptional and in a sense universal mission—something allying him to the prophets without making him a prophet in the strict sense of the word; in our times of confusion, distress, and doubt, he was the saintly "verifier" of forms and the "revealer" as it were of their single truth. This function is sufficient in itself, and it excludes in any case the establishment of an organization seeking to represent a "super-religion"; the assertion of the spiritual equivalence of the great revelations cannot become the basis of a system and even less of a method, for this would be a contradiction and pleonasm. What should have been done was to gather together the spiritual heritage of Ramakrishna in its strictly Hindu form while at the same time expressly maintaining, as characteristic of the saint, the idea of traditional universality; what should have been done was to establish the *ashram* at Dakshineswar near the temple—now said to be in a dilapidated state—and near the *panchabati*, the grove planted by the *Paramahamsa* and sanctified by his meditations and visions. This hallowed spot could have become a place of pilgrimage consecrated to the cult of the "Mother" and the veneration of the great foreign *Avatāras*: the Buddha,[2] Christ, the Prophet.[3]

*
*   *

The danger for the *Paramahamsa* lay in the following factors: first a *jnāna* that was in fact too experimental and therefore poorly structured extrinsically—whence an inadequate integration of the mind in his perspective—then a universalism that was purely "bhaktic" and therefore too easygoing, and finally the dissolving influence of modernism. If there was in him something like a partial error, a fatal imperfection, this is where it lay, and it found something like a center in the person of Narendra (Vivekananda): each of them was the ideal and the victim of the other. Narendra maintained that he loved nothing more than absorption in *samādhi*; he wished for nothing else, and no one could blame him for that; but the universalism of Ramakrishna was seeking for other modalities: with the extraordinary plasticity of his genius, the *Paramahamsa* wished to realize himself indefinitely through all possible modes; he wished to turn Narendra into an unlimited being because he believed he had discovered in the substance of the disciple and in the complementary polarity of their common substance a token of universality and limitlessness. Narendra "incarnated" in a natural, not a superhuman, way all that was humanly lacking in the tender and fragile Ramakrishna, unlettered country brahmin that he was; Narendra was the complement, the *alter ego*, the *shakti*.

*
*   *

Ramakrishnian *jnāna*, for which a lack of intellective aptitude is not an obstacle, is not strictly speaking *jnāna* as such. And in this lies the

---

[2] The Buddha is "foreign" in the sense that he stepped out of the Hindu framework and that his radiance, with certain exceptions, embraces only the people of East Asia.

[3] We name only those with whom Ramakrishna was concerned and who govern what are by far the most important religions.

vulnerability of his perspective: in his almost exclusive faith in the spiritual omnipotence of love. Fundamentally he does not pose the question whether men are in "truth" or in "error", but he asks instead: do they love God? In short, he becomes a *jnānin* by love or, in a more profound sense, by a thirst for reality, limitlessness, the Infinite—not by "knowledge" in the direct sense. He shatters the image of the Mother, the supreme "illusion", because he "wills" to do so, not because he "knows"; he "knows" in a sort of *a posteriori* manner, and not *a priori* like the pure *jnānin*. This weak point is not in itself a defect, provided the homogeneity of the spiritual system is maintained; nonetheless this weakness in the Ramakrishnian perspective—namely, its single-minded faith in the salvific power of *bhakti* at the price of doctrinal guarantees—was bound to lead to another weakness: underestimating the powers of illusion. There is nothing in the Ramakrishnian perspective that requires us to suppose it was completely impervious to illusion at the level of facts; the malleable, ingenuous, and cheerful temperament of the saint serves only to underscore this point.[4] But it must be added that these illusions would have remained harmless in the closed system of a pure Hinduism, and one may even ask oneself whether—within this framework—the things we can recognize in hindsight as having been illusory would not have revealed themselves as real thanks to an appropriate spiritual climate.

Another aspect of the enigma of Ramakrishna is his universalism; here again there existed a fatal antinomy, for integral universality, which leaves no dimension outside itself, requires the prophetic function by its very nature. Ramakrishnian universality was a universality without prophecy. A deviation was inevitable the moment people sought to give this unique universalism a collective and quasi-religious expression; nothing could have been more contrary to the spirit of Ramakrishna.

---

[4] We must never forget the disproportion that exists between spiritual reality and individuality. From a strictly spiritual point of view no illusion was possible for Ramakrishna. "To claim that 'I am He' is not a healthy attitude. Whoever entertains this ideal without first having overcome the consciousness of the physical ego suffers great harm, his progress is slowed, and little by little he is dragged downwards. He deceives others and deceives himself, remaining as he does in absolute unawareness of his own lamentable state" (*The Gospel of Sri Ramakrishna*).

Then there came a final fatality: the modernist influence, which is decisive. The insufficiently doctrinal character of Ramakrishnian *jnāna* and his lack of discernment with regard to conceptual forms—which did not seem to exist for him—then his ill-defined and somewhat imprudent universalism, and finally the dynamic and sentimental tendencies of Vivekananda: all this would have been free from danger within the framework of a Hinduism that was complete, closed, free from fissures; the environment would have rectified, neutralized, and counterbalanced whatever there might have been that was "subjective", "fragile", and "hazardous" in certain attitudes of the *Paramahamsa*.[5] Furthermore an integral or total Hinduism would not have allowed Vivekananda to open his mind to Western influences, which were unknown and incomprehensible to Ramakrishna but which stimulated in the disciple exactly those tendencies whose development had at times been feared by the master.[6] Everywhere in the master's life there were interferences—abnormal and incalculable in relation to the possibilities of the Hindu world—coming from the modern West, starting with the Arya Samaj and the Brahmo Samaj;[7] quite against his

[5] Monotheistic religions, with their invariable dogmatism and formal homogeneity, have a real advantage here in the sense that their very structure opposes the deviations to which *bhakti* is liable. The structure of Hinduism is too primordial not to be terribly vulnerable in such a period as our own; it is almost impossible for contemporary *bhakta*s to remain fully orthodox.

[6] On the subject of Narendra the master had two certainties: that of his spiritual possibility and that of his activity in the world; but he had no certainty as to the actualization of this possibility nor as to the quality of this activity among men, in spite of certain partial intuitions that were unilaterally and "subjectively" interpreted. Had Ramakrishna possessed this certainty, there would have been nothing to fear; now "Narendra was a skeptic, with no faith in the Hindu gods. He laughed at many of the injunctions of the Hindu scriptures. Yet Sri Ramakrishna instructed him with the infinite love and patience of an ideal teacher. He was full of admiration for Narendra's pure character and strength of mind. But he had apprehensions for him in one respect. He knew that the boy was endowed with rare potentialities, a fraction of which were sufficient to make him a powerful figure in the world, but if his tremendous energy was not directed into a spiritual channel, it might be misused: he might become the founder of a new sect or party, even though this was not his mission" (*Life of Sri Ramakrishna*, published by Swami Vireswarananda).

[7] A characteristic feature: his rejection of the Brahmo Samajist heresy had no doctrinal rigor but remained rather vague and instinctive. Where a Shankara or Ramanuja would have felled the Brahmo Samaj with one blow, Ramakrishna frequented these

inclination and moreover quite unsuspectingly, the *Paramahamsa* thus found himself at the crossroads of two worlds between which there was no common measure. His altogether primordial simplicity and candor, even his modesty, were not "up to"—we ought to say "down to"—dealing with these conditions; he grasped in them neither the principle nor the complexity.

It is here that Ramakrishna reveals a disturbing misapprehension: in wanting Narendra to "go beyond *samādhi*", not to be content with "so limited an ideal", and to be—like his master—"at once *jnānin* and *bhakta*", Ramakrishna attributed to his disciple a genius for ontologically metamorphic realization he neither possessed nor could have possessed; in order to realize *jnāna* Narendra would have had to begin with an intellectual comprehension of traditional doctrine instead of interpreting the *Vedānta* in terms of modern concepts and tendencies;[8]

---

sectaries as friends. If there was generosity in this attitude, there was also a measure of unconsciousness, which the sages of old would have labeled "culpable"; on the other hand this "tolerant" view can be explained by a presentiment of an inevitable adaptation of India to the modern world.

[8] Narendra might have been a born *bhakta*, but one accidentally deformed by a faulty education in school; he could not in any case have been a *jnānin* who had perfected his realization (*sādhana*) in a previous existence, and to discover this there was no need to plunge him into a passive state of *samādhi* in order to question him; it would have been sufficient to take account of natural criteria, the obvious and indisputable data. A sage who has perfected his *sādhana* and who is therefore born with "innate wisdom" proves his spiritual nature by accepting every manifestation of Truth at the first opportunity, and with the alacrity of genius; a man who, like the young Narendra, "missed no chance of turning the doctrine of Advaita to ridicule" (*Life of Sri Ramakrishna*), could not be a *jnānin* "incarnate". But this argument is altogether superfluous if one knows the writings of Vivekananda, which contain such things as this: "Jesus was not perfect because he did not give woman a place equal to that of man. Women did everything for him, and yet he was so much the slave of Jewish custom that not one of them was made an apostle." "The visions of Moses are more likely to be false than our own because we have more knowledge at our disposal and are less subject to illusions" (*Inspired Talks*). "The Buddhas and Christs we know are second rate heroes compared with those greater ones of which the world knows nothing. Hundreds of these unknown heroes have lived in every land" (*Karma-Yoga*). "We have seen that the theory of a personal God who created the world cannot be proven; is there still today a single child who could believe in it? . . . Your personal God, Creator of this world, has he ever helped you? This is the challenge now flung down by modern science!" (Lecture on *Vedānta*). "The totality of all living beings is the personal God" (Letter to Sister Nivedita). Such absurdities as these would be inconceivable in a Hindu who was not already modernized, just as they would be in

unlike his master, whose spiritual plasticity was of a miraculous order, he was not able to realize *jnāna* in what amounted to a "bhaktic" way—or rather in an ontological, hence extradoctrinal, way. But there is something else: this perfect simultaneity of *jnāna* and *bhakti* indicates a universality characteristic of prophets: if Ramakrishna judged "samadhic" contemplation too limited for Narendra, this means that he wished to make him into a prophet, at least practically speaking, for beyond sanctity there is only prophecy;[9] in order to be able to accomplish his mission a prophet alone has need of all the spiritual modes. It is true that such universality can also be found in the case of a saint who has no prophetic mandate, but this is exceptional, and it always implies a mission similar to that of prophecy within the religion from which the saint has sprung; such precisely was the case with Ramakrishna—and with him alone in the Hindu world of our times.

There was thus with Ramakrishna something like an unconscious encroachment on the prophetic function; nonetheless he never pretended to be the founder of a religion, quite the contrary; at the same time he did not prevent such a thing from taking place in his name: his excessive independence with regard to orthodoxy was bound indirectly to bring about this error[10]—an independence that suited the function of a prophet precisely; only a prophet has nothing to learn and must offer himself as a blank and untouched page to the divine Pen.

---

an orthodox Christian. Ramakrishna could not foresee effects whose causes he had not even imagined; what would he have said if he had known about the opinions quoted—and many others—which are so perfectly contrary to his own teachings? No euphemism can diminish the brutality of these contradictions.

[9] Prophecy is not a degree of sanctity; sanctity may be supreme without the prophetic office being added to it; on the other hand prophecy always presupposes supreme sanctity.

[10] We know there are contemplatives of the line of Ramakrishna whose spirituality is impeccable, whatever their opinions with regard to Vivekananda. Already in Vivekananda's day, Swami Brahmananda was teaching a perfectly regular doctrine; if he nonetheless admired the books of Vivekananda, perhaps for the simple reason that he admired the man, it was with that strange faculty for paradox that characterizes partially Westernized Orientals and renders them capable of thinking as if with two distinct brains, combining in this way a genuine depth with an astonishing superficiality.

*

* *

It would be possible to find an explanation of the Ramakrishna-Vive-
kananda enigma in the fact that the rise of Hindu nationalism was
inevitable and that Vivekananda was its predestined inspirer, that in
order to be able to play this part he needed the dynamic quality of
the West and thus certain of its ideological premises, that seen from
this angle his exaggerations and errors were only provisional, and that
in this consists the meaning of the master's prediction, and of others
like it: "Naren will shake the world to its very foundations." If one
assumes that for a Hindu the world is India, then Ramakrishna saw
aright: Vivekananda did give an impulse to Indian nationalism, which
might otherwise have had a materialistic and satanic character. In
"modernizing" Hinduism Vivekananda at the same time "Hinduized"
modernism, if one may put it this way, and by this means he neutralized some of its destructive impetus; in a word, if it was inevitable
that India would become a "nation", it was preferable for it to do so
in some way under the distant auspices of a Ramakrishna rather than
under the sign of a modernism that would brutally deny everything
India had stood for throughout the millennia.[11]

In the life of Vivekananda there is an almost continual struggle
between his powerful, proud nature and the "presence" of Ramakrishna, that is, the spiritualized psychic force the master had transmitted to him, which actualized itself one last time in Vivekananda
during the hours before his death. The master owed him this final

---

[11] Gandhian nationalism—with its pure and ascetic form, moderate character, and a
style that is basically Hindu compared with materialistic and mechanistic national-
isms—was able to develop as it did thanks to the Vivekanandian impulse; this was
a two-edged sword, as it were, but India had no choice; and after his own fashion
Ramakrishna seems to have had a presentiment of this. No doubt some will object
that any modernization, "Hinduizing" or not, will by its very nature always end in
a loss of spiritual values; this is true, but an influence that for any reason slows this
process has its usefulness nonetheless; it is clearly impossible to liken a Vivekananda
and a Gandhi to the creator of the "New Turkey" or any of the other protagonists of
extreme modernism. From another point of view, if one considers the lack of a sense
of proportion that seems to be the price paid for every form of *bhakti*, Vivekananda's
"shaking of the world" could also mean the celebrity he enjoyed outside of India.

grace—the master who had chosen this turbulent and haughty substance and touched it with his blessing, only then to set it adrift in the vortex between two worlds that were colliding and penetrating each another.

*

*   *

In Sri Ramana Maharshi one meets ancient and eternal India again. Vedantic truth—that of the *Upanishads*—is reduced to its simplest expression but without any betrayal: it is the simplicity inherent in the Real, not the artificial and quite external simplification that springs from ignorance.

The spiritual function that consists in an "action of presence" found its most rigorous expression in the Maharshi. In these latter days Sri Ramana was as it were the incarnation of what is primordial and incorruptible in India in opposition to modern activism; he manifested the nobility of contemplative "nonaction" in opposition to an ethic of utilitarian agitation, and he showed the implacable beauty of pure truth in opposition to passions, weaknesses, betrayals.

The great question "Who am I?" appears in his case as the concrete expression of a "lived" reality, if one may put it this way, and this authenticity gives each word of the Maharshi a perfume of inimitable freshness—the perfume of Truth, which incarnates itself in the most immediate way.

The whole *Vedānta* is contained in Sri Ramana's question: "Who am I?" The answer is the Inexpressible.

V

KNOWLEDGE AND LOVE

1

Whence does certainty come to saints and prophets regarding their supernatural inspirations? Why did Joan of Arc believe in her voices? It is because there is ontological evidence in the inspirations themselves: believing in them is as obvious as believing in one's own existence.

The same is true of ordinary inspirations, which are "natural" in their mode, that is, related to intellectual intuition and not revelation: metaphysical truths are accepted not merely because they are logically evident but because they are ontologically evident; being logically evident is only a mental trace.

Ontological evidence is part of our very existence, part of the universe, part of God.

*

*   *

The theological distinction between faith as belief, hence as a relative darkness, and the certainty of the blessed in Paradise is analogous to the distinction between theoretical knowledge and a knowledge that is effective, "concrete", "realized".

*

*   *

Christ's words to the Apostle Thomas could not mean that those who do see are not blessed; otherwise the elect of Heaven, who see God, would be deprived of beatitude. The blessedness of those who do not see and yet believe lies in the future, like the blessedness of those who mourn and will be comforted; but the blessedness of those who see and thus have no more need to believe is in the present, and this is why it is not mentioned in the Sermon on the Mount.

*

*   *

A man may have metaphysical certainty without having "faith", that is, without this certainty residing in his soul as a continuously active presence. But if metaphysical certainty suffices on doctrinal grounds, it is far from being sufficient on the spiritual plane where it must be completed and brought to life by faith. Faith is nothing other than the adherence of our whole being to Truth, whether we have a direct intuition of this Truth or an indirect notion.[1] It is a misuse of language to reduce "faith" to "belief"; it is the opposite that is true: belief—or theoretical knowledge—must be changed into the faith "that moves mountains".[2] For the Apostles there was no difference in practice between an idea and its spiritual validation; they did not separate theory from realization, hence the word "love" as a way of indicating all conformity to divine Truth.

He who has faith acts as if he were in the presence of what he believes—or knows—to be true. One can neither cast doubt on the fact that simple belief is already an adherence to Truth nor affirm that metaphysical certainty by itself implies an adherence of our whole being; for every man, whether he "knows" or "believes", perfection is "to worship God as if you saw Him, and if you do not see Him, He nonetheless sees you".[3]

---

[1] Evagrius Ponticus teaches that when faith is fortified by the other virtues (fear, temperance, patience, and hope) it engenders "apathy", spiritual indifference or impassibility, which in turn engenders charity, the gateway of contemplation; he also says that "apathy" precedes charity, and charity precedes knowledge. Let us add that, according to the Hesychasts Barsanuphius and John, "continual prayer measures itself against 'apathy'".

[2] This is the *credo ut intelligam* of Saint Anselm.

[3] This saying of the Prophet is considered the very definition of Sufism. For Saint Simeon the New Theologian, faith must live in works of holiness, hence in every-thing leading to contemplation, and he therefore concludes that the saints alone are effectively baptized. Far from wanting to replace Baptism by an initiation that would go beyond it, Saint Simeon wants on the contrary to make baptismal grace come alive again through spiritual tears and diverse disciplines and benedictions, and he founds his teaching on these words of Christ: "He that believeth on me, out of his belly shall flow rivers of living water." Now it is clear that this formula does not institute any rite. "According to Saint John Climacus, 'Repentance is a renewal of Baptism, but the well of tears after Baptism is a greater thing than Baptism.' This judgment may seem paradoxical if one forgets that repentance is the fruit of baptismal grace; this same grace, if only it is acquired and appropriated by the person, becomes in itself the 'gift of tears', a sure sign that the heart has been melted by Divine love" (Vladimir Lossky,

*

*　*

There is a longstanding illusion that consists in wanting to approach the Absolute with the aid of the mind, as if there were not a measureless discontinuity between the most refined concept and Reality. The furthest tip of a concept, a doctrinal symbol, far from touching Reality, is like a needle pointing toward limitless space. A theoretical conception may acquire an infinite complexity as a result of intellectual intuitions: it is nothing by comparison with the Real. And yet this speculative meditation is everything for the man who, with the help of a revealed idea and by assimilating its deepest aspects, puts himself into the required state of readiness in order that the miracle of intellection might be accomplished; now this state of readiness essentially implies faith and therefore the virtues that express and nourish it.

Even if it is only belief, faith always contains some measure of certainty, and in metaphysical certainty there is always a measure of faith: faith is a luminous obscurity, certainty an obscure light.

*

*　*

What God requires from man primarily is faith: an attachment with the very depths of our being to the Truth that transcends us; now this Truth is invisible to human nature as such.

If faith is the adherence of our whole being to Truth, then the trials of life will have the divine and spiritual function of proving the quality of our faith and increasing our faith by purifying it; suffering, "trial", thus becomes the criterion of our real attachment to immutable, divine Truth, that is, of the integral and fundamental nature of our adherence. In relationship to this function, the trial is essentially "sent by God"; in other words it is considered from the standpoint of its divine cause in connection with our spiritual weakness.[4]

Essai sur la théologie mystique de l'Église d'Orient).

[4] The Bible—especially the Book of Job—the Koran, and other revealed Scriptures clearly show this link between "trial" and "faith"; the Koran says: "Do men imagine that they will be left in quiet if they say, 'We believe'? And that they will not be put

It is fire that "tests" the true quality of metals; because of its incorruptible purity, fire has the function of divine criterion.

*

*   *

The great requirement of Islam is to believe in God, who is One. The question Sufism asks is this: "What does it mean to believe in God?" To believe is to prove one believes: to prove it to God, in whom one believes, and to prove it to oneself, hence to him who believes.[5] And it is proven by the participation of our whole being in the conviction of the mind—"as if you saw Him, and if you do not see Him, He nonetheless sees you".

Trials, which are sent by God, have a similar function, though it is in a sense the opposite since the initiative, if one may put it this way, begins with God; He tests the faith of man, which man must prove.

Sincere, integral faith always implies renunciation, poverty, and privation since the world—or the ego—is not God.

God tests by removing; man proves by renouncing. The renunciation may be inward and independent of facts; in this case it is detachment. He is detached who never forgets the ephemeral nature of the things he possesses and who considers them loans, not possessions.

Faith, trial, patience, sincerity: the virtue of patience (the *sabr* of the Sufis) remains meaningless without faith and trial; it is the criterion of sincerity (*sidq*).

*

*   *

to the test?" (*Sūrah* "The Spider" [29]:2). "And We (God) will test you by fright, by hunger, by loss of goods, of lives and harvests" (*Sūrah* "The Cow" [2]:155). "We shall alternate such days (of misfortune) among men that God may know which are those that believe . . . in order that God may test those that believe" (*Sūrah* "The Family of Imran" [3]:140-41).

[5] "Faith (*īmān*) is a confessing with the tongue, a verifying with the heart, and an act with the arms and legs" (*hadīth*). "He has the greatest perfection in faith who has the most beauty of character" (*hadīth*)—or according to another saying, "who most fears God".

The annoyances or adversities that come to man always have three causes: man himself, the world, God. Depending on the point of view adopted, we may take into consideration one or another of these causes, but we cannot deny any of them.

Man is the author of his misfortune to the extent it is experienced as suffering; the world is its author to the extent the misfortune seeks to keep man in cosmic illusion; and God is the Author to the extent the misfortune comes to man as a sanction, though also as a purification, hence a trial.

The same thing is true *mutatis mutandis* of happy events: we can never say they do not come from God or that they do not come from the cosmic surroundings or that they do not result from our own nature. These events are also trials in their character of temptation;[6] the corresponding virtue is renunciation or detachment (*zuhd*). The spiritual "traveler" (*sālik*) should be not only "patient" (*sabūr*) but also "detached" (*zāhid*).

*
*   *

It is clear that suffering does not necessarily have the character of a trial; the impious man may suffer, but in his case there is nothing spiritual to be tested.

According to Meister Eckhart—who was nonetheless far from regarding ascetic practices as anything other than a quite contingent, preparatory means—there is nothing nobler than suffering; this is the doctrine of ascetics and martyrs because it is the doctrine of Christ: "And he that taketh not his cross, and followeth after me, is not worthy of me."[7]

It is this spiritual dimension of suffering that made it possible for Buddhism also to be founded on the experience of distress.[8] Other

---

[6] "And We shall test you by ill and by good in order to try you, and you will return to Us" (*Sūrah* "The Prophets" [21]:35).

[7] "For as the sufferings of Christ abound in us, so our consolation also aboundeth by Christ" (2 Corinthians 1:5).

[8] Buddhism is a kind of "Hindu Christianity", and this doubtless explains the interest it has for Westerners; but it goes without saying that in other respects—precisely

perspectives are founded on the experience of beauty and sometimes even on the experience of earthly love;[9] everything that has an aspect of nobility or limitlessness can by definition be a vehicle for spiritual development.

*
*   *

The negation of pleasure, the world, or manifestation amounts to an implicit affirmation of the Principle, which in relation to the world is "void" (*shūnya* in Sanskrit) and "not this" (*neti*). Suffering transposes the problem to the plane of what is most intimately human; it is for man like a fissure in his existential illusion.

There is no spirituality that is not founded in one of its constituent elements on the negation of this dream; there is no spirituality devoid of ascetic elements: even simple mental concentration implies sacrifice. When the concentration is continuous, it is the narrow path, the dark night: the soul itself, this living substance full of images and desires, is sacrificed.

Distress affirms the Principle by denying manifestation, but noble enjoyment affirms the Principle by direct analogy and becomes in this way a possible channel for intellection. The question of what is opportune arises only on the level of individual applications.

*
*   *

The cult of suffering or of what is disagreeable is a different thing from the spiritualization of suffering: it is the error of believing that suffering is the only thing that brings one nearer to God. In a certain sense this is true when suffering or martyrdom is given a universal meaning. In this case it is true that man draws nearer to God only

---

because it is Hindu and not Western in origin—it is much further from Christianity than are Judaism and Islam.

[9] This is the story of Majnun and Layla, of a love that pierced through appearances to the infinite Essence of all beauty. A similar example is that of the role of Beatrice in the life of Dante.

through suffering—that is, through sacrifice, renunciation, poverty, extinction, loss of self.

Clearly what matters is not that man should suffer but that he should think of God. Suffering has a value only to the extent it provokes, deepens, and perpetuates this thought; now it plays this role for every man who believes in God and the immortality of the soul.

An enjoyment that brings man nearer to God by virtue of its symbolism, its nobility, and the contemplative quality of its subject is no less profound than suffering, and perhaps in some respects even more profound; but this possibility requires rare qualities of nobility and contemplative penetration, of intuition of the universal essences.

*

*   *

The fact that spiritual causes can engender darkness in no way signifies that darkness always has spiritual causes.

The criterion is in the nature of the darkness in question and in the way in which it is experienced. A spiritually necessary form of darkness is passive and never destroys continuity of judgment or humility; it gives rise to suffering, not error; it cannot tarnish the life of a saint. Man has a right to grief but never to sin: lacking light is a different thing from putting out the light one already has.

2

Metaphysical certainty is not God, though it contains something of Him. This is why Sufis accompany even their certainties with this formula: "And God is more wise" (wa 'Llahu a'lam).

The cult of intelligence and mental passion distances man from truth: intelligence narrows as soon as man puts his trust in it alone; mental passion chases away intellectual intuition just as the wind blows out the light of a candle.

Monomania of the mind, with the unconscious pretension, prejudice, insatiability, and haste that are its concomitants, is incompatible with sanctity; indeed sanctity introduces into the flux of thought an element of humility and charity, hence of calm and generosity; far from interfering with the spiritual momentum or the sometimes violent force of truth, this element delivers the mind from the vexations of passions, guaranteeing both the integrity of thought and the purity of inspiration.

According to the Sufis mental passion must be ranked as one of the associations with Satan, like other forms of passional "idolatry"; it cannot directly have God for its object; if God were its direct object, it would lose its specifically negative characteristics. Furthermore it does not contain within itself any principle of repose, for it excludes all consciousness of its own destitution.

*

*   *

We must beware of two things: first of replacing God—in practice if not in theory—with the functions and products of the Intellect or considering Him only in connection with this faculty; second of putting the "mechanical" factors of spirituality in place of human values—the virtues—or considering virtues only in relation to their "technical" utility, not their beauty.[1]

---

[1] According to Eckhart's conception, the sufficient reason for the virtues is not primarily their extrinsic usefulness but their beauty.

*
* *

Intelligence has only one nature, luminosity; but it has diverse functions, different modes of working that appear as so many particular intelligences. Intelligence with a "logical", "mathematical"—one might say "abstract"—quality is insufficient for reaching all aspects of the real; it is impossible to insist too often on the importance of the "visual" or "aesthetic" function of the intellective faculty. Everything in reality resembles an interplay of alternatives between what is determined in advance—starting from principles—and what is incalculable and in some way unforeseeable, and we must come to know this by concrete "assimilation", not abstract "discernment".[2]

In reflecting upon formal elements it would be a serious disadvantage to be deprived of this aesthetic function of the Intellect. A religion is revealed not only by its doctrine but also by its general form, which has its own characteristic beauty and is reflected everywhere, from "mythology" to art. Sacred art expresses the Real in relation to a particular spiritual vision. Aesthetic intelligence sees manifestations of the Spirit in the same way the eye sees flowers or jewels: for example, in order to understand Buddhism in depth—if one is not born a Buddhist—it is not enough to study its doctrine; it is also necessary to penetrate the language of Buddhist beauty as it appears in the sacramental image of the Buddha or in such features as the "Flower Sermon".[3]

*
* *

The aesthetic function of intelligence—if we may call it that for lack of a better term—enters not only into the form of every spiritual

---

[2] This is the perspective of Chaitanya and Ramakrishna, who would fall into ecstasy (*samādhi*) on seeing a beautiful animal. In Sufism similar examples of "spiritual aesthetics" are to be found in Omar ibn al-Farid and Jalal al-Din Rumi.

[3] Without saying a word the Buddha lifted a flower, and this gesture was the origin of Zen. Let us recall here that the Buddhas save not only by their teaching but also by their superhuman beauty, which is perpetuated—in a manner half concrete, half abstract—in sacramental images.

manifestation but also into the process of its manifestation: truth must be enunciated not only with a sense of proportion but also according to a certain rhythm. One cannot speak of sacred things in just any manner, nor can one speak of them without moderation.

Every manifestation has laws the intelligence must observe when manifesting itself, or else truth will suffer.

*

*   *

The Intellect is not cerebral nor is it specifically human or angelic; all beings "possess" it. If gold is not lead, this is because it "knows" the Divine better; its "knowledge" is in its very form, and this amounts to saying that the form does not belong to it in its own right since matter cannot know. Nonetheless we can say that the rose differs from the water lily by its intellectual particularity, by its "way of knowing", and thus by its mode of intelligence. Beings have intelligence in their forms to the extent they are "peripheral" or "passive" and in their essences to the extent they are "central", "active", "conscious".

A noble animal or a lovely flower is "intellectually" superior to a man who is base.

God reveals Himself to the plant in the form of the light of the sun. The plant irresistibly turns itself toward the light; it could not be atheistic or impious.

*

*   *

The infallible "instinct" of animals is a lower "intellect"; man's Intellect may be called a higher "instinct". Reason stands in a certain sense between instinct and Intellect and owes its misfortunes to the fact that it constitutes a sort of "Luciferian" duplication of the divine Intelligence, the only intelligence there is.

*

*   *

Knowledge of facts depends upon contingencies, which cannot enter into principial knowledge. The plane of facts is in certain respects opposed to that of principles in the sense that it includes modes and imponderables that are at the opposite extreme from the wholly mathematical rigor of universal laws; at least this is so in appearance, for it goes without saying that universal principles do not contradict themselves; even beneath the veil of the inexhaustible diversity of what is possible, their immutability can always be discerned, provided the intelligence finds itself in suitable circumstances.

*

* *

Although the Intellect is, so to speak, sovereign and infallible on its own ground, it can exercise its discernment on the level of facts only in a conditional manner; moreover God may intervene on this level with particular and at times unpredictable manifestations of His will, and this is something principial knowledge can verify only *a posteriori*.

*

* *

Hidden causes—whether cosmic or human—must be acknowledged wherever their intervention results from the nature of things, but not for the sake of satisfying a postulate whose metaphysical basis and practical bearing have been lost from view. When we see a waterfall, we have no reason for thinking it is moved by a magical force, even when a saint is drowned in it. The fact that there are some men who produce evil more consciously than others does not authorize us in thinking that all human evil is a conscious production with regard to its scope and repercussions and still less that every work having a negative aspect was undertaken for the sake of this aspect. Human evil is intentional in relation to its immediate object but not in relation to its cosmic significance; if this were not the case, evil would end up being dissolved in knowledge. If Voltaire had foreseen the ills of the twentieth century, he would have become a Carthusian.

A true principle always corresponds to a necessity, and on the other hand it never excludes a possibility; every postulate is false if it does not refer to a necessity that is divine, natural, traditional, or spiritual—according to the case or point of view—or if it excludes some possibility inherent in the order with which it is concerned.

From another angle the principial truth of a postulate must not be confused with some particular factual application even when this represents a relative norm. Reality is differentiated, comprising diverse combinations; one can never escape the necessity of a direct insight into the spiritual or cosmic factors whose nature one seeks to define.

*

*   *

What is better in principle does not always appear so in fact; the virtuous act of a simple and ignorant man may have a secret quality that makes it more pleasing to God—not more than metaphysics in itself, certainly, but more than the soul of some particular metaphysician.

In a general way the plane of facts has a tendency to escape the determinism of principles, and this is because of the limitlessness of universal Possibility. This truth provides a safeguard against illusions and creates an atmosphere of circumspect humility, which alone allows us to concern ourselves with wisdom fruitfully and with impunity.

When a fact seems to contradict a principle, it is actually manifesting another principle, which of necessity corroborates the first and is therefore an aspect of it.

To interpret facts in relation to principles is quite a different thing from distorting them in order to adjust them to preconceived conceptions.

*

*   *

The Biblical idea of "justice" sums up the fundamental qualities of a man centered on God. This justice is made of intelligence and generosity: the primordial object of intelligence is Divinity, and the object of generosity is man, the neighbor.

Generosity may be a matter of sentiment just as intelligence may be a matter of thought, but intelligence unaccompanied by generosity becomes fallible, and generosity lacking in intelligence becomes arbitrary. True knowledge does not dry up the soul, and true charity does not dissolve truth.

What is human must never be confused with what is spiritual: one who finds that he is the receptacle of the Spirit of truth should never forget that the receptacle is not the Spirit. It is true that the Spirit may burn and consume the recipient, but only if he is not closed to the influx of Light. "God alone is good."

*

* *

In order to be protected against unconscious presumption, a man may begin with the idea that the human recipient is bad, the Spirit alone being good. But he may also begin with the idea that the recipient is whatever he pleases—"good" or "bad" or both at once—and that the Spirit alone is real, or truly the "Self".

The unconscious presumption of an intelligent man often has its occasional cause in the unintelligence of other people, which he is bound to observe and from which he is bound to suffer. But he must never forget that the one-eyed man is king among the blind.

*

* *

The spontaneous manifestation of truth implies an aspect of incorruptibility and an aspect of generosity: without the first truth is engulfed and finally dissolved in some absurdity or other, and without the second it loses the grace that nourishes it and ends by giving rise to error.

It could also be said that truth includes an aspect of self-respect and an aspect of humility.

*

* *

Doctrine, in relation to which individuals are of no account, must not be confused with doctrinal functions involving the individual substance. Light is colorless in itself, but it may be transmitted through a crystal that is more or less transparent or through a crystal that is either white or colored.

*

*   *

Strictly speaking, doctrinal knowledge is independent of the individual. But its actualization is not independent of the human capacity to act as a vehicle for it; he who possesses truth must nonetheless merit it even though it is a free gift. Truth is immutable in itself, but in us it lives because we live.

If we want truth to live in us, we must live in it.

*

*   *

Knowledge saves only on condition that it engages all that we are: only when it constitutes a path that works and transforms and wounds our nature as the plough wounds the soil.

This means that intelligence and metaphysical certainty alone do not save and do not of themselves prevent titanic falls. This explains the psychological and other precautions with which every tradition protects the gift of doctrine.

*

*   *

When metaphysical knowledge is effective it produces love and destroys presumption. It produces love: that is, the spontaneous directing of the will toward God and the perception of "myself"—and of God—in the neighbor.

It destroys presumption: for knowledge does not allow a man to overestimate himself or underestimate others; by reducing to ashes all that is not God, it orders all things.

Everything Saint Paul says about charity concerns effective wisdom, for this wisdom is love; he opposes it to theory to the extent this theory is considered a human concept. The Apostle desires that truth should be contemplated with our whole being, and he calls this totality of contemplation "love".

Metaphysical knowledge is sacred. It is the property of sacred things to require of man all that he is.

*

*   *

Intelligence, as soon as it distinguishes, perceives proportions—if one may put it this way. The spiritual man integrates these proportions into his will, his soul, his life.

All defects are disproportions; they are errors that are lived. To be spiritual means not to deny with one's "being" what is affirmed with one's "knowledge", that is, what is accepted by intelligence.

Truth lived: incorruptibility and generosity.

*

*   *

Since ignorance is all that we are and not merely our thinking, knowledge will also be all that we are to the extent our existential modalities are by their nature able to participate in truth.

Human nature contains obscurities that no intellectual certainty could *ipso facto* eliminate.

*

*   *

The knowledge man enjoys—or can enjoy—is at once animal, human, and divine: animal insofar as man knows through the senses; human when he knows by reason; and divine in the contemplative activity of the Intellect. Now man cannot be divine without first being human; the Intellect, in the direct and higher meaning of the word—for the reason and senses are also, though indirectly, derived from the Intellect—cannot be actualized in a being that does not possess what is supplied by reason in the human domain. In the same way the uncreated Intellect, of which Meister Eckhart speaks, is not accessible to man without the created Intellect, which far from being identical with the rational faculty is as it were its center and secret, the fine point turned toward the infinite Light.

Man knows through the senses, brain, and heart, which correspond respectively to his animality, humanity, and divinity.

Reason is like air, without which fire—intellection—cannot manifest itself discursively, but which can extinguish this same fire.

*

*   *

One must distinguish between intellectuality and intellectualism: intellectualism appears as an end in itself; it is an intelligence contented with its multiple visions of the true and forgetful that it is not alone in the world and that life is passing; it practically makes itself God. The intellectualist acts as if he had concluded a security pact with the Eternal.

Intellectualism cannot fail to engender errors. It confers self-complacency and abolishes fear of God; it introduces a sort of worldliness into the intellectual domain. Its good side is that it may speak of truth; its bad side is the manner in which it speaks of it. It replaces the virtues it lacks by sophistries; it lays claim to everything but is in fact ineffectual.

In intellectualism a capacity to understand the most difficult things readily goes hand in hand with an inability to understand the simplest things.

*

*   *

Pure intellectuality is as serene as a summer sky—with a serenity that is at once infinitely incorruptible and infinitely generous.

Intellectualism, which "dries up the heart", has no connection with intellectuality.

The incorruptibility—or inviolability—of truth involves neither contempt nor avarice.

*

*   *

What is the certitude possessed by man? On the plane of ideas it may be perfect, but on the plane of life it rarely pierces through illusion.

Everything is ephemeral; every man must die. No one is unaware of this, and no one knows it.

*

*   *

A man may have a completely illusory interest in adopting the most transcendent ideas and readily believe himself to be superior to someone else who, not having this interest—perhaps because he is too intelligent or noble to have it—is sincere enough not to adopt them, though he may all the same be better able to understand them than the one who does adopt them. Man does not always accept truth because he understands it; often he believes he understands it because he wants to accept it.

People often discuss truths, whereas they should limit themselves to discussing tastes and tendencies.

*
*   *

It is possible to speak of "intellectual pride"—although there is a contradiction in this expression[4]—when a man imputes disproportionate virtues and rights to his intelligence and when acuteness of intelligence provokes in the mind a passional activity contrary to contemplation, cutting it off from the remembrance of God.

Acuteness of intelligence is a blessing only when it is balanced by greatness and gentleness of soul; it should not appear as a disruption of equilibrium, an excess splitting a man in two. A gift of nature requires complementary qualities permitting its harmonious manifestation; otherwise there is a risk of the light becoming mingled with darkness.

---

[4] Strictly speaking, we should call this "intellectualist pride".

3

There is something in man that is in opposition to God and something that is in accordance with Him: on the one hand the impassioned will, and on the other the pure Intellect. For paths founded on the first aspect, the conversion of the will—asceticism—is everything, and doctrinal truth is a background. For those founded on the second element, it is the Intellect—thus intellection—that is everything; asceticism is an auxiliary.

But these two perspectives give rise to indefinitely varied combinations in keeping with the inexhaustible diversity of spiritual and human possibilities.

*

* *

The excellence of *gnosis* results from the very nature of God, who is Light, and also from the primordial—and essential—nature of man: "The dignity of man", says Saint Gregory of Nyssa, "lies in his intelligence."[1]

*

* *

In intellection it is God who is the "subject", for man as such cannot bring an activity to bear upon God, who alone is pure Act; the creature is always passive in relation to the Creator and His graces. It is impossible for God to be the object of a knowledge of which He is not the subject; the answer to the objection that God is finally the subject of all real knowledge is that God is the indirect subject to the extent

---

[1] According to Saint Maximus the Confessor, "It is intuition that unites man to God." "You worship," he says, "in the inmost sanctuary—not in the atrium of sensory knowledge or the temple of reason—when you give yourself up exclusively to the supernatural activity of the intelligence." Meister Eckhart said similarly that he would rather abandon God than Truth, and he adds: "But God is Truth." Again, Ramakrishna said one day that he could give back everything to Kali, even love—everything except the Truth.

the knowledge is indirect and the direct subject to the extent the knowledge is direct; now pure intellection is distinguished precisely by its directness, although here as well there are degrees.

*

*　*

Sometimes, though quite mistakenly, the label "natural mysticism" is given to a spirituality not explicitly founded on the idea of grace, even though it appears as a method necessarily leading to the *fiat lux*; now grace and method are not antagonistic principles but two poles as it were of the same reality; there is a predominance of one over the other depending on the perspective, not a reciprocal incompatibility.[2] A methodic perspective—*yoga*, for example—can easily conceive of grace, whereas a devotional perspective seems to be ignorant of the "supernatural" character implicit in method; this is especially surprising in that sacraments also make the "supernatural" rest upon elements that are precise, necessary, and infallible.

Method itself is already a grace, freely given by the fact of its revelation but, like sacraments, necessarily efficacious in its modes of operation—with this difference, however, that it requires more complex conditions. If one believes in absolute gratuitousness, is it not contradictory to speak of "means of grace"?

On the other hand it is scarcely logical to insist on the importance of "gratuitousness" while also protesting on every occasion against "easy solutions", whether real or apparent; there are elements in *gnosis* that inevitably elude the devotional perspective. Moreover, if "gratuitousness" is conceived as an exclusive dogma, this amounts to attributing arbitrariness to God while denying Him the perfection

---

[2] The spiritual line of Ramanuja is divided into two schools; the first of these, the "Northern" (*Vadakalai*), holds that grace is not given except to one who actively collaborates with it, whereas the other, the "Southern" school (*Tenkalai*), begins with the idea that man is incapable of collaborating with grace and must therefore have trust in God, allowing himself to be carried along by His mercy. The first of these points of view is even more prominent in the school of Shankara; as for the second, it gave rise in the Christian world to the quietist deviation. In Japanese Buddhism the school of "Pure Land" (*Jōdo*) distinguishes between a way of "individual power" (*jiriki*), hence of "effort", and a way of the "power of another" (*tariki*), that is, of grace.

of necessity: if God is perfect, He must be both free and necessary; this truth appears in all domains. Human activity is simultaneously free, since man is not under complete constraint, and predestined, since God is not ignorant of what—in human terms—is the future. Perfection is made of geometry and beauty, rigor and radiation, the absolute and the infinite; geometry is in the method, and beauty is in the grace.

The use some people make of the term "supernatural" may appear to others a negation of the metaphysical homogeneity of the cosmos, a negation that explains the reduction of man to his volitive and rational aspects. It goes without saying that a distinction between the "natural" and the "supernatural" is fully valid on the plane of human experience, but this plane itself has only a very relative validity.

*
*   *

In comparison with the element of absoluteness in intellection, the facts of our will amount to nothing, strictly speaking; it is therefore absurd to speak of "easiness" when it is a question of knowledge.

Since the will is essentially a relative thing, its necessity cannot be absolute in relation to intellection.

*
*   *

Grace is an intrinsic aspect of intellection; it is not something separate as it is on the moral plane; its gratuitousness is that of knowledge.

To "provoke grace": this is certainly an ill-sounding phrase, but it does not prevent grace from always being accessible in pure intellection to the extent intellection itself is accessible. What is perhaps most shocking to partisans of spiritual "difficulty" and "gratuitous grace" is that intellection, when it is in fact accessible, can be actualized through sensory supports by reason of the law of hierarchical analogies.

*
*   *

A philosopher has said that saints contemplate not in order to know but in order to love. This opinion is not only contrary to the teachings of the Fathers but also self-contradictory, for contemplation is an act of knowledge.[3]

Polemics against knowledge in the name of love are like wanting to put out the light of one fire by the heat of another.

*
*   *

Love has man for its subject; it begins with man and converges toward God, and it becomes "enlightened" to the extent it conforms to its divine Object. By contrast, knowledge—that is, the intellective identification of the subject with the object—has the Self for its subject; it realizes love by ontological necessity as a result of returning to its own root, its essence: the Self, which is the divine Subject and which is Beatitude.

For love man is the subject and God the Object.

For knowledge it is God who is the Subject and man the object.

*
*   *

A follower of the affective or volitional way will say that love is more than knowledge because love engages the whole of man's being, all our "life", whereas knowledge concerns only the mind, thus only "thought"; he will make a connection between love and the heart, on the one hand, and between knowledge and the brain, on the other, in

---

[3] "Love is inseparable from knowledge, *gnosis*. It provides an element of personal consciousness, without which the way toward union would be blind and lacking a certain goal, an 'illusory asceticism', according to Saint Macarius of Egypt. The ascetical life 'apart from *gnosis*' has no value, according to Saint Dorotheus. . . . This consciousness in spiritual life is called knowledge. . . . It is fully manifested in the higher stages of the mystical way as perfect knowledge of the Trinity. This is why Evagrius Ponticus identified the Kingdom of God with knowledge of the Holy Trinity—consciousness of the object of union" (Vladimir Lossky, *Essai sur la théologie mystique de l'Église d'Orient*). According to Evagrius, "Everything that exists exists for the sake of the knowledge of God." "Christ himself is the Intellect of all intelligent beings." "Faith is the principle of charity, and the end of charity is the knowledge of God."

keeping with his individual starting point; the follower of the cognitive way will say, however, that the heart represents the Universal,
knowledge,[4] and the brain represents what is human and "subjective",
the ego. For the spiritual man of an affective temperament, to love is
to be and to know is to think; the heart represents the totality, the
very depths of the being, and the brain the fragment, the surface. But
for the spiritual man of an intellective temperament, to know is to
be and to love is to will or feel; the heart represents universality, the
Self, and the brain individuality or the "I". Knowledge starts from the
Universal and love from the individual; it is the absolute Knower who
knows whereas it is the human subject, the "creature", who is called
to love.

*
*   *

Knowledge is one and indivisible; the superimposed planes that
proceed from sensory knowledge up to the infinite resplendence of
the Self truly exist according to the "horizontal" degrees of cosmic
reality—or unreality—but not according to the essential Reality,
which is "vertical" and "continuous". This is why knowledge, intellective light, which is "uncreated" in its "created" reflection, reaches
all things and is sufficient unto itself.[5]

---

[4] According to the Hesychasts, the essence of the Jesus Prayer is the "descent of the
intelligence into the heart".

[5] "But God hath revealed them unto us by His Spirit: for the Spirit searcheth all
things, yea, the deep things of God. For what man knoweth the things of a man, save
the spirit of man which is in him? even so the things of God knoweth no man, but
the Spirit of God" (1 Corinthians 2:10-11). "And all such things as are either secret or
manifest, them I know. For wisdom, which is the worker of all things, taught me: for
in her is an understanding spirit, holy, one only, manifold, subtle, lively, clear, unde-
filed, plain, not subject to hurt, loving the thing that is good, quick, which cannot be
letted, ready to do good, kind to man, steadfast, sure, free from care, having all power,
overseeing all things, and going through all understanding, pure, and most subtle,
spirits. For wisdom is more moving than any motion: she passeth and goeth through
all things by reason of her pureness. For she is the breath of the power of God, and a
pure influence flowing from the glory of the Almighty: therefore can no defiled thing
fall into her. For she is the brightness of the everlasting light, the unspotted mirror
of the power of God, and the image of his goodness. And being but one, she can do

*

*   *

Man is a state of hardening. The man of an affective temperament pulverizes this hardness with the help of noble errors—or half-truths—such as the idea of being the vilest of men; the intellective man dissolves this hardness with the help of objective and impersonal truths. Such at least are the extreme positions.

God comes to meet the affective man, who hammers at the ice of his hardness, just as the sun comes to melt ice and makes hammering superfluous. As for the intellective man, God is already in his method, one might say, for if God resides indirectly in virtue, He resides directly in knowledge. When a body is dissolved in a chemical solvent, the dissolving power is already in the solvent and does not have to come from outside.

In practice it is always necessary to take into account the indefinitely varied combinations of these two attitudes; it is rare if not impossible for them to appear in isolation. In principle the affective attitude concerns the man who has a passional disposition and the intellective attitude the man in whom pure intelligence predominates.

*

*   *

Why is the volitive perspective, generally speaking, also an affective perspective? It is because the will inevitably becomes negative in the sphere of its earthly ends if it is directed toward God; now this negative character must be balanced by a positive factor, for an individual cannot live on negations; and this factor is love. If this factor were knowledge, there would no longer be a volitive perspective; the will would simply find itself integrated into the intellectual perspective.

all things: and remaining in herself, she maketh all things new: and in all ages entering into holy souls, she maketh them friends of God, and prophets. For God loveth none but him who dwelleth in wisdom. For she is more beautiful than the sun, and above all the order of stars: being compared with the light, she is found before it. For after this cometh night: but vice shall not prevail against wisdom. Wisdom reacheth from one end to the other mightily: and sweetly doth she order all things" (Wisdom of Solomon 7:21-8:1).

*
*　　*

When man is reduced to his will, intellection can hardly be looked upon as something human.

The will can determine and vitiate reasoning but not intellectual intuition, which it can at most only paralyze in certain cases. As for reason, it may be either humble or proud since its domain is that of opinions; it is a kind of intelligence degraded by the initial luciferian quality of the will. Reason can exaggerate and falsify, distorting proportions without being illogical in the actual mechanism of its working; Intellect on the other hand can only perceive, and if it acts it is not through restrictive movements but through the principial activity of its very substance.

*
*　　*

In doctrinal formulations those of an affective temperament (the *bhaktas*) tend to adopt individual and rational modes of thought, and being more or less aware of the limitations this implies, they attribute them to man as such.

For Shankara theory is an objectification of Reality, which is the Self; for Ramanuja theory is a dialectic—even an apologetic—destined to prepare the ground for the way of love.

For the affective man knowledge results from love as a gift; for the intellective man, the gnostic (the *jnānin*), love results from knowledge as a necessity.

*
*　　*

In order to escape all danger of deviation the way of love (*bhakti*) needs an external protection that is impersonal in character, namely, the general traditional environment; gnosis (*jnāna*) on the other hand requires an inner axis of a personal kind, namely, the effort of realization. In other words, if the affective way cannot subsist without the static, objective element that the traditional framework provides, the intellective way cannot subsist without the dynamic, subjective element provided by the personal will for actualization. Love possesses this element by definition just as *gnosis* necessarily possesses the discernment of essential forms, to the extent at least that such forms may concern it.

The relationship often established between intelligence and pride, while absurd from the standpoint of principles or essences, has a certain human—one might say moral—justification insofar as intelligence produces arrogance if it turns aside from Truth and refuses to retrace the course of its ontological process: the intelligent man who does not realize while he is contemplating that God alone contemplates ends up making himself into God.[6] Pure intelligence implies by definition the realization of its single Essence and thus the forgetting—or surpassing—of the cosmic accidentality that is the thinking ego: intelligence "serves God", one might say, by "becoming what it is"; it is "impious" when it deliberately remains an individualized vision committed to nothing, constituting an end in itself, and excusing man from any obligation. Although intelligence is in itself contemplation and thus "nonacting", it requires of man an inward act that is total, and this act is "love".

*
* *

If as Saint Thomas said "love of God is better than knowledge of God", this is primarily for the following reason: in principle knowledge is more than love, but in fact—in the world—the relationship is the reverse because of the law of analogy between the principial and manifested planes; love, the will, or the individual tendency is in practice more important than knowledge since for the individual as such knowledge can only be theoretical.

Even so there is not only inverse analogy but also direct or parallel analogy, by virtue of which—and this is the "essential" or "vertical" perspective—knowledge always remains what it is by its metaphysical nature; this is the point of view of *gnosis*.

---

[6] Theologically, one would say that man should always be aware that intelligence is a gift of God.

*
*   *

The Gospel saying: "Blessed are they that have not seen, and yet have believed" not only concerns "faith" in the usual sense of the word but also refers to a general human reality independent of the distinction charity-*gnosis*: in other words individuality as such will always be a veil before the divine Reality; the individual as such cannot "know God". The Intellect, whether understood in its "created" aspect or in its "uncreated" reality, is not the individual; the individual experiences it as a fulgurating darkness; he grasps only the flashes, which enlighten and transfigure him.

*
*   *

What is "love" at the outset will appear finally as "Knowledge"; and what is "knowledge" at the outset will appear finally as "Love".

Perfect Love is "luminous", and perfect Knowledge is "warm", or rather it implies "warmth" without being identified with it.

*
*   *

In God Love is Light, and Light is Love. It is irrelevant in this case to object that one divine quality is not another, for here it is not a question of qualities—or "names"—but of the divine Essence itself.

God is Love, for by His Essence He is "union" and "gift of Self".

*
*   *

The spiritual man of an affective temperament knows God because he loves Him.

The spiritual man of an intellective temperament loves God because he knows Him, and in knowing Him.

The love of the affective man is that he loves God.

The love of the intellective man is that God loves him; that is, he realizes intellectively—not simply in a theoretical way—that God is Love.

The intellective man sees beauty in truth whereas the affective man does not see this *a priori*. The affective man leans upon truth; the intellective man lives in it.

*

*   *

To love God is to attach oneself to Him. The spiritual man of an affective temperament arrives at the *vacare Deo* through love; the intellective man arrives at love in the *vacare Deo*, and this emptiness is the fruit of his science, not of his fervor as with the affective man. True science is fervent in a secondary manner, however, since it involves the entire being, and true fervor is conscious, lucid, active in its very center, where it is attached to truth.

*

*   *

Christianity emphasizes the aspect "love"; Sufism for its part emphasizes—though in a different way—the aspect "beauty". The Arabic words denoting virtue (*ihsān*) and the virtuous (*muhsin*) contain the root *husn*, "beauty". According to Ibn Arabi, God loves the beauty of forms because form reflects the beauty of God, just as this beauty reflects Being. A *hadīth* says, "God is beautiful, and He loves what is beautiful." Here beauty appears as the sufficient reason for love; in love of the neighbor, which for Sufis is charity in action, it is God who is loved through man; divine beauty, which the *muhsin* attains through the creature, is reflected in him in purity and generosity of soul. Virtue makes the soul a mirror of divine beauty.

*

*   *

Why is Christianity not able to speak about "knowledge" without meaning "love" when—in the *Vedānta* for example—knowledge seems sufficient in itself? It is because in Christianity—also in Buddhism—everything *a priori* converges toward man's spiritual realization; *gnosis* is considered with reference to its "realization" by the human being, not in its divine essentiality.

Among Shivaite Vedantists knowledge is considered above all in itself, its subject being by definition the Self, not the human being; in this perspective there is no starting point, no springboard: its logical center is "everywhere and nowhere", and its doctrinal form is not anthropocentric.

For some men knowledge and love are complements, which means that each term is regarded from the standpoint of what distinguishes it from the opposite term; for others knowledge is unique; it is not the complement of anything, and it thus contains love; for still other men there is only love, and this contains wisdom, which is actualized to a degree corresponding to the "quality" the love attains.

*
*   *

"God is Light" (1 John 1:5)—hence Knowledge—even as He is "Love" (1 John 4:8). To love God is also to love the knowledge of God.[7] Man cannot love God in His Essence, which is humanly unknowable, but only in what God "makes known" to him.

In a certain indirect sense God answers knowledge with Love and love with Knowledge,[8] although in another respect—in this case direct—God reveals Himself as Wise to the wise and as Lover to the lover.

*
*   *

---

[7] Evagrius Ponticus says that "charity is the higher state of the reasonable soul in which it is impossible to love anything in the world more than the knowledge of God" (*Centuries*). And the same Father calls charity the "gate of *gnosis*", which clearly points to the transcendence of knowledge in relation to love.

[8] If Saint Maximus the Confessor says that "charity brings about knowledge", it must be understood in this indirect sense, for it is clear that nothing "outside" knowledge can be the cause of knowledge.

160

Intellective contemplation is "contained" in the "peace" Christ gave the Apostles: "It is thus"—says the *Century* of the monks Callistus and Ignatius—"that our merciful and beloved Lord Jesus Christ . . . bequeathed to his own these three things [his Name, his Peace, and his Love]." This "peace" is analogous to the Hindu *shānti*, spiritual ataraxia, and to *Shānta*, the Infinite conceived in its calm and profound nature, which is "nonagitated" because it is "nonexteriorized" (or "nonmanifested"); and this *shānti*, this "peace" or "serenity", is closely related to pure, intellective contemplation;[9] "peace" therefore indicates an attitude of intellection in Christian mysticism as well.[10] This element of *gnosis* is likewise found in the apophatic and antinomian theology of the Fathers, a doctrine crystallized in Palamite teaching.

From the affective point of view peace is connected with trust and hope, that is, with the "sentimental certitude" that must compensate for what is "obscure" in faith.

Peace implies satisfaction or possession just as agitation implies privation or separation. The trace of intellective contemplation in the affective soul is reassurance and also, in a certain sense, trusting abandonment or hope.

*

* *

Peace is the absence of dissipation. Love is the absence of hardness. Fallen man is hardness and dissipation; the hardness appears in indifference toward God, an attitude poles apart from spiritual impassibility,

---

[9] This ontological connection between knowledge and peace—or contemplation and immobility—is expressed in many inspired writings: according to Saint James, "The wisdom that is from above is first pure, then peaceable" (James 3:17). Evagrius Ponticus says that "the divine Intellect is an Intellect calmed from all movement." Again, according to Nikitas Stithatos, "He [the Holy Spirit] gives them intelligence that is peaceful and sweet in order to understand the deep things of God."

[10] This is the *gnosis* of the Alexandrians. This term is scriptural in any case and does not properly belong to any school. As for the "holy silence" of the Hesychasts, this fundamentally designates the same thing though it puts the accent on the aspect of "peace"; it is the state of *samprasāda*, the "serenity" in which Truth appears without veils and which resembles, according to Shankara, a flame that does not flicker.

and the dissipation appears in curiosity, preoccupation, anxiety with regard to the world, an attitude the very opposite of vigilance of mind. In the peace of the Lord the waves of this dissipation are calmed, and the soul is at rest in its primordial nature, its center; through love the outer shell of the heart is melted like snow, and the heart awakens from its death; hard, opaque, and cold in the fallen state, it becomes liquid,[11] transparent, and aflame in the divine Life.

Peace is contemplation in opposition to action;[12] it is therefore also intellection. Love is the spiritual will in opposition to natural inertia; but it is also in a higher sense the content of contemplation, the immutable intoxication of union.

Peace is first of all the calm that truth confers, then its direct contemplation; when the mind is perfectly calm—or perfectly simple—Truth is mirrored in it just as objects are reflected in calm water.[13] Love is primarily the will turned toward God, then the bliss God gives us in return.

*

*   *

Every spiritual path begins with an inversion with regard to the preceding state: the profane soul finds itself in a state of "hardness", for it is closed to God, who shines "outside". This hardness reveals itself by indifference toward God, then by egoism, greed, anger, distraction; spiritual conversion will therefore involve fervor, goodness, renunciation, peace: the soul must "melt" before Truth so that the divine presence may henceforth be felt as "inward" and "central". One can

---

[11] This "liquefaction" of the heart is mentioned by many different Christian writers: the Greek Fathers, Saint Thomas, Angelus Silesius, the Curé d'Ars, to name but a few; and it is closely related to the "gift of tears". According to Silesius, who was also an alchemist, the tears of Saint Mary Magdalene at the Savior's feet represent her "melted heart" (*sind ihr zerschmolzen Herz*).

[12] Strictly speaking, the relationship is just the opposite: it is action that in a certain manner opposes contemplation, for having no opposite contemplation does not oppose anything.

[13] A Chinese Buddhist master told us in a letter, "Serenity leads to higher knowledge." This expresses not only the relationship between calm and contemplation or peace and *gnosis* but also that between virtue and intellection.

legitimately call this conversion "love", for where there is no longer any hardness, no longer a constricting coil around the ego, the distinction between "I" and "thou" is abolished; within there is bliss, and outwardly there is goodness; there is a gentle warmth like spring sunshine,[14] comparable to the joy of love. It is for this reason that there is no spirituality without love; no spirituality is possible in a heart that is hardened and at the same time dissipated.

This aspect of spirituality calls for another, apparently its opposite but in reality complementary: this is incorruptibility, the cold and hard purity of the diamond.

*

*   *

Charity has two meanings in the doctrine of the ante-Nicene Fathers and their spiritual heirs: first, it is "a good disposition of the soul, which makes it prefer the knowledge of God above all things" (Saint Maximus the Confessor);[15] and second, it is the beatitude inhering in this knowledge by virtue of its Object, for "God is Love"; in the first sense charity is in man, and in the second it is in God.[16] In principle

---

[14] "When man discovers in the intelligent soul a tender feeling, completely calm and pure as day, let him recognize that it is the quality of ascending perfection"—*sattva*, conformity with Being, *Sat* (*Mānava Dharma Shāstra*, 12).

[15] "If the life of the spirit is the illumination of knowledge and if it is the love of God that produces this illumination, then it is right to say: there is nothing higher than the love of God" (*Centuries on Charity*). According to Evagrius Ponticus, "Holy knowledge draws the purified spirit even as a magnet, by the natural force it possesses, draws iron" (*Centuries*).

[16] These considerations show that the hymn of praise to charity in the First Epistle to the Corinthians should also be understood in a sense conformable to the intellectual perspective. In this connection we may quote the following passage from our book *L'œil du cœur* ("Modes of Spiritual Realization"): "The use . . . of the term 'love' to designate an intellectual reality is explained by the fact that sentiment, while inferior to reason on account of its 'subjectivity', is nonetheless symbolically comparable to what is higher than reason, namely, the Intellect; this is so because sentiment is not discursive but direct, simple, spontaneous, limitless, like the Intellect, to which it is in a sense diametrically opposed; compared to reason sentiment appears free from form and fallibility, and that is why the divine Intelligence can be called 'Love' and even really is Love in a transposed sense compared with the poor human intelligence; there is here a simultaneous application of direct and inverse analogies, which at one and

love is as it were enveloped in knowledge, for God is Love "in being" Light or "because He is" Light, if one may so express it; but on the level of facts effective knowledge is as it were enveloped in love, for man as such is will[17] "before" he knows what surpasses him.

*

*   *

The will cannot act without the collaboration of the intelligence or sentiment, or both together; now insofar as a mystical "voluntarism" is not linked to a truly intellectual perspective, it is necessarily allied to an affective element.

This is what allows us to see a form of "love" in every volitive attitude and thus to realize love through the will. It is in the will, in asceticism, that love and knowledge most visibly meet; all spiritual paths, from the most modest to the loftiest, converge upon one and the same act of will, the rejection of the world and the search for the Divine.

*

*   *

Intelligence is the noblest thing in the world precisely because it represents "something of God", being a ray of the "Self"; it is by intelligence, even if it is only virtual,[18] that man surpasses the other creatures on earth and not by reason, which is only the specifically human mode of intelligence and which characterizes man insofar as he is a "thinking animal"; and it is again by virtue of his intelligence that man falls to a lower level than that of other creatures when he betrays this intelligence by turning it away from its proper object, although

---

the same time link and separate the divine and cosmic orders."

[17] An Upanishad says that "the essence of man is made of desire", hence of "will".

[18] This reservation is necessary because a noble animal has a more adequate knowledge of God—although completely indirect and passive—than does a man whose spirit is blinded and paralyzed by error; but this man nonetheless retains the possibility of a relatively direct and active knowledge, which is lacking in the animal.

this fall always retains a specifically human form, that is, a mental or rational form, which makes for an illusion that is even more satanic.

The "active" or "direct" intelligence of which mankind is the beneficiary is therefore a "nobility that imposes demands"; it may thus seem surprising that there are spiritual paths that appear to exclude it or in any case to assign it a secondary and indirect role. Even for these "voluntarist" paths, however, it is still always intelligence that matters, though understood in connection with its volitive function, and in this case it is free choice that constitutes the nobility of the human being: it is by free will that man surpasses the animals, by it that he resembles God, and by it that he returns to Him.

*
*   *

In order to purify and save man the intelligence does not have to become something other than it is; it only needs to conform to its own nature. The will, however—if it seeks to bring man back toward his origins—must contradict itself. The will has the freedom to do evil, but the intelligence does not have the freedom to err; in evil the will remains itself whereas intelligence becomes stupidity when it is in error, whatever the appearances. When the will conforms to its true end and thus realizes its primordial movement, it is absorbed into the intelligence; it can then be called "love". Love is the will reintegrated into Truth.

Having become "knowledge" by its application to the "object" inherent in it, which is its normal goal, the intelligence also determines the will. The opposite is true only indirectly: though the will inevitably carries with it a certain illumination, it nonetheless acts on the intelligence only in a roundabout and quite relative way; the will is incapable of producing knowledge; all that it can do is remove obstacles.

*
*   *

When the object of the intelligence is God—and to the extent it is—intelligence becomes "love", and this is because of the essentially attractive nature of the Divinity; intelligence becomes purely "itself"

165

only through the "object", God, which "qualifies" it. From this point of view the intelligence as such is without quality; it is a human fact. The Hindu—or Alexandrian—perspective is more direct: the intelligence is considered *a priori* in its universal Essence, not in its human modes, and it is for this reason that it is "knowledge" by definition; it is not by virtue of an object imposed on it apparently *ab extra* that it constitutes truth, but thanks to the elimination of the microcosmic accidents veiling its true nature in an illusory manner. In other words the intelligence is "qualified" by its own supernatural essence, and its inherent object, which it includes by definition, is the divine Reality, even if microcosmic accidents veil this object and reduce it to the appearances of the world.

Knowledge is holy when it is the knowledge of God; it then possesses love. Only that knowledge is holy which in this way is love, for it alone is the knowledge of God.[19]

*

* *

Knowledge does not abolish faith but gives it a more inward meaning. He who "knows" theoretically does indeed enjoy metaphysical certainty, but such certainty does not yet penetrate his whole being; it is as if, instead of believing a description, one saw the object described but without the sight of it implying either a detailed knowledge or a possession of the object, for a single visual perspective does not of course teach us the whole nature of the thing seen; thus there is certainty regarding the object as such in this case, but uncertainty regarding its integral nature. To "know" an object perfectly means to "possess" it, "become" it, "be" it; if the sight of an object is very much more than an abstract belief in its existence, the realization of the object will likewise be infinitely more than the sight of it; metaphysical certainty thus stands in a sense between belief—"faith" in the ordinary sense of the word—and the realization of union. As long as a man is not delivered from the chains of existence, there is always

---

[19] Al-Hallaj calls wisdom "that of which the tiniest atom surpasses in its beauty and extent the two worlds [the earthly and the heavenly]".

an element of "faith" in his "knowledge"; otherwise there would be nothing separating him from the Reality "known" or "to be known".

"Blessed are they that have not seen, and yet have believed." Metaphysical truths in their deepest sense are never "visible" to the "soul-desire"; otherwise they would immediately perfect it. The soul-desire—the man who rejoices and suffers—must therefore "believe" the truths that are evident to the Intellect. In metaphysics faith is the assent of the whole being.

*

*   *

The difference between the affective and intellective ways can also be defined in the following manner: the first proceeds essentially in an "objective" or "dualistic" way whereas the second, though it does not lack an appropriate "objective" perspective, is able to proceed in a "subjective" way:[20] this means that in the first case God is objective, outward, and that in the second case He can be conceived as subjective, inward; He is the "Self".

Each of these perspectives must take account of the other's reality: the "lover" knows that God—from whom he is separated since the Beloved is "other" in relation to the lover—is also "within" him; and the "gnostic" knows that the Self—which is his own essential Reality—appears as "objectivity" because egocentric objectification, the illusion of "I", is produced by existence itself; it follows that for man as such, whether *jnānin* or *bhakta*, God will always be "external", "objective", "other"—infinitely "other" in relation to human nothingness.

*

*   *

[20] In the current sense of the word, "subjective" means what is colored by the limitations of the ego; in reality, however, the ego is not a pure subject, but an objectification; only the divine Intellect is absolutely Subject. The "subjective" way spoken of here can base itself on the scriptural formula: "The kingdom of God is within you."

The renunciation of the contemplative does not at all have the aim of accumulating merits for the sake of individual bliss; by means of what one might call radical measures, it serves to put the soul into the most favorable possible state for realizing its own infinite Essence.

Love of God, far from being essentially a sentiment, is what makes the wise man contemplate rather than do anything else.[21]

The virtue of the contemplative is that he makes his virtues into a grace for others; in the final analysis his positive virtue is that of God, which he realizes in his vision.

*
* *

For certain people the intention of loving God brings with it an inability to love men; now the second of these things destroys the first. In an ordinary soul concern for spiritual love and mortification may bring with it an icy egoism and sometimes also a curious hatred of animals as "useless" beings, to say nothing of a no less curious aversion to beauty; beauty, with its breath of infinity and generosity, breaks down the fixed attitudes and closed systems of this supposedly spiritual egoism.

Beauty is an aspect of love, and conversely; it is utterly contradictory to seek to realize love in ugliness and avarice.

*
* *

Charity is first of all the faculty of putting God before the world and then the faculty of putting oneself in the place of others. When Saint Louis urged his friends to thrust their swords into the body of anyone

---

[21] For Shankara *bhakti* is what Muslims call *himmah*—spiritual fervor; for Ramanuja it is continuity or perpetuity of contemplation; for Chaitanya it is limitless love, though this is but the means and not yet the end: the goal is *prema*, divine Love, Beatitude. For Origen, "The whole life of a saint should be a single and continuous great prayer; what commonly bears this name is only a part of this great prayer, a part one should perform no fewer than three times a day" (*De Oratione*). "He who truly celebrates the feast does what he should and prays without ceasing, continually offering bloodless victims in his prayers to God" (*Contra Celsum*).

168

who made impious remarks in their presence, he was in no way for-getting that one must love one's neighbor as oneself; he would have wished to be struck through with a sword himself had he pronounced a blasphemy; he loved his neighbor as he loved himself, neither more nor less; and since society is also—and even *a fortiori*—one's neighbor, charity impelled him to seek to rid it of a harmful virus. There are alternatives no virtue can escape.[22] Love of the neighbor may sacrifice the individual to the collectivity; it should never sacrifice the quali-tative collectivity to the individual as such any more than it should sacrifice the qualitative human person to the quantitative and crude collectivity.

For the mother who loves her child more than herself—by nature and not supernaturally, for otherwise she would have no reason for preferring her own child to those of others—the child is an exten-sion of the "I"; it is only partly the "neighbor"; it is nature that loves through the mother even as it loves through lovers or spouses. This love is nature's egoism, but love of the neighbor—if one may put it this way—is the "egoism" of God.

Without charity it is not possible to see the total truth or even the complexity of partial truths.

*
*   *

In the final analysis charity is to make a gift of God to God by means of the ego and through other beings. It communicates a blessing whose source is God, and it communicates it to the neighbor, who is God's representative insofar as he is the object of love.

In giving God to our neighbor we give ourselves to God.

---

[22] "For it cannot be that he who loves God does not love himself. Indeed he alone knows how to love himself who loves God. Doubtless whoever is careful to do the good that is sovereign and true loves himself in sufficient measure" (Saint Augustine, *The Customs of the Church*). Origen notes that according to the Gospel it is God alone whom we must love "with all our heart"; and just as we must not love ourselves with all our heart since we are not God, neither should we love our neighbor in a manner suiting God alone. As for our enemies, Origen adds, we should love them by abstaining from hating them. According to Richard of Saint Victor, only God should be loved without measure; the neighbor should be loved with measure, as we should love ourselves; and the enemy should not be hated.

4

The infinity of God requires His affirmation: the Word. The affirmation requires manifestation: the world, the apparent "going forth" of the Divine "outside" itself. Manifestation requires limitation or diversification, without which it could not subsist "outside" of God, at least from the point of view of its own illusion. Manifestation requires negation since it is not God: hence imperfections and destructions on the one hand and spiritual liberation on the other.

A perspective holding that the world "necessarily emanates" from God will also hold that beings "return" to God, but a perspective for which the world is "freely created" out of "nothing" cannot accept the opposite and correlative process, for this would require the immortal person to become "nothing" again. And yet there is here only a difference of words: the first perspective starts from the idea that the world is in God, whence a certain spiritual continuity, and the second starts from the idea that God is not in the world, whence the dogma of exclusive discontinuity.

*

*   *

"God doeth what He will": this does not mean that He displays the capriciousness of a tyrant, but that universal Possibility is limitless and incalculable, of such complexity that human understanding can no more analyze it than one glance can take in the extent and complexity of a virgin forest or star-spangled sky. If there are holy men who appear to be limited and limited men who only appear to be holy, and if there are fish that fly and birds that swim—if God loves in His creation this interplay of compensations and surprises, this game of hide-and-seek, in which anything can be anything—this is by virtue of His infinity, which cannot stop at any limits.

If God is the Absolute, there is nothing that could be He: God is continually shattering whatever in creation appears to assume an absolute or infinite character. Were it not so, the relative would itself be God.

*

*   *

That we are conformed to God—"made in His image"—this is certain; otherwise we would not exist.

That we are contrary to God, this is also certain; otherwise we would not be different from God.

Apart from analogy with God, we would be nothing.

Apart from opposition to God, we would be God.

*

*   *

The separation between man and God is at one and the same time absolute and relative: were it not absolute, man as such would be God; were it not relative, there would be no possible contact between the human and the Divine, and man would be an atheist by ontological definition, thus irremediably so. The separation is absolute because God alone is real, and no continuity is possible between nothingness and Reality, but the separation is relative—or rather "nonabsolute"—because nothing is outside of God.

In a sense it might be said that this separation is absolute from man to God and relative from God to man.

*

*   *

God as such does not have the possibility of not being God: He has this possibility only in the world and through the world. But the world is not in reality outside of God, or else it would limit Him.

One of the mysteries of the "Word made flesh" is that "God made nothingness": the world. To say that God made the world "from nothing" is to say that He made Himself "nothing"—and also that the world "is" not.

*

*   *

The notion of the radical otherness of creation in relation to the Creator—or manifestation in relation to the Principle—does not do justice to the total nature of this manifestation; from the point of view of absolute Truth it is not enough to define the created as "infinitely other" in an exclusive manner, although this is obviously the case with regard to its existential separation.

The Infinite is what is absolutely without limits, but the finite cannot be what is "absolutely limited", for there is no absolute limitation. The world is not an inverted God; God is without a second.

*
* *

A mere "resemblance" is nothing in relation to God. If the finite is absolutely distinct from the Infinite—and it is so with regard to the limitation that defines it, its "nothingness", though not with regard to its "qualitative content"—then it cannot draw near the Infinite; the disparity will always remain incommensurable.[1]

The human substance is only a veil. Nothing "returns" to God except what "pre-exists" in Him.

*
* *

If the only thing distinguishing man, supremely beatified, from God were the "human substance"—in other words if the "resemblance" were such that only the "human substance" prevented there being "identity"—then man would have something more than God has, namely, this very substance; he would then be more than God. But since "God alone is good", the substance in question is necessarily privative. Now if the human substance is less than God, it cannot subsist, we do not say in man, but in absolute Reality.[2] If the "content"

---

[1] It goes without saying that from the standpoint of its existence qualitative content—beauty, for instance—is itself also "absolutely other" than God. Words cannot adequately express these things; they cannot simultaneously grasp all aspects of the real.

[2] According to Saint Basil, "Man has received the order to become God." Saint Cyril

is God alone, what does the "container" matter? If the "container" is privative, how can the "content" be God? Only the doctrine of the degrees of Reality can account for this mystery.

Apophatic and antinomian theology conforms to the inward incommensurability of dogma. Thus it acknowledges simultaneously the imparticipability and the participability of the divine Nature: the soul is not God, and according to Saint Macarius of Egypt, "there is nothing in common between their natures"; in another respect, however, there is a "transmutation of the soul into the divine Nature". If theology never makes use of direct expressions of the doctrines of identity—such as those of the Shankarian *Vedānta*—it is because it looks at everything in relation to man; for theology identity comes under the heading of the inexpressible.[3]

*
* *

The most explicit metaphysical doctrine will always take it as axiomatic that every doctrine is only error when confronted with the divine Reality in itself, but a provisional, indispensable, salutary "error", containing and communicating the virtuality of Truth.

The Divinity is beyond "knowledge" insofar as this implies a subject and object; for this reason the divine Essence is "unknowable".

---

of Alexandria expresses it thus: "If God has become man, man has become God." According to Meister Eckhart, "We are wholly transformed into God and changed into Him in the same manner as the bread is changed into the body of Christ in the sacrament. Thus I am changed into Him because He makes me one with His Being and not simply like it. By the living God it is true that there no longer remains any distinction." Angelus Silesius says, "Man does not have perfect bliss until Unity has swallowed up alterity." And again: "The blissful soul no longer knows alterity; it is one single Light with God and one single Glory."

[3] According to the Sufi Hasan al-Shadhili, "The desire for union with God is one of the things that most surely separate us from Him"; in this case it is a question of the desire—understood as something individual—to be united to God as an individual. On the other hand desire for "deliverance" is permissible, since this is liberation from a privation.

*

    *   *

The human "I" reflects the divine "I"; and yet the human "I" represents an inverse principle in relation to the "I" of God. All exoterism stops at this aspect of inversion and ignores the aspect of essential identity; exoterism, which is by definition formal, does not have the capacity—or the duty, of course—to combine antinomic aspects of the Real in a direct and nonformal vision of things.

    To say, "He alone is real, the ego is not" and to say, "I am not other than 'I' (the Self)" amount to exactly the same thing.[4]

*

    *   *

In Monotheism religious dogmatism excludes nondualistic formulations of union; no formulation can go against dogma, which is of necessity dualistic. Now this dualism, like that of the Vishnuites, says that human nature is human nature and the divine Nature is the divine Nature, and nothing else. From the point of view of dogmatic language, nondual union belongs to the domain of the inexpressible; it is as though, being unable to say that a plant is green, one said that it was at the same time yellow and blue, and neither one nor the other. Created nature assuredly remains what it is: no one has ever maintained that the created as such is transformed into the Uncreated.

*

    *   *

The man still undelivered is in truth a delivered man who does not know it.

    The bridge from the finite to the Infinite is this: that the finite is infinite in its center and essence—that the finite as such is not.

    When the sun rises, the night has never been.

---

[4] According to an expressive phrase of the Shaykh Ahmad al-Alawi, "The invocation of God is like a movement to and fro, which maintains an increasingly complete communication until there is an identity between the glimmer of consciousness and the dazzling fulguration of the Infinite."

*

* *

Spiritual doctrines allow for "union" or "identity" according to whether they consider a being from the point of view of creation or from that of the divine Reality. From the standpoint of creation nothing can "become God" or "become nothing"; in the divine Reality the world has never been, and therefore the creature could never cease to be. Now the intelligence that is plunged in God sees according to the divine Reality; otherwise it would not truly see God. In the final analysis everything is reduced to a question of terminology: the unconditional affirmation of identity by Shankara—not by all Vedantists—necessarily results from the perspective of the absolute Subject. For Ibn Arabi it is not a question of "becoming one" with God: the contemplative "becomes conscious" that he "is one" with Him; he "realizes" true unity. In Christianity "deification", the necessary complement of "incarnation", does not imply any "identification" on the same plane of reality; that man as such should literally "become" God would imply that there was a common measure and a symmetrical confrontation between God and man; no doubt it was this reservation Shankara had in mind when he maintained that the delivered one (*mukta*) is without the creative power of *Brahma*. Be that as it may, there is no more reason to reject the expression "to become God" than to reject Shankara's formula of "identity", for they retain all their antinomic and elliptical value.

*

* *

Inevitably, a dialectic conforming to transcendent wisdom is not only apophatic and antinomic but also elliptical.

"He (the delivered one) is *Brahma*" is an elliptical formula, and the same is true of the most controversial of Eckhart's formulations, such as his teaching about the uncreated and deifying character of the Intellect "in the soul". Retraction was easy, since the formula in question—*aliquid est in anima quod est increatum et increabile . . . et hoc est Intellectus*—when not regarded as elliptical, is erroneous by reason of the fact that it seems to affirm immanentism pure and simple; in reality it implicitly affirms the created intellect as the vehicle of the uncreated Intellect, but it does not put this into words since spiritual vision is "vertical" and "essential", not "horizontal" and "analogical".

*

*   *

The opposition of Creator and creature, of Lord and servant, is irreducible because man cannot be God.

The essential identity of manifested intelligence and principial Intelligence is necessary and metaphysically clear because the microcosmic subject cannot be of another essence than the absolute Subject, the Subject as such, the Self. There is only one single Subject; the rest is blindness.

We may thus differentiate between perspectives that are objective and outward, where the divine Objectivity confronts the individual subject, and a perspective that is subjective and inward, where the universal Subject is considered without regard to possible degrees of objectification.

The monotheistic religions are objective perspectives; now it is not possible to set forth directly, in "objective" terms, the "subjective" truth[5] of the essential identity between the objectified subject and the pure Subject; the extinction of the microcosmic subject in the metacosmic Object[6] is not strictly speaking a formula of identity, although the reality thus expressed is the same.

Objective perspectives start from the irreducible distinction between the subject and the Object; subjective perspectives do not see the object except as a function of the one and exclusive reality of the Subject.

---

[5] It goes without saying that the terms "subject" and "object" are being used here only with the strictly logical and universal meaning they have in themselves, and not in the least "psychologically".

[6] Al-Ghazzali speaks of "those who are consumed by the splendors of the sublime Face (the Essence) and who are submerged by the majesty of the divine Glory to such an extent that they are effaced and brought to nothing, and there is no longer any room for contemplation of themselves since they no longer have anything to do with the soul. Nothing remains except the One, the Real" (*Mishkāt al-Anwār*). Monotheistic dogmas do not exclude formulations that are "subjective" in their mode, however, and the Hallajian *anā'l-Haqq* is an example of this.

*

* *

There are three great, divine mysteries: the world, Being, Non-Being.

In the world no quality is another quality, and no quality is God. In Being no quality is another quality, but each of them is God. In Non-Being—Beyond-Being—there are no qualities; but since Non-Being is transcendence and not privation, having no qualities because it is beyond all diversity, it can be said that in it every quality is every other and that their nondistinction—or their transcending—is God.

What reason cannot comprehend is how the world can be metaphysically reducible to God and how God can be Non-Being, or better Beyond-Being. The world exists, but it "is" not. When the divine Reality is considered in its totality, God "is" not, but He "possesses Being": God-Being is in reality only the Being of God. Nonetheless it is not false to say that God "is" in relation to the world; humanly speaking, it can even be said—though the expression is incorrect—that God "exists" in order to specify that He is not "nonexistent", that is, that He is "real", "positive", "concrete".

*

* *

Analogy is a mode of identity; otherwise there would be only an absolute difference, an irreducible opposition, between the two terms of comparison: now such an opposition would reduce one of the terms to nothing. Man is "nothing" in the context of his separation, but not from the standpoint of analogy.

Man is made "in the image" of God. This is what allows him to "become" what he "is".[7] The word "become" is here entirely approximate and provisional, for there is no real continuity between "what should be" and "what has never been".

*

* *

[7] Meister Eckhart said that the image—the Son—expresses "identity" (*Gleichheit*) with the Father.

Creatures are good or bad; in created things there are qualities and defects, perfections and imperfections. Everything that is good in one way or another "pre-exists" in God; otherwise there would be perfections whose source or cause was other than divine. Everything that is good is good because God is good; hence no quality, no perfection, can be lost; God can never be something "less" in relation to the world. For this reason one may say that what is "lost" before God is "found again" in Him.

*
*   *

God is said to have created the world "by an absolutely gratuitous act"; He was not "obliged" to create it. This amounts to saying that necessity is an imperfection and arbitrariness a perfection; one might as well say that God is perfect by caprice since He is not "obliged" to be so. Is it not its necessity that constitutes the perfection of a geometrical figure? God possesses two complementary perfections in an absolute fashion, liberty and necessity, each in a different way: liberty refers to the Infinite, necessity to the Absolute. The absolute character of God is not an imperfection any more than His justice. God creates because He is God—there is no place here for arbitrariness—but in His creation He gives free rein to all the imponderables of His infinite liberty. The creative act is derived from divine necessity, the created content from divine liberty. God could refrain from creating a particular being, but He cannot not create at all since He cannot not be God.

*
*   *

Human liberty is necessary since it is determined by God, the Cause of all.

Divine necessity is free since it has no cause outside itself.

Human necessity is doubly necessary: first of all divinely and then humanly; the impossibility of man's changing his form has both a metaphysical cause and secondarily a physical cause. As for the divine liberty it is doubly free, above all in itself and then with regard to the world.

But the divine necessity is not free with regard to the world; otherwise it would contradict itself and create the impossible. And

178

conversely: human liberty is not necessary with regard to God because in this respect it participates in the absolute, divine liberty.

Man's freedom to choose God is already something of the freedom of God.

*
*   *

Between the human microcosm and the divine Metacosm there stands the macrocosm, which represents "the Principle manifested" or "the manifestation of the Principle" in relation to the human subject. There is no common measure between man and God, the "I" and the "Self": in order to become conscious of the "Self" the "I" needs the Intellect, which is its direct manifestation in man. In a similar fashion what necessarily stands between the formal creation and the Uncreated is the supraformal or non-formal creation, the world of the Spirit.

There is no common measure between manifestation and the Principle, and for this reason there cannot be an intermediate point situated as it were "mathematically" at the center; this center exists only in relation to the world, in a purely symbolic manner. It appears either as "the Principle manifested" or as "the manifestation of the Principle"; it has no existence apart from these two "poles" but may be reduced to either one: it is either "Principle" or "manifestation". Between God and the world stands the "avataric", Christic, prophetic mystery: the mystery of the human God or the divine man.

Man cannot know or meet God if he has not known or met Him in the world; he is separated from God if he denies revelation or if he does not see God in his neighbor. In a certain sense everything that comes into contact with man acts as "neighbor"—and thus indirectly as God—in an appropriate manner. In the neighbor God wishes to be loved and heard: He wishes to be loved through the charity we practice toward men and to be heard in the teachings they give us either directly or indirectly; He is hidden in the neighbor, either in the perfections that teach the truth or in the misfortunes that call forth charity.

If a man does not trample on a flower without reason, it is because the flower is something of God, a distant effect of the infinite Cause; whoever despises a flower indirectly despises God. If a good man had the power to destroy a stone, he would nevertheless not do so without a motive, for the existence of the stone—this quasi-absolute something that distinguishes it from nothingness—is a manifestation of the Principle; it is therefore sacred. In every neutral contact with matter—and this is all the more true of contact with one's fellow men—a man should either not leave any trace or else leave a beneficent trace; he should either enrich or pass unperceived. Even when there is a need to destroy—in which case the destruction is divinely willed—a man should destroy in conformity with the nature of the object, which then objectifies human nothingness to the extent the man is the agent of a celestial will. The life of man being sacred, the destructions it inevitably requires are also sacred.

The ternary "ego-world-God" or "I-Intellect-Self", or again "form-spirit-Cause", is found analogically in the ternary "humility-charity-truth" as well as in the three great stages of the spiritual life: purification, perfection, union.

*
*   *

Life is the passage of an individual dream, a consciousness, an ego through a cosmic and collective dream. Death withdraws the particular dream from the general dream and tears out the roots the former has thrust into the latter. The universe is a dream woven of dreams; the Self alone is awake.

The objective homogeneity of the world does not prove its absolute reality but rather the collective nature of the illusion, or a particular illusion, a particular world.

For the ego the world is not a subjective state; it is an objective and polyvalent reality; but for the divine Self the world—or a particular world—is a subjective unity like a particular soul. When the Intellect, which is as it were hidden within us and in which we can participate under certain conditions of realization and grace, has seen the Self and has penetrated us with this vision, then the world will appear to us a precarious and fugitive substance—thus a dream—and it is our spiritual consciousness that will be revealed as polyvalent and stable, whether one calls this realization grace, knowledge, or something else.

VI

THE SPIRITUAL VIRTUES

1

Setting aside the purely formal factors of the contemplative life, which do not directly engage the intellectual and moral worth of man, we can say that spirituality stands in a sense between metaphysical truth and human virtue, or rather that it has an absolute need of these two, though it can be reduced to neither. The presence in our mind of metaphysical truth is by itself inoperative as far as our final ends are concerned. Similarly, virtues sundered from truth do not have the power to raise us above ourselves—if indeed they can still subsist—for only the truth can surpass the level of our nature.

Truths make us understand virtues, giving them all their cosmic amplitude and their efficacy. Virtues for their part lead us to truths and transform them for us into realities that are concrete, seen, and lived.

*
*   *

Everything revolves around truth and the will; the one must penetrate the other. Truth illumines the will, which, when illuminated, vivifies the truth. From the point of view of fallen man truth is dead, and the will is blind. Truth is life, but in human consciousness it appears *a priori* as a dead letter.

Intelligence is nothing without truth, and without virtue it is unable to contain truth in a really adequate and absolutely stable way. As for the will it is nothing without virtue, and without truth it cannot realize virtue in a profound and total manner.

Truth is what we must know: the Absolute and the relative and, at their points of contact—if one may speak in this way—the divine will in all its complexity. As for virtue, it is humility[1] and charity. Truth includes something of both humility and charity in its manifestation;

---

[1] This word is taken in its etymological sense, which is independent of the sentimental flavor it has in fact acquired. In itself the word "humility" expresses a fundamental attitude independent of any particular sentimentality, and this amounts to saying that the emotive concomitants of this attitude may differ according to the point of view.

183

humility is false if it has neither truth nor charity, and charity is false if it has neither truth nor humility. The virtues condition one another.

Truth becomes virtue when it appears on the level of our will, and it is then veracity and sincerity.

*

* *

The three fundamental virtues—veracity, charity, humility—must penetrate even into our thinking since this thinking is an act. There is no plane of activity where the virtues should not intervene. When pure truth manifests itself, it cannot do so without the virtues, for manifestation is an act.

Humility means looking at oneself in the limiting state of individuation; it means turning one's gaze on the ego, limitation, nothingness. Charity means looking around oneself: it means seeing God in one's neighbor and also seeing oneself there, though this time not as pure limitation but as a creature of God made in His image. Veracity means looking toward Truth, submitting and attaching oneself to it, and becoming penetrated by its implacable light. Each of the three virtues must be found again in the others; they are the criteria of one another.

*

* *

Charitable humility will avoid causing scandal and thus injuring one's neighbor; it must not be contrary to self-effacement, which is its sufficient reason.

Truthful humility will avoid overestimation: virtue must not run counter to truth. But it can be more "true" than some outward and sterile truth; in this case it is virtue that is truth, and the contradiction is only apparent.

Humble charity will avoid exhibiting itself without any useful purpose; man must not pride himself on his generosity: "Let not thy left hand know what thy right hand doeth." The gift of self should be above all inward; without this gift outward charity is devoid of spiritual value and blessing.

Truthful charity is conscious of the nature of things: I am not less than my neighbor since I too exist and have an immortal soul. On the other hand it may be that some higher interest takes precedence over some particular interest of the neighbor; in a general way spiritual interest takes precedence over temporal interest whether it is a question of the "neighbor" or "oneself".

Humble veracity will not hide our ignorance; to pretend to a knowledge we do not possess is harmful to the knowledge we do possess.

Charitable veracity will neglect nothing in order to make the truth understood; if truth is a good, it should also be a gift.

Effacement of ego, gift of self, realization of truth. It could be said that these attitudes correspond respectively to the stages—or states—of purification, expansion, union. They are the three "dimensions" of perfect *gnosis*.

*

*   *

A spiritual virtue is nothing other than consciousness of a reality; it is natural—but immaterial—if it is accompanied by feeling. When virtue is purely sentimental, in the sense of being ignorant of the reality to which it relates, it may have a relative utility, but it is nonetheless a spiritual obstacle and a source of errors.

*

*   *

If metaphysics is sacred, this means it cannot be presented as though it were only a profane philosophy sufficient unto itself, that is, not surpassing the sphere of mental operations. It is illogical and dangerous to talk of metaphysics without concerning oneself with its moral concomitants, whose criteria for man are his behavior in relation to God and his neighbor.

*

*   *

The key to understanding the spiritual necessity of the virtues lies in the fact that metaphysical truths are reflected in the will and not just in the Intellect and reason. To a given principial truth there corresponds a specific volitional attitude; this is a necessary aspect—or a consequence—of the principle that "to know is to be".

*

*   *

To meditate on the divine qualities is at the same time to meditate on the virtues—and consequently the vices—of human beings. Spirituality includes concentric circles and radii, modes of analogy and modes of identity: virtues and intellections. When intellections are replaced by rational operations, it is the virtues in their turn that appear as modes of identity, as "relatively direct" participations in the divine Being.

*

*   *

We must clearly distinguish between natural qualities and spiritual virtues, although the appearances may be the same and although, in principle, the first constitute qualifications for the second; we say "in principle" because in fact natural qualities may give rise to a moral idolatry that prevents the passage to a higher plane and can even provoke spiritual falls. In other words natural qualities do not necessarily retain their efficacy on the spiritual level; this is also true of a purely mental—or "worldly"—intelligence, though not of metaphysical intuition when it is predominant, for metaphysical intuition by definition belongs to the domain of the spirit and therefore to the domain of the immutable.

There are vices that appear in certain men only on the spiritual, or so-called spiritual, level; and from this results the paradox of men who are naturally intelligent and spiritually stupid or modest on the surface and fundamentally proud. As soon as a man tries to go beyond himself the qualities that are linked strictly to his earthly nature and not anchored in his spiritual essence become more or less inoperative.

In some cases mental intelligence is the normal expression of the Intellect, but in others it is the opposition between the natural and the supernatural intelligence that manifests itself.

*
*   *

If qualities may be only apparent and not real, the same must be true of certain defects.

False qualities are always superficial and fragmentary, hence inoperative beyond certain limits; they are not false on their own level of manifestation but in relation to the sum of the characteristics that make up the individual. The same thing is true *mutatis mutandis* of superficial defects: they are situated on the surface of the soul and cannot indefinitely resist the contrary—and fundamental—tendencies of the soul itself; and this implies that such defects—like the qualities of which we have just spoken—always remain within certain limits.

It is the overall nature of man that decides his intrinsic worth: if there is incompatibility between a quality and a defect, this means that they are not situated on the same level and that one of the two characteristics is only superficial; thus the criterion lies in their respective scope, so that some essential aspect of the soul—one that is decisive by its nature—will be the key for evaluating all the other aspects. It goes without saying that there are qualities and defects that are too important to be merely accidental; it is also evident that a great good excludes a great evil of the same order, and conversely; hence they cannot both be found in the same individual.

*
*   *

Strictly social morality does not permit psychological or spiritual complications, and in this it is right in view of its practical bearing; on the other hand it is improper to attach an absolute value to this point of view and to apply it to the intrinsic nature of man. Narrow-minded moralists do not like complications, and they think this is because of their own "straightforwardness", thus absolving themselves of the need for reflection. Nonetheless complexity is to be met with everywhere in the world: there are mammals that live like fish and others that live like birds, just as there are winged creatures adapted to the water and others adapted to the land. There are men whose qualities are genuine only at the level of profane life and others whose defects result only from ephemeral conditions on this same level.

Normally a man's evident qualities should manifest his fundamental worth, but it may happen that such qualities merely compensate for latent defects that are themselves fundamental; where there is analogy there may also be opposition. Every human quality may either express or contradict a divine perfection: it expresses it thanks to its analogy with this perfection and contradicts it because of its own relativity, which then—despite its positive content—sets it in opposition to its celestial prototype. To speak of expression is to speak at the same time of analogy, relativity, opposition.

A quality has a definitive value only through its inward humility—its position before God. False virtues are those that man alone enjoys without God being able to delight in them.

*
*   *

The world is woven of analogies and oppositions in relation to God; either of these can be real or merely apparent. This is why the world is full of paradoxes, for both good and ill.

*
*   *

The disproportion between the natural virtues and those having a supernatural essence or between those tainted by a secret vanity and those that are pure and deep implies that virtues of the second category may be at times less apparent than those of the first and that a certain spiritual modesty may even conceal them. It may also be that some inner reality, misunderstood from without, may seem to contradict them.

In a similar manner *gnosis* sometimes gives rise to paradoxical expressions, which in reality indicate the qualitative separation between the profane and spiritual planes; but this discontinuity is only one aspect alongside another that is more important, that of analogy and essential continuity.

*

*   *

A virtue is a token of immortality only on condition that it is founded on God; this gives it a character at once impersonal and generous. A quality that is purely natural—and not validated by a spiritual attitude infusing it with divine life—has no more importance for God than "sounding brass".

*

*   *

There are men who are virtuous in a conventional way, on the surface of their being and for the sole reason that their habitual environment imposes certain styles of action on them; this does not at all mean that such virtues are without merit at a particular level, however small the merit might be. There are other men who are incapable of being virtuous in a purely conventional way and without a deep understanding of the nature of things, but whose virtue would on the contrary be unshakeable given such an understanding.

A virtue that is purely natural, that is, independent of any acceptance of truth and any movement toward God, is like a crystal with which a man might try to light a darkened room; the crystal is naturally luminous, but its properties of purity and transparency and its power to focus luminous rays are inoperative without the presence of light, which in our example is nothing other than humility or perfect objectivity toward the ego and its infirmities. Or likewise: the color white is certainly luminous when set beside black, but it cannot light up a dark place; similarly a quality is certainly good when set beside a vice, but if it is not accompanied by a true, inner effacement before God and before the merit of our neighbor, it will be drowned in the blackness of hidden vanity just as the color white is drowned in darkness. One other example: without any question a horse in itself represents a force, but when two elephants pulling in the opposite direction are harnessed to the other end of a vehicle, the strength of the horse becomes inoperative even though it does not for a moment cease to exist. It is the same with the force or merit possessed by a strictly human virtue, one not illumined or transfigured by a spiritual development, by a real victory over our nature, by a gift of our being to God.

Virtue in itself is necessary, for light does not pass through an opaque stone and barely illuminates a black wall; man must therefore become like crystal or snow but without maintaining that snow is light.

On the other hand even fire loses its brilliance before the sun; it is thus that in knowledge—or perfect love—the virtues lose their separate existence and human conditioning.

*
*   *

God at times permits weaknesses in order to be able—by means of the contrast between these accidental infirmities and the essential being—to awaken virtues that are all the more profound. Qualities that have grown up from the compost of some affliction are as it were endowed with consciousness; in a concrete way they know the vanity of error.

At times God reinforces the appearance of the natural in order to be able to make the supernatural all the more evident, or He permits weakness in order to bring out the radiance and transcendence—or the gratuitous nature—of grace all the more fully, and this is without prejudice to the fact that in a general way God brings the receptacle into conformity with the supernatural gift, for these two possibilities are combined in different ways.

Too great an indulgence toward others is often caused not by an innate weakness of character but by an actual inability to conceive the frailty of men and the malice of the devil. Human beings have a tendency to believe only what they see; now there are men who *a priori* see God rather than the secret evil of creatures.

*
*   *

Scandal mongering is an evil because one who is absent cannot defend himself and the divulging of an unfavorable fact may injure him and also because man naturally tends to overestimate his own power of judgment. From the point of view of simple logic it is normal for a

190

man to report facts that surprise him or make him suffer since in principle he always has the right to ask for advice and assure himself of the correctness of his own feeling; but this depends on the accuracy of the facts and the impartiality of the witness as well as the moral dignity of the interlocutor, quite apart from safeguarding those who are absent. Now in practice there is no means of guaranteeing that these conditions are always completely fulfilled, and indeed in nine cases out of ten they will not be; insofar as it concerns the collectivity the moral law is therefore obliged to sacrifice the exception to the rule and the particular truth to the general expediency.

As for calumny, it consists in peddling inaccurate and unfavorable facts and in interpreting unfavorably things that are susceptible to a favorable interpretation, making no distinction between what is certain, probable, possible, doubtful, improbable, and impossible. Calumny is not a matter of accidental mistakes but of systematic passion.

*

* *

In psychology as elsewhere we must differentiate between accidental essences and essences as such; thus the fact that a human being is young or is a woman constitutes a kind of essence for the person—the will cannot change it in any way—but its character is accidental, for age is fleeting and a person's sex neither adds nor takes away any fundamental human value. On the other hand there are also essential accidents, that is, accidents that manifest an essence: for example, a very unusual destiny that would be incompatible with a different essence, the mortal sin of a man who is damned, the sudden conversion of a dying man, or a crucial fact determining the life of a saint.

Experience can teach us that a man who is apparently quite imperfect may in time reveal very solid virtues, or conversely. The supernatural alone guarantees the stability of human values.

*

* *

A thought that is in itself passionate and self-interested, and "juridical" instead of "just" in its external functioning—its logic lacking a sense of proportion and thus what one might call "the aesthetic dimension" of intelligence—cannot encompass all aspects of truth; it is a thought that "argues" and does not "listen".

Pure intellectuality depends upon thought, which in itself is contemplative, hence as completely disinterested as the act of seeing, and which in its outward functioning employs a logic that is not artificial or somehow mechanical but consonant with the real nature of things.

We could almost speak of a "moral dimension" of intelligence: moral elevation, which has nothing to do with external laws but depends upon beauty of soul, excludes an arbitrary functioning of the mind; if "beauty is the splendor of the true", it is also in a sense its criterion and guarantee, though in a subtle manner that cannot be comprehended by means of a purely theoretical knowledge; otherwise the idea of beauty would automatically confer beauty on the soul. It is true that every man has a tendency to attribute to himself what he is merely able to conceive: there is no proud man who does not deem himself humble, assuming he admits that humility is a virtue.

If truth is a constituent element of beauty, beauty is in turn a necessary factor of intellectual manifestation. There is no error without some ugliness: like every form thought is made up of conformities and proportions.

*

* *

There are men who believe themselves to be without passions because they have transferred their whole passional life to the mental plane, which becomes "egoistic".

"Wisdom after the flesh" is among other things mental passion with its compensating complement, petrifaction; it is the thought of a "hardened heart".

Since he transcends the mind, the sage loses his concepts in contemplation; he is always being born anew. Charity is to lose oneself.

*

* *

To take fallen man as the human norm is to end up idealizing not man but the human animal, the thinking beast.

Men who spiritually speaking are "fools" are often more cunning than wise men; hence their conviction, which is sustained by a certain practical experience, that they are more intelligent than such men. But this experience is limited by their very ignorance and therefore furnishes only a quite specious argument.

There are modes of intelligence that are more or less mutually exclusive in their development; this becomes very apparent when a comparison is made between the Middle Ages and the modern era or between the traditional East and the "progressive" West.

*

* *

In the normal state of the world the intelligent man possesses intelligence, and the fool is without it, but in our period of the "realization of impossibilities"—if one may venture such an elliptical definition—we see everywhere fools who are accidentally intelligent and intelligent men who are accidentally fools.

Among our ancestors intelligence had a sort of artlessness; being at once contemplative and practical, it was not projected in its entirety onto the plane of discursive thought and hardly needed external complications. In our day the opposite occurs: what characterizes our period is not so much stupidity in itself as intelligent stupidity.

In former times the devil would have had every reason for showing himself in his characteristic guise, for in this form he fascinated and intimidated the weak and perverse; indeed he was obliged to reveal himself in this manner because faith in God was everywhere. But today it is the devil who is everywhere, and he therefore no longer has any reason for showing himself as he is, nor does anything any longer oblige him to do so; on the contrary he has every reason to make people deny him since, in order to be able to make them forget God, the devil must himself be forgotten.

*

* *

"Be ye therefore wise as serpents", says the Gospel, not "be ye therefore cunning as foxes". Wisdom or prudence is defensive and is based on generosity; but cunning is aggressive, and its basis is a glacial egoism.

True intelligence has no need of cunning, for it has a sense of proportion. With cunning man falls "intelligently" into error, but with a sense of proportion he remains "naively" in truth.

Every man must resign himself to the thought that he is of necessity a little foolish; humility is not a luxury.

Most of our contemporaries would rather appear bad than naive; and yet God is indulgent toward a sincere naiveté and even has a tenderness for it, but He always hates pretentious cleverness and spitefulness or arrogance.

*

* *

A tendency toward suspicion is no more a normal mode of intelligence[2] than is guile. If suspicion is legitimate when it arises incidentally—and exceptionally—from an accurate impression, it is illegitimate as soon as it becomes a tendency and a kind of principle, for it then engenders a sickness of the soul that is incompatible with virtue and hence with sanctity.

But suspicion not only feeds on subjective illusions: it also lives on objective appearances, which are just as illusory but nonetheless rooted in facts. Indeed suspicion, which essentially ignores the laws of coincidence and paradox, often finds itself corroborated by appearances that the environment seems to create quite wantonly, and this is by no means the least of the aspects of cosmic illusion; these possibilities—accumulations of coincidences, of appearances contrary to the reality they hide—are necessary applications of the principle of contradiction, which is included in universal Possibility. Sometimes the paradox is intentional on man's part, as is shown by the classic example of Omar Khayyam, whose wisdom clothed in frivolity is

---

[2] A *hadīth* says: "Keep yourselves from suspicion, for suspicion is the most deceitful thing the soul can hold out as an enticement to man." Another says: "Do not make investigations and do not spy." The police mentality is in fact closely linked with a suspicious and corrosive moralism and even with a certain mania of persecution.

opposed to a Phariseeism clothed in piety; if religious hypocrisy is possible, the contrary paradox must be equally so.

It is sometimes necessary for the good to show itself under the accidental appearance of evil, and conversely—a superficial illusion, which would always be discernible if self-interest did not prevent man from perceiving the truth.

*

* *

In certain respects every human manifestation, every thought, is an "evil" before God since every manifestation of oneself is an affirmation "alongside" God and in "opposition" to Him; in other respects every thought is inevitably a form of egoism because it does not confer a blessing on one's neighbor; finally every thought indicates a sort of illusion insofar as it does not act as a vehicle of Reality. Our nature lives on forgetfulness.

To efface oneself, to bless one's neighbor, to contemplate Truth: three ways of remembering.

There are evils that are inevitable, that are inherent in existence and individuation, and that are therefore capable of being the vehicles of a good; in this case they lose, if not their limitative character, at least their poison; but as soon as they become the vehicles of an evil, their own wretchedness reappears before God; they again become evils.

2

The spiritual necessity of the virtues is founded not only on the analogy between the human and the Divine but also on the complementary relationship—in the microcosm—between the center and the totality; this is because it is not possible for man to realize in his heart-intellect what he conceives in his mind without making the whole of his being participate in this realization. The intellective center of a being is not reached without involving his volitional circumference: he who wants the center must realize the whole; in other words he who wants to know with the heart-intellect must "know" with the whole soul, and this entails the purification of the soul and therefore the virtues. When the mind is purified by doctrinal truth and the whole being is purified by virtue, Truth can reveal itself in the heart with the help of God.

Virtue is "moral"—and therefore volitive—"truth"; it concerns not only action but all of life. The center of man cannot see as long as his periphery is blind.

Virtue is the abolition of egoism. Why? Because the ego is error: it is a principle of illusion, which falsifies the proportions of things in relation to both God and one's neighbor.

*

*   *

The spiritual importance of the virtues is apparent in the fact that there are inner obstacles that come only from the falsity—or from the ugliness, which amounts to the same thing—of certain human attitudes. At the moment man wants to draw near to God the ugliness of his attitude toward others turns against him.

To know God with all that we are: the very infinity of the object of knowledge requires the totality of the act of knowing, and this totality requires the essential virtues.

It is always these essential virtues we have in view and not the qualities required by secondary human functions, such as courage and diligence. In appropriate circumstances qualities such as these obviously combine with the fundamental virtues, which in principle they depend upon. But this in no way concerns a moralism that sees in the most contingent quality an end in itself.

*
* *

It is abundantly clear that virtue, in the general and ordinary sense of the term, is by no means a guarantee of spiritual knowledge, for the thinking of a man who is "normally" virtuous may—barring pure and simple ignorance—be steeped in mental passion and unconscious presumption. In order to awaken intellection virtue must penetrate even into thought, just as knowledge should penetrate into inward and outward actions to be complete.

When virtue reaches the innermost regions of the soul, it gives rise to illumination; when the wall of a darkened room is broken, light cannot fail to enter. Complete virtue is the elimination of everything that constitutes an obstacle to *gnosis* and love.

Actions are not only superficial manifestations of the individual but also criteria of his heart, hence of his essence and of his knowledge or ignorance. To watch over one's actions is therefore not only an individual preoccupation; in some cases it is also a pursuit of purity of heart for the sake of the knowledge of God.

This confers on the theory of sin, on the examination of conscience, and on penitence a significance that goes further than any religious individualism, making them compatible with pure spirituality: in Muslim esoterism as in Christian mysticism, this strictly alchemical way of regarding actions, whether good or bad, goes hand in hand with selfless contemplation of God.

*
* *

On the plane of activity everything is a matter of proportion and equilibrium: individualistic or sentimental deviations are always possible but cannot discredit action as such. If action directly or indirectly exteriorizes what the heart contains and what the individual "knows"—or does not know—of God, it may also and conversely act upon the heart: it purifies the heart for the sake of knowledge or else hardens and darkens it; it may be either virtuous or sinful.

It is in this sense that there exists a necessary connection between action and virtue.

*

* *

If "beauty is the splendor of the true", then it can be said that moralism consists in sundering beauty from truth. Without truth beauty cannot exist, and this explains the ugliness associated with moralism. It replaces knowledge of the true by idolatry of a "good" that is often arbitrary and cramped.

In the very nature of things moralism is ignorant of both truth and beauty: it cannot avoid being hypocritical in relation to the former and a mockery in relation to the latter.

One of the most salient criteria of moralism is calumny of the object on account of the corruptibility of the subject.

The opposite error, intellectualism, consists in sundering truth from beauty—not truth as such, which is sufficient unto itself, but truth as it is reflected in us and transmitted by us. The question of beauty does not arise for pure truth, but it does arise for the human receptacle—for the substance it gives to the lightning flashes of the spirit.

*

* *

Spirituality has for its object not man but God; this is something a certain moral absolutism seems to forget.

Spirituality has a negative condition: the absence of error and vice; and it has a positive object: contemplation of the Divine. Vice—passion—clouds the organ that should contemplate God, and this organ is the whole man.

*

* *

In esoteric doctrines it always comes about that things "worshipped" on one plane are "consigned to the flames" on another; hence the apparent rejection of the virtues—by the Sufi Ibn al-Arif or by Buddhists, for example.

"God alone is good." All that is not God can in principle be rejected on one ground or another. The setting of the sun is only an appearance but an appearance imposing itself on all men and thus having nothing fortuitous about it: the sun must set because it is not God, or again as the Prophet said, "It must prostrate itself every evening before the Throne of *Allāh.*"

*

*   *

If it is true that virtue is the absence of vice, it is even truer that vice is the absence of virtue. Virtue exists before vice because God is before the world; vice is the privation of virtue since the world is in a certain sense the privation of God. If one begins with the fallen nature of man, it is legitimate to say that virtue is in practice the absence of a vice even though in reality the relationship is just the opposite; but the realization of God is the negation of the world only insofar as the world is the negation of God. Considered independently of human imperfection virtue obviously reflects a divine perfection by its intrinsic quality.

*

*   *

The vulgarization of spirituality—inevitable within certain limits— carries with it a predominance of moral injunctions over considerations of spiritual alchemy: the dynamism of the will is preached, and the good residing in the very nature of things is neglected; the "duty of doing" is insisted on, and "being" is forgotten.

Intellective contemplation goes straight to the existential roots of the virtues; it finds the virtues again, beyond moral effort, in the nature of things.[1]

---

[1] The *Philokalia* says, "When the wise soul is in the state that is natural to it, virtue is necessarily found in it. The soul finds itself in its natural state when it remains as it has been created. . . . The soul is just when its knowledge remains in the state that is natural to it. . . . This is why virtue is not a difficult thing; when we remain as we have been created, we are in a state of virtue. . . . If we had to seek for virtue outside ourselves, this would certainly be difficult; but since it is within us, it is enough to avoid evil thoughts and to keep our soul [as it is *a priori*] turned toward the Lord."

But since man is not pure contemplation, effort is also required of him.

*
*   *

Intellection and virtue: everything is there.

Intellection refers to the divine "I", to the pure and absolute Subject, to "Consciousness" that is absolutely non-objectified, to God-Intellect: divine Knowledge.

Virtue refers to divine "Being", to pure and infinite Objectivity, to Reality free of all individuation, to God-Being: divine Qualities.

The way of intellection, the way of virtue: one does not go without the other, but one or the other predominates in keeping with human temperaments.

If "the soul is all that it knows", one may also say in another respect: "the soul knows all that it is".

3

In Hindu morals—*yama* and *niyama*—humility appears as "modesty" (*hrī*); spiritual, or one might say esoteric, humility is "childlikeness" (*bālya*) or, in its highest sense, "extinction" (*nirvāna*). An attitude that is in a sense intermediate—between *hrī* and *bālya*—is that of devotion to the master (*guru*).

Among Asians sentimentality is certainly not absent, but it lies less deep in them than in most Europeans.

Divine revelation always conforms to the human receptacle. Thus it is said that angels speak to each man in the appropriate tongue.

*

*   *

The acceptance of injustice may have a spiritual meaning: humility then consists in having recourse to divine justice alone at the price of earthly rights; human justice may in fact become a pretext for egocentrism or, in Vedantic terms, for the superimposition of an "I" on the "Self".

*

*   *

Man is "made in the image of God"; to humiliate this image may be a profanation. Likewise the intelligence cannot humble itself in its impersonal essence or transcendent principle; one must not seek to humiliate the Holy Spirit along with man.

One thing remains intact in our fall, and this is the Intellect. Moral requirements therefore do not account for the whole of man; if the difference between primordial man and fallen man were absolute, they would not be the same being; only one would be human. But there is something unalterable in man, and this can be a spiritual starting point, like the abyss of the fall.

The element in man that becomes aware that he is despicable cannot itself be what is to be despised; what judges cannot be what is judged.

*

*   *

Ramakrishna, when speaking of a certain show of humility—an unbalanced humility one might say—rightly remarks that people who are forever comparing themselves to the lowest animals end by becoming as feebleminded as they. A purely moralistic humility blindly imitates a virtue that is in itself lucid, and it paralyses not only the knowledge but even the love of God; false humility never has its roots in truth. Virtue can be a form of idolatry like anything else.

Man needs humility to the extent that he does not think of God—to the extent that he does not forget himself in thinking of God.

*

*   *

It is possible for a man not to know he is nothing and yet cultivate a feeling of humility. He may believe he is far more than he is in reality and cultivate a sentimental humility.[1]

It is possible not to know that the "neighbor" is "myself" and yet cultivate a feeling of charity. One may be an egoist and at the same time cultivate a sentimental charity.

To know "I am nothing" is perfect humility; to know the "neighbor is myself" is perfect charity. What is rooted in existence is perfect, not what depends upon action.

*

*   *

When humility assumes a quasi-unique form in the sense that it obliges a man to believe he is literally and individually the worst of sinners, it has something in common with what the same individualistic perspective refers to as "pride"; the opposite of such "pride" does

---

[1] Certain suspicions on the part of theologians regarding a Saint Bernadette or a Saint Teresa of the Child Jesus show to what confusions the purely moralistic conception of humility can give rise.

not in fact consist in believing oneself to be for one reason or another a unique being but rather in knowing oneself to be an insignificant accident amid an indefinite number of such accidents. The Word humbled itself not by becoming Jesus but by becoming man.

Nirvāna, extinction: extinction of the "sin" of existence. He who literally believes himself to be the worst of sinners is not even close to being extinguished.

*
*   *

If it is illogical to believe oneself "the worst of men", it is not only because the worst of men would not take himself to be the worst—for if he did he would not be—but because so unique an individual does not exist any more than does "the most beautiful of women"; if beauty has by definition an infinity of equivalent modes, which are reciprocally incomparable, the same is true of every other quality and also every vice.

The most perfect—or least imperfect—of ascetics can realize humility only in certain respects; otherwise he would end by sinning from humility.[2] This proves that humility, in the exclusively ascetic meaning of the term, is of value only in a very conditional way—that it is relative like all penitence. It is not on the ascetic level that humility can be total.

Instead of seeking the Absolute beyond himself, the exclusive moralist projects a kind of absolute into his own relativity by concerning himself indefinitely with the perfection—metaphysically impossible moreover—of what is only an instrument or support: the individual, the human. It is as if, instead of accomplishing a work with a usable instrument, a man devoted his whole life to making this instrument better.

It will be said that all our apparent qualities come from God and not from ourselves. This is perfectly true, but by the same token it removes from our neighbor all merit and from ourselves the possibility

---

[2] The concept of a "sin from humility" or of achieving humility through sin did indeed exist among certain Russian heretics; detached from its sufficient reason, the notion of humility is then reduced to absurdity.

of being worse than he; in other words it takes away from us the possibility of believing ourselves to be the vilest of men or at least of suffering from such a conviction.

*
*   *

The conviction of being the basest of men may determine a movement toward God; it may open a fissure in our darkness and thus allow grace to flow in.

But from a more profound point of view the question of knowing whether a man is "high" or "low" is a matter of complete indifference. What it is important to know is that every being, every relativity, is a limitation, hence a "nothingness".

Even on the earthly plane the nothingness of the "creature" is tangible in an altogether immediate way: in space as in time we are nothing; the two "infinities" crush us on every side. If the earth is a speck of dust in the measureless gulf of space and if life is an instant between two incalculable abysses of time, what remains of man? Man cannot add one inch to his stature nor one instant to his life; he cannot be in more than one place at a time; he can live only in the moment destiny has prescribed for him, unable to turn back or fly forward; and with all his vain glories man is physically just an animal, who hides his wretchedness with great difficulty.

*
*   *

We should never lose sight of the fact that a quality may be either the opposite of a defect on the same plane where this defect manifests itself or the absence of a defect by way of the elimination of this plane; pride is not the deepest root of evil, but egocentrism—whether "proud" or "humble"—which is itself the cause of all pride. It is true that this egocentrism is called "pride" in Christian terms, and the spiritual elimination of this illusion is called "humility".

An affected and as it were expansive humility is not the same thing as an absence of pride. In the case of such humility, which disregards intelligence, one never knows whether one is required to be

204

stupid or virtuous; in other words one never knows whether stupidity is a virtue or whether virtue is a form of stupidity.

*
* *

Individualistic, sentimental, and penitential humility is opposed to pride in the same way the color green is opposed to the color red; it is always an affectation, either useful or harmful as the case may be, and it is incompatible with a path that does not permit subjective positions contrary to objective truth.

Insofar as it is a spontaneous expression of virtue, humility is distinguished from pride in the same way white is distinguished from red; it is not an affectation, but a natural, or more exactly a primordial, state. It is in no way opposed to a sane affirmation of oneself or to an objective knowledge a man may have of his own worth;[3] on the other hand it does not constitute a path but is found in every good man.

Insofar as it is knowledge, humility is distinguished from pride in the same way pure light is distinguished from every color; it belongs to paths that exclude individualistic sentimentalities or to states that have passed beyond such a level.

*
* *

Men are very often prone to deem themselves exempt from the obligation of humility because they know their own qualities; they form an opinion of themselves according to their consciousness of some particular personal merit and not according to the balance of their nature as a whole. What they forget is that this merit may be diminished or even reduced to nothing by a flaw of which they are unaware or to which they attach no importance.

Knowledge is never illegitimate in itself; what is illegitimate are the improper conclusions drawn from it by human egocentrism, and

---

[3] Dante knew he was the greatest poet after Virgil and even the last great poet of that line; no moral reasoning forced him to be mistaken about himself, and history has confirmed his judgment.

it is for this reason that the qualities a man is conscious of do not in themselves constitute for him a guarantee of overall worth. The good resides in the qualities themselves, and the evil comes from the consciousness we have of them; this consciousness is an evil, however, only when the good is drowned in it.

*
*   *

The possibility of our becoming aware of our personal merits with impunity is connected to our effective capacity for knowing our limitations and destitution, for a man must be immunized against himself: he cannot really know himself without being penetrated by lights that wound him, the price of which is therefore high. Nonetheless, although our nature always obliges us to take account of the danger of illusion, it is not possible to legislate about knowledge, the rights of which remain by definition inalienable.

*
*   *

Man sees in himself alternatives and efforts, abysses and conflicting possibilities, which another does not see and which he himself does not see in another; the will, which to an outside witness is something already set and intelligible, is itself in a state of constant fermentation even if the agent is able in large measure to assume the point of view of a spectator.

This is why, subjectively, no one can be good. Or again: while knowing we are not evil in one respect, relatively speaking, we are ignorant of what we are in another respect—at least to the extent "we are", that is, to the extent the individuality finds itself in act.

Spiritually speaking, to know oneself is to be conscious of one's limitations and to attribute every quality to God.

*
*   *

Habitual readiness to criticize other people presupposes a kind of blindness in a man regarding his own state, but at the same time it provokes this blindness through an inevitable concordant reaction.

Whoever is obliged to criticize through force of circumstances, that is, for the sake of truth, should show himself all the more humble and charitable and capable of penetrating the secret good in creatures.

*

* *

Humility toward men may be an aspect of humility toward God, but it may also be the opposite insofar as there is an antinomy between the human order and the divine Order; it will then be said that a man must humble himself before God and not before men, while being free from all pride. One must distinguish moreover between humility and humiliation.[4]

If "he that humbleth himself shall be exalted" and conversely, this cannot be taken to imply a purely sentimental attitude that excludes more serene and profound applications. If humility is an essential attitude, it cannot be limited to sentimentality, ascetic or otherwise. Humility is profound to the extent it is lucid; the more intelligent it is the greater will be its detachment from forms.

Humbling oneself with zeal but without intelligence in order to be exalted: is this truly being "humble"?

*

* *

From the psychological point of view, humility is essential because it is logically impossible to be in potency and in act at the same time and in the same respect or to be simultaneously subject and object, and therefore to be judge in one's own cause. Man cannot "be" good and "define himself" as good at one and the same time: he cannot bring his mind to bear at one and the same time on a particular content of his

---

[4] Ibn Arabi says that the loftiest of the virtues, humility, is too noble to have to manifest itself as humiliation before men.

knowledge and on the act of knowing; the eye cannot see itself. "Let not thy left hand know what thy right hand doeth."

Virtue implies a kind of incessant movement since it involves our will; there is no life—and consequently no virtue—without continual renewal. Now to attribute a particular quality to oneself amounts to a fixation—or crystallization—of the inner flux that makes the quality live; the result is to make it sterile. In a similar fashion praise is unhealthy for the one who receives it and is not above it, for then it kills the good—which is never perfected since it must continue to live and renew itself—by a sort of anticipation calculated to exhaust its possibility, exactly as too much talk before an action compromises its realization in an almost magical way.

Nonetheless, if we say that knowledge always remains inalienable, this means that God can make known to us what we are, whether by the Intellect or grace. God knows the qualities—the "talents" of the parable—He has entrusted to us, and insofar as we know that "God alone is good" we can participate in this knowledge, the real subject of which can only be God Himself. This is an instance of the reciprocity between God and man: what man cannot know about himself as logical "subject", he can know through God, for whom man is "object"—on condition that he gives up making himself into God on the human plane.

*

*   *

We can understand without difficulty the meaning of humility before God; but what is the objective value of humility with regard to our neighbor? It resides in the fact that our neighbor can always teach us something even if only in a quite indirect way; in this respect he assumes a function that is quasi-divine.

Since every man has limitations, either fundamental or accidental, and since men are by definition different, there is every chance that our neighbor will not be limited in exactly the same fashion as ourselves and that he will therefore be free of limitations at the point where we are limited; in this respect he is our master.

In a certain sense the neighbor is the criterion of our sincerity toward God.

*

*   *

Pride consists in taking ourselves for what we are not and disparaging others; self-respect is knowing what one is and not allowing oneself to be humiliated. Self-respect does not prevent a man from humbling himself before what surpasses him; it is far from being the opposite of true humility, whatever the more superficial moralists may say.[5]

Modesty may be a quality or a defect according to whether it springs from veracity or weakness; but even in the latter case it is nearer virtue than vice, for weakness is preferable to presumption.

*

*   *

According to Saint Augustine, "The other vices attach themselves to evil in order that it may be done; pride alone attaches itself to the good in order that it may perish."

According to Boethius, "All the other vices flee from God; pride alone rises up against Him."[6]

*

*   *

Spiritually speaking, pride consists in attributing to oneself what is due to God. It poisons and kills every value, for as soon as man claims a good in its cause and essence, it is transmuted into evil: it embraces the limitations of the creature and engenders limitations in turn; pride appropriates the divine gift and then strangles it. A good vivifies

---

[5] To the question "Do you believe in God?" Joan of Arc replied: "Better than you!" Another instance of humble self-respect is this reply of a Hindu *guru* to a worldly traveler: "I am not worthy to be your master, and you are not worthy to be my disciple."

[6] The Hasidim Cabalists relate the following saying of their master, Baal Shem: "Pride is more serious than any sin. For it is in relation to sinners that God designates Himself [in the *Torah*] as 'He who dwelleth amid their impurities'. But as the wise men [of the *Talmud*] teach, God says of the proud man: 'I and he cannot dwell together in the world.'"

insofar as it comes from God, not insofar as it is handed on by man nor above all insofar as it is usurped by him.

Man deems himself good even before God, who is Perfection, and when he endeavors to recognize his wretchedness he again deems himself good on account of this effort.

*

* *

The existential drama has as it were three movements: adoration of God, adoration of the world, and adoration of self; the last is "pride" whereas all other vices belong to the second category.

Adoration of the world inevitably brings with it in some degree adoration of self, so that it is legitimate to attribute "pride" to every man, if only potentially so. In its universal sense "humility" is thus a *conditio sine qua non* of all spirituality: as soon as a man tears himself away from adoration of the world, he must pass through the temptations of "pride" in order to approach God; for the "I" wants to appropriate this approach and to glory in it to the detriment of what is its sufficient reason.

When the proud man learns that humility is a virtue, he wants to claim it for himself because he cannot bear to be inferior to others. If humility is the concealing of the virtues one has, hypocrisy is the counterfeiting of the virtues one does not have.

In general men readily believe they possess virtues simply because they are able to conceive of them.

*

* *

In every manifestation there is an element capable of leading one away from the Principle, and it is upon this element that "pride", which is the error that subjectively brings about this distancing, is grafted.

This "demiurgic"—and virtually "luciferian"—element enters into the very definition of the created.

Pride: the "something" that prevents a man from "losing his life" for God.

*

*   *

The spiritual man does not rejoice at his progress but at the disappearance of the old self; human perfection is the norm, not a peak.

After purifying oneself from one's defects one must purify oneself from one's virtues, say the Buddhists. Everything must be brought back to the divine Cause; this is the perfection of humility.

To think "I have" a given virtue is almost as false as to think "I am" God.

*

*   *

In a sense knowledge does not and cannot have any direct relationship with strictly human attitudes, but in another sense—that of manifestation—it is inseparable from them: in the first case it shows its absolute transcendence by the fact that it appears as a "free" gift or "grace"; in the second case it appears on the contrary as a function of the receptivity—thus the "simplicity" or "humility"—of the individual. These two aspects are always linked to some degree.

*

*   *

The loftiest *gnosis* and the most perfect humility go together: the one is knowledge of the Divine and the other knowledge of the human.[7] Pride is to treat the human as the Divine, and conversely; it is therefore to be ignorant of both the one and the other.

What the proud man readily forgets is that human virtue could never overtake either Unicity or creative Power.

---

[7] Diadochos of Photike distinguishes two humilities: the first comes from earthly troubles and "most often includes grief and despondency"; the second comes from an illumination of the Intellect in which "the soul possesses humility as by nature" and "judges itself beneath everything because it participates in the divine equity"; this humility includes "joy with a wise reserve".

*

*   *

Humility is a state of emptiness in which our thoughts and actions appear foreign to us, so that we judge them as we judge the thoughts and actions of others.

Pride is a blind plenitude that monopolizes everything.

*

*   *

Basilian spirituality includes four principal elements: separation from the world, purification, meditation on the sacred Scriptures, and continual prayer. The first element cuts man off from the current of profane life; the second empties the soul of illusory contents; the third infuses the discursive intelligence with divine Light; the fourth essentially brings about deification. This could be formulated as follows: in renunciation the soul leaves the world; in purification the world leaves the soul; in meditation God enters the soul; in continual prayer the soul enters God.

Here humility is not conceived as a "ladder"; it does not constitute the path as such but is in a sense at one and the same time its condition and its effect. Humility is *vacare Deo* in all its aspects, and for this reason it is perfect simplicity and primordial purity of the soul before the divine influx. On the one hand it conditions incessant prayer, and on the other it is conditioned by it. He who is not humble, that is, simple and pure—we would willingly say "impersonal" and "objective"—cannot persevere in this prayer, and he who does persevere in it cannot remain in the imperfections that are contrary to simplicity, purity, humility.

*

*   *

Saint Bernard defines humility as "a virtue through which a man who has true knowledge of himself becomes contemptible in his own eyes".[8] And he adds that "the Lord, who is gentle and just, gives men the law of humility in order that they might thus return to knowledge of the truth". This means that knowledge of oneself is indispensable for knowledge of God. This is also the meaning of the Prophet's teaching: "He who knows his soul knows his Lord."

Saint Bernard connects humility with truth; he understands it in a sense that has nothing exclusively moral about it, and this appears even more clearly when he speaks of the third degree of truth, which is "to purify the eye of the heart to contemplate things celestial and divine".

*

*　*

Meister Eckhart says that humility[9] consists in "being below", for otherwise it is impossible for God to give; hence a lack of humility—egotism for example—does violence to the nature of God, which consists in giving.

*

*　*

Christ said to Saint Catherine of Siena in a vision: "I am He who is; thou art she who is not." This is the metaphysical foundation of all humility expressed in direct terms.[10]

For Thomism humility is the measure of our nothingness before God.

---

[8] For Ibn Arabi likewise, humility is the sincere conviction of being a vile object in the eyes of God; perfect humility belongs only to the Sufi. The Prophet said: "Whoever has pride in his heart, if only a rice grain, cannot enter Paradise." At the beginning of one of his treatises Sri Shankaracharya designates himself as "I, who am without worth"; likewise Sri Chaitanya desires the *bhakta* "always to look upon himself as inferior to a wisp of straw" and to be "humble like grass". It would be easy to multiply examples to show that humility is far from being unique to Christianity.

[9] Etymologically, the virtue of being like the soil (*humus*).

[10] It will be noted that these terms are Vedantic, which means they are esoteric.

*

* *

"Humility," says Saint Teresa of Avila, "is to walk according to the Truth." For Saint Ignatius Loyola as well, humility is first of all the simplicity of soul that makes a man submit himself quite naturally to the divine Law,[11] then indifference with regard to worldly things,[12] and finally the ascetic will to live in privations—material and moral—for the sake of God.[13]

[11] Al-Qushayri: "It is to submit oneself to the direction of God." The same writer also gives this definition: "It is melting and contracting of the heart when subjugated by the Truth."

[12] According to al-Tirmidhi, "Man is humble when the blazing of the fire of desires has ceased" (*fanā'*, "extinction").

[13] Al-Ghazzali has been criticized for bringing the Aristotelian "measure" into his doctrine of humility instead of understanding the quasi-infinite character of virtue; this "measure" does not show that the Muslim conception stops halfway, but that al-Ghazzali's exposition gives only its purely social application (*adab*).

4

There is an inner dignity and an outer dignity just as there is an inner humility and an outer humility.

Dignity is the ontological awareness an individual has of his supra-individual reality.

The criterion of true humility is its truth and dignity.[1]

The criterion of true dignity is its truth and humility.

*
*   *

There is no legitimate connection between humility and a mere leveling down, for such a leveling is a form of pride since it denies the natural hierarchy of values and men; by this negation it is also opposed to dignity. Humility—or simplicity—is never a synonym for egalitarian mediocrity or weakness.

*
*   *

The spiritual content of dignity, unlike that of humility, is not accessible to all men even though in principle every man possesses the same dignity of being made in the image of God, of being the vicar of God on earth and having access to the Divine.

Dignity is opposed to vulgarity, frivolity, or curiosity as contemplation is opposed to agitation or as "being" transcends "doing". It is the "motionless mover" incarnate in movement, the "being" that shows through "acting", the contemplation affirmed in action; it is the integration of the periphery in the center as well as the revelation of the center in the periphery.[2]

---

[1] Or its force, according to Saint Francis of Sales. It was said of the Curé d'Ars that humility had "a certain element of unction and dignity" in him. The same saint said of humility that "it is to the virtues what the thread is to the rosary: take away the thread, and all the beads escape; take away humility, and all the virtues disappear".

[2] The "non-action" (*wu-wei*) of the Far Eastern tradition will be recalled here; these

Dignity is a universal possibility because it refers to Being, the Cause, the Principle. It appears in every realm of nature: an animal or plant such as the swan or water lily expresses a folding back of the created upon its immutable Principle.

Sacerdotal functions imply in a certain sense a way of dignity. To act in the place of God, as does the officiating priest, is to act with dignity, to act divinely; it is to be central in the periphery or immoveable in movement.

*
*   *

Dignity is a way of remembering the divine presence by means of the body; it requires effacement just as self-respect requires humility. More precisely, effacement is already included in dignity and humility in self-respect. If there could be a humble pride, it would be self-respect.

Dignity is consciousness of a universal quality. Effacement is consciousness of our nothingness.

Sentimental humility individualizes this nothingness, and in this lies its contradiction. The same applies to affected dignity: it individualizes the theomorphism of Adam, which is just as contradictory, for it is not the individual who resembles God but man as such, the human form, which includes all individuals.

Dignity is a repose, not an activity like affectation; it is not an individual affirmation but on the contrary a retreat toward the impersonal center.

Dignity reflects the sacred aspect of man.

---

two syllables were written above the throne of the Emperor, "Son of Heaven" and personification of this "non-action".

5

The idea of sin presupposes the fact of the "fall", in other words—as Maimonides says—the passage from "necessary knowledge" to "probable opinions": before the fall Adam distinguished the true from the false; after the fall he distinguished good from evil. In the beginning will was inseparable from intelligence; the fall is a scission between the two. The distinction between what is "good" and what is "evil" is made by a will that has fallen into the void, and not by the Intellect, which is fixed in the immutable.

The good is a possibility of action; the true is not a possibility of knowing but knowledge itself. Evil is a "willing", but error is not a "knowing": it is a form of "ignorance". In other words evil is an act of the will, but error is not an act of the intelligence. Unlike the will, intelligence is not free through its possible action; it is free through its very substance and thus through the necessity of its perfection.

*
* *

Sin concerns every man to the extent that individual liberty maintains itself outside divine liberty, but this in no way means that every spiritual perspective must begin with the act of sin; to identify man with sinful action is to create a danger of individualism.

Hindus believe in hell; it cannot be denied that they therefore possess the notion of sin, but since their disciplines have ignorance—and not sin—as their negative starting point, they do not suffer from a guilt complex. Sin appears to them as a form of imprudence or stupidity and in any case as a form of ignorance; it is characterized less by its form than by its inner process.

*
* *

There is a saying of Saint James that indicates how the contemplative ought to look upon sin and in what sense he is obliged to look on himself as a great sinner: "Therefore to him that knoweth to do good, and doeth it not, to him it is sin." This definition of sin goes far beyond the social level; it concerns the essential morality that is inseparable from spirituality, and its scope therefore embraces humanity in general and not the specifically Judeo-Christian part of it.

Far from being a mere sentimentality the voice of conscience is the inner criterion of our vocation—on condition, however, that we dwell in the truth as it relates to God, the world, and ourselves.

*
* *

In the thought of a Saint Benedict or a Saint Bernard, the idea of "the greatest sinner" is equivalent to a definition of sin itself: the slightest inadvertence of our will is "sin" as such and without epithet, for in sin there is always something incommensurable because of what it denies, which is the primordial conformity of our will to God. If intellective knowledge has total Truth for its object, free will has supreme Good for its goal; knowledge liberates whereas the will binds for the sake of liberty. Like knowledge the will is "perfectly itself" through its primordial object since absolute liberty exists only in God.

If as Saint James says every omission of a good—hence of a movement of our will toward God—is a sin or "sin as such", this is because even the slightest inclination of the will that is not in accord with the meaning or goal of our existence is either directly or indirectly—and in any case logically if not effectively—contrary to the highest Good. This way of looking at things in light of an individual alternative reveals a perspective that places the human problem on the plane of the will and therefore identifies man with will; the idea of redemption requires in fact the idea of the fall; if redemption is everything, the fall must also be everything.

*
* *

"The worst of sinners": this is a subjective reality expressed in objective terms. I am necessarily "the worst", "the most vile", since I alone am "I".

Metaphysically the obstacle separating man from the Infinite is the ego, that is, the principle of individuation or the "passion" engendered by "ignorance", as Hindus would say. For individualistic mysticism the obstacle is not the ego as such but a mode of it, namely, the extreme—and subversive—point of individuation: pride, which rears itself up against God and men, against Truth and destiny.

A doctrine like that of Christianity, which must take account of every level of understanding and all the human possibilities of spiritual realization, will designate the higher term by the lower, with the lower symbolizing the higher and not conversely; it is thus, practically and methodically, that the ego becomes "pride".

*

* *

The ordinary notion of "sin" is founded on action; other conceptions, in particular the idea of sin as "ignorance", place the accent on the root of evil and let action as such keep its inner indetermination. Action in fact can have divergent meanings; only the intention behind it can place it decisively in the hierarchy of values. Although action is everything from a social point of view, where the criterion lies in collective expediency, it may in itself be equivocal and enigmatic, whereas the root of evil, ignorance—and the passion resulting from it—does not give rise to any doubt or error of interpretation.

*

* *

According to some Muslim theologians there are in practice no small sins, for the transgression that is considered small by man will be considered great by God whereas the small fault that man considers great will be counted as small; just as the Christian deems himself "the greatest of sinners", the Muslim sees "the least sin rise up before him like a mountain", according to an expression of the Prophet. In Muslim esoterism sin is essentially to forget God, and this forgetting has about it something symbolically absolute because of the infinity of Him who is forgotten; from this point of view there can be no little sins. In the same way "the greatest of sinners" means, spiritually speaking, that there cannot be a greater sinner than he who commits "the greatest sin", which is none other than pride, the sin of Lucifer, who wished to be like God.

*

* *

Like "idolatry" or polytheistic "association", or again like "ignorance" (*avidyā*), pride is a cosmic tendency—in one sense "demiurgic" and in another "satanic"—which insinuates itself into all manifestation; this explains why he who knows himself knows he is "the greatest of sinners"—that is, "completely a sinner", for the negation of God contains something "relatively absolute"—and it also explains in what sense there is "no greater fault than existence", according to a saying of the Prophet.

This perspective makes it possible to understand why in Islam humility is founded less on consciousness of sin than on consciousness of powerlessness before God. In this connection the following sentence from the Koran is very revealing: "Walk not on the earth in a proud manner, for in truth thou canst neither cleave the earth nor attain the mountains in height" (*Sūrah* "The Night Journey" [17]: 37). Here the source of humility is the daily experience of our physical limitations, a meaning that also appears in the rite of ablution—the occasional cause of which is impurity of the body—and that is contained as well in the word *bashar*, "man": this term designates the human being not in his more or less theomorphic aspect—for in this case he is called *insān*—but in his aspect of mortality, powerlessness, and impurity.

Setting aside the fact that humility has the same fundamental reasons everywhere, we can say in a relative sense that the Christian is humble because he knows himself to be a sinner and the Muslim because he can neither displace the moon nor abolish death.

*

* *

If a spiritual man of an affective temperament can look upon himself as the greatest of sinners, an intellective can look upon himself—with the same logic and the same illogicality—as the most ignorant of the ignorant. With the same logic: if our fall is a state of revolt, it is also and with greater reason a state of ignorance. With the same illogicality: if it is inconsistent to hold that the greatest of sinners is the man who takes himself to be such—sin *par excellence* being pride, which excludes the recognition of its own baseness, precisely—it is just as inconsistent to regard oneself as the least wise of men since the man who knows he is ignorant cannot be more ignorant than one who does not know this.

*
* *

From the Judeo-Christian point of view death proves the wrath of God; Edenic immortality proves that man was not yet under this wrath. For the Hindu there is a difference here only of degree; the fall was contained in the possibility of man, and this God "knew".

Man could not not fall since God "could not not create".

God "created" by reason of His infinity: the Infinite requires its own affirmation, which is Being; Being requires creation; creation requires limitation and diversity; these in turn require negation and contradiction, and therefore evil. He who wants a world perfect in virtue and happiness therefore also wants an imperfect world full of sin and misfortune. The only choice is between the world and God; there is no choice between an imperfect world and a perfect world. In a similar way there is no choice between a fallen Adam and an incorruptible Adam; there is only a choice between man and God, hence the attitude of the saint who regards himself as "the greatest sinner" and, at the spiritual antipodes of this perspective, the idea of non-duality, identity in the absolute Subject.

*
* *

Modern man always begins with the idea of his axiomatic innocence: he is not the cause of existence, he did not want the world, he did not create himself, and he is responsible neither for his predispositions nor for the circumstances that actualize them; he cannot be culpable, which amounts to saying that he has unlimited rights. The consequences of such an attitude are evident: it opens the door to all the vices of human nature and unleashes the downward force of its fall; this is enough to prove it false.

Every man who is injured in his elementary rights assumes the existence of responsibility and culpability in others; he should therefore admit the possibility of culpability in himself; he should also recognize the existence of culpability as such, hence in relation to God. And such culpability incontestably exists, for every man freely does things the responsibility for which he casts upon Heaven; every man, within the limits of his freedom, does what he reproaches God for having done in the universe. The opposite attitude is to ask pardon of God; the response, if one may put it this way, is that God asks pardon of man: this is salvation.

Spiritual contrition—the moral form of emptiness—has its full justification not in the moral and relatively superficial idea of remorse but in the essential nature of things, in our metaphysical knowledge of the universe and the empirical consciousness of our destitution. God alone possesses Being; He alone is Plenitude; if man asks pardon of God it is finally in order to conform to a normative reality or simply to truth; it is because man exists without being able to move the sun or create one grain of dust, because he usurps the existence that belongs to Him who creates and who orders the stars, because he desires and accomplishes this usurpation within the limits of his freedom and on the plane of his life.

*

*   *

The fear of God is not in any way a matter of feeling any more than is the love of God; like love, which is the tendency of our whole being toward transcendent Reality, fear is an attitude of the intelligence and the will: it consists in taking account at every moment of a Reality which infinitely surpasses us, against which we can do nothing, in opposition to which we could not live, and from the teeth of which we cannot escape.

6

No "egoism" is possible in the attitude of the pure contemplative, for his "I" is the world, the "neighbor". What is realized in the microcosm radiates in the macrocosm because of the analogy between all cosmic orders; spiritual realization is a kind of "magic", which necessarily communicates itself to the surroundings. The equilibrium of the world requires contemplatives.[1]

To lose oneself for God is always to give oneself to men. To reduce all spirituality to social charity not only means putting the human above the Divine but also deeming oneself indispensable and attributing an absolute value to what one is capable of giving.

Why is social benevolence not a virtue in itself, and why does it not bring knowledge of God with it? It is because it can perfectly well go hand in hand with complacency, which annuls its spiritual quality. Without the inner virtues, such as humility and generosity, good works have no connection with sanctity; they may even indirectly take man further away from God.

According to circumstances virtue is possible without good works, but from the point of view of the love of God good works are nothing without intrinsic virtue, just as—in another order of ideas—detachment is possible without renunciation whereas renunciation is meaningless except for the sake of detachment.

*

* *

Certain Hindus of old blessed our epoch not because it is good but because, being bad, it includes by way of compensation spiritual graces that make easy what is in itself difficult, provided man is sincere, pure, humble, and persevering. In former ages the spirit was more or less ubiquitous but was more difficult to reach and realize just because it

---

[1] It is a question of a relative equilibrium consonant with particular cyclic conditions. Saint John of the Cross said, "A spark of pure love is more precious to God, more useful for the soul, and more rich in blessings for the Church than all other works taken together, even if to all appearances one does nothing".

was present everywhere: its very boundlessness precluded easiness. It was there but had a tendency to disappear; today it is hidden but has a tendency to give itself.

There is an economy of mercy even though mercy in its essence goes beyond any economy, for principially it comes before justice. Mercy is not measured except in its outward aspect; justice, which is neither the first nor the last word of God, limits it only accidentally and with respect to a particular plane of existence.

Apart from compensatory graces, which are in themselves independent of the evil of our times, there are advantages in this evil itself: the world has become so emptied of substance that it is hard for a spiritual man to be too attached to it; for this reason the man of today, if he is contemplative, is already half broken. In former times worldliness was all the more seductive for having aspects of intelligence, nobility, and plenitude; it was far from being wholly contemptible as it is in our day; no doubt it made possible in the souls of the elite— who alone concern us here—a sort of guileless and total attachment, which required a corresponding renunciation; the evil of the world did not yet make itself felt in the actual appearance of the world.

*

*   *

Why is man unable to enter into contemplation as long as his heart is full of anger against his neighbor? It is because he is unable to go beyond his "I"—his individuality—unless he sees it as individuality as such without any distinction of person.

Before sacrificing, says the Gospel, man must be reconciled with his brother; a saint—we do not remember who—said that it is just as absurd to want to contemplate God with one's heart full of bitterness against one's neighbor as it is to pluck out one's eye in order to see better.

In this case moral imperfection is simply the human expression of an incompatibility of perspectives. Hatred of a particular person—or a collectivity, which amounts qualitatively to the same thing—is inconsistent with love of the totality; and it is the totality that one must love in order to be able to love God. Perfection requires one to love man, not a particular man.

*

*   *

Spiritual realization is theoretically the easiest thing and in practice the most difficult thing there is. It is the easiest because it is enough to think of God; it is the most difficult because human nature is forgetfulness of God.

Sanctity is a tree that grows between impossibility and a miracle.

*

*   *

Love is in the depths of man even as water in the depths of the earth, and man suffers from not being able to enjoy the infinity that he bears in himself and that he is made for.

It is necessary to dig deep into the soil of the soul through layers of aridity and bitterness in order to find love and to live on it.

The depths of love are inaccessible to man in his state of hardness but reveal themselves externally through the language of art and also through that of nature. In sacred art and in virgin nature the soul can taste, by analogical anticipation, something of the love which lies dormant in it and for which it has only nostalgia without experience.

*

*   *

In this low world in which we live there is the immense problem of separation; how can one make men understand that in God they are separated from nothing?

Our formal—or separative—world appears to the angels as a pile of debris: what is united in reality is separated in form and by form. The formal world is made up of congealed essences.

Man escapes from form—and separateness—in his own supernatural center, on the shore of eternal and blissful essences.

*

*   *

The soul is a tree whose roots are deeply embedded in the "world"—in things, whether in ourselves or around us, that are capable of being felt, tasted, lived; the "world" is diversity as well as the passional movements that respond to it, whether in the flesh, in sentiment, or in thought.

The "one thing needful" is to transfer our roots into what appears to be nothingness, emptiness, unity. Since the soul cannot plant its roots in the void, the void is "incarnated" in the symbol; it is in everything that brings us nearer God.

*

*   *

There is one great certainty in life, and this is death; whoever really understands this certainty is already dead in this life. Man is hardly at all preoccupied with his past sufferings if his present state is happy; what is past in life, whatever its importance, no longer exists. Now everything will one day be past; this is what a man understands at the moment of death; thus the future is already part of the past. To know this is to be dead; it is to rest in peace.

But there is yet another certainty in life—whether we can have this certainty depends only on ourselves—and it is the certainty of living in the divine will; this certainty compensates for that of death and conquers it. To put it another way: when we have the certainty of being in conformity with the divine will, the certainty of death is full of sweetness. Thus the meaning of our life on earth can be reduced to two certainties: the ineluctability of our destiny and the meaning or value of our will. We cannot avoid the meaning of life any more than we can avoid death; this great departure, which cannot have a shadow of doubt for us, proves to us that we are not free to act no matter how, that from this present moment we ought to conform to a will stronger than our own.

*

*   *

In his empirical existence man finds himself in contact with God, the world, the soul, and the neighbor. On each of these levels it might be said that God speaks a different language: in the world He touches us through destiny, which is in time, and through the symbols that surround us, which are in space; in the soul He is truth, which is objective, and the voice of conscience, which is subjective; in our neighbor He appears as the need we must satisfy and the teaching we must accept: the divine function of the neighbor is at once passive and active.

One cannot serve God without also seeing Him in destiny, truth, the neighbor.

*
*   *

What are the great misfortunes of the soul? A false life, a false death, a false activity, a false rest.

A false life: passion, which engenders suffering; a false death: egoism, which hardens the heart and separates it from God and His mercy; a false activity: dissipation, which casts the soul into an insatiable vortex and makes it forget God, who is Peace; a false rest or false passivity: weakness and laziness, which deliver up the unresisting soul to the countless solicitations of the world.

*
*   *

To this false life is opposed a true death: the death of passion; this is spiritual death, the cold and crystalline purity of the soul conscious of its immortality. To false death is opposed a true life: the life of the heart turned toward God and open to the warmth of His love. To false activity is opposed a true rest, a true peace: the repose of the soul that is simple and generous and content with God, the soul that turns aside from agitations and curiosity and ambition in order to repose in divine beauty. To false rest is opposed a true activity: the battle of the spirit against the multiple weaknesses that squander the soul—and this precious life—as in a game or dream.

To false knowledge, vain thought, is opposed a manner of being: that of the spirit united to its divine Source, beyond discursive thought, which is scission, indefinite dispersion, movement without issue. To false existence, crude and blind fact, is opposed true knowledge, true discernment: to know that God alone is absolute Reality, that the world is only through Him and in Him, and that outside Him I am not.

*
*   *

To think of God: in the mind the divine presence is like snow; in the heart—as existential essence—it is like fire. Freshness, purity, peace; warmth, love, bliss. The lily and the rose.

The divine presence penetrates the soul—the existential ego, not thought in itself—like a gentle heat; or it pierces the heart—as intellective center—like an arrow of light.

*
*   *

Prayer—in the widest sense—triumphs over the four accidents of our existence: the world, life, the body, the soul; we might also say: space, time, matter, desire. It is situated in existence like a shelter, like an islet. In it alone we are perfectly ourselves because it puts us into the presence of God. It is like a diamond, which nothing can tarnish and nothing can resist.

*
*   *

Man prays, and prayer fashions man. The saint has himself become prayer, the meeting place of earth and Heaven; he thereby contains the universe, and the universe prays with him. He is everywhere where nature prays, and he prays with her and in her: in the peaks, which touch the void and eternity; in a flower, which scatters its scent; in the carefree song of a bird.

He who lives in prayer has not lived in vain.

APPENDIX

Selections from Letters and
Other Previously Unpublished Writings

1

Difficulties resulting from contacts between whites and Indians are easy to understand. In the first place the white man does not have a sense of the sacred to the extent he is a modern man, and almost all whites are modern men; if he asks an Indian questions he usually does so out of curiosity, without realizing that the Indian has no motive for responding to an interrogation he considers indiscreet and pointless.

To say that modern man does not have a sense of the sacred amounts to recognizing that he is full of false ideas; intellectually and morally he is unaware of the axioms of the traditional spirit—in other words of spirituality as such; he does not know about metaphysics, cosmology, mysticism. Metaphysically modern man is unaware that everything is a manifestation of the Self, which is at once transcendent and immanent; he knows nothing of the doctrine of *Ātmā* and *Māyā* even if he has read some Hindu books, for in this case he thinks it is merely a question of concepts having a historical, psychological, or phenomenological interest—in short, things that can be put aside. Cosmologically he does not realize that the world is made of a hierarchical series of regions—beginning with the Self and extending to matter—and that the evolutionist error is simply a "horizontal" substitute for "vertical" emanation, which begins unfolding with the archetypes and passes through the animic or subtle world. This being the case, modern man also knows nothing of the sacred and its laws or of the psychology that is derived from it and bears witness to it.

Question: how can one study the metaphysics, cosmology, and spirituality of a people without having any idea what it means? This is the whole problem. And this is why people go around in circles indefinitely while developing by way of compensation finely drawn or charitable considerations that are beside the point. I repeat: the white man does not offer the Indian a sufficient, satisfying, or acceptable motivation for answering the questions he asks, nor in the eyes of the Indian does he exhibit a state of spiritual readiness meriting the answers he seeks. From the point of view of any traditional discipline, one does not have the right to speak of sacred things without a sufficient reason or outside the relationship between a master and his disciple; besides, there are things that lose their "power" if discussed without a plausible motive.

But there is more: beyond the fact that the Indian has no motive for answering questions whose justification he does not perceive, he cannot see the value of the white man's need for logical explanations; and if in spite of this the Indian answers, he is unable to do so by means of the abstract categories of classic, European dialectic. He therefore responds in a symbolic language that the white man in turn cannot comprehend, for the modern mind does not understand symbolism, its principles, and its methods. If the Indian has gone to a university, there is a very good chance he will have accepted uncritically the errors and mental habits of white people and that the abstract and differentiated language he avails himself of will therefore be of no use to him when explaining the Indian mysteries. In a similar way there are Orientals who think with two separate brains, a traditional one and a modern one, so that their thinking is either impeccable or absurd depending on the brain they are using.

One might object that academics who study the Indians are no longer so ignorant because of the work of Eliade and others; I reply that they remain ignorant and incompetent enough to meet the description I gave above, if only because they draw no serious conclusions from whatever real knowledge they may possess.

2

There are three fundamental, essential colors: Red, Blue, Yellow: Red and Blue are heavy, so to speak; Yellow is light; Red and Yellow are warm; Blue is cold. The mixed colors are Green, Orange, Violet; Green comes first because its components, Blue and Yellow, are complementary rather than irreconcilable opposites; then come Orange and Violet, the first light and the second heavy.

As for the symbolism of colors, everyone agrees on the following meanings: Red represents intensity as well as aggressiveness; Blue represents calm, profundity, and contemplativity; Yellow should naturally be felt as a symbol of radiation or joy, but too often a malefic sense is attributed to this color: falseness, envy, hatred; this is a patent example of pseudo-symbolism.

Among the mixed colors Green represents contemplative joy, hope; Violet represents sadness and, on another plane, sacerdotal gravity as well as old age; Orange represents emotion that is lively, joyful, vital, hence also youth.

3

Poetry is the "language of the gods", and *noblesse oblige*; what I mean by this is that the poet has certain responsibilities. In poetry the musicality of things or their cosmic essentiality erupts onto the plane of language; and this process requires the grandeur, hence the authenticity, of both image and sentiment. The poet spontaneously intuits the underlying musicality of phenomena; under the pressure of an image or emotion—the emotion, moreover, being naturally combined with concordant images—he expresses an archetypal beauty; without this pressure there is no poetry, which means that true poetry always has an aspect of inward necessity, whence its irreplaceable perfume.

I am rather hostile to poetry because hardly anyone knows how to write it—spiritual motives notwithstanding—and also because most true poets are the dupes of their talent and get lost in prolixity instead of letting the muse take over, for the muse is sometimes very parsimonious, which is saying something! This implies that there is an inward pressure that tolerates no vagueness or chitchat, and this pressure must be the result of a certain order of grandeur, whence the "musical crystallinity" of poetry, the convincing power of its inward necessity. There is no beauty without grandeur; these two qualities must be in the soul of the poet as well as in the form that he knows how to impart to language. Gem of perfection and vibration of infinitude.

4

Guénon was right to specify that the *Vedānta* is the most direct and in a certain respect the most assimilable expression of pure metaphysics; no non-Hindu traditional affiliation could oblige us to ignore this or pretend to ignore it. Within the Semitic monotheistic religions there

233

is an esoterism "in fact" and another "by right"; now it is the second that is equivalent to Vedantic wisdom; *de facto* esoterism results from what has been said or written—with the veilings and detours at times required by a given theological framework and above all by a given religious *upāya*. Doubtless it was in thinking of *de jure* esoterism that certain Cabalists were led to say that if wisdom were lost the sages could reconstitute it.

The monotheistic Scriptures each manifest an *upāya*, a religious perspective that is particular and characteristic by definition, and hermeneutics in general is affected accordingly; this is not the case for the fundamental formulations or symbols of the religions, which in themselves are not limitative in any way. For example, the *Shahādah*—"the most precious thing I have brought to the world", according to the Prophet—expresses total metaphysical truth in a most direct and limpid manner; in Hindu terms I would say it is at once an *Upanishad* and a *Mantra*; and the second *Shahādah* is the complement of the first, which means that the mystery of immanence is joined to the mystery of transcendence. In Christianity the Patristic formula of saving reciprocity is a priceless jewel: "God became man that man might become God"; it is a revelation in the full sense, at the same level as the Scriptures; this may seem surprising, but it is a "paracletic" possibility, examples of which can be found—very rarely, it is true—in all traditional worlds. The sentence *anā'l-Haqq* of al-Hallaj is a case of this kind; it is the Sufic equivalent as it were of the Vedic *aham Brahmāsmi*; al-Hallaj himself affirmed the possibility of post-Koranic sayings situated at the level of the Koran, something for which other Sufis did not pardon him, at least not in his time.

But there are not only formulas; there are also theophanies. Christ, understood as universal symbol and regarded from the point of view of esoteric application, represents first of all the *Logos* in itself and then the immanent Intellect—*aliquid est in anima quod est increatum et increabile*—which at once illuminates and liberates; the Holy Virgin personifies the soul in a state of sanctifying grace or this grace itself. There is no theophany that is not prefigured in the very constitution of the human being, for man is "made in the image of God"; now esoterism aims at actualizing the divine content that God places in this mirror of Himself called man. Meister Eckhart spoke of immanent sacraments; analogous natural or "congenial" things may serve as sacramental supports, he said, for the same reason as sacraments in the proper sense of the word.

Thus one must distinguish between an esoterism that is more or less founded on a given theology and bound up with the speculations provided *de facto* by the traditional sources—and it goes without saying that these doctrines or insights may be of the greatest interest—and another esoterism resulting from the truly fundamental elements of the religion and for this reason from the simple nature of things; the two dimensions may of course be combined, and in fact they often are; but it is a question of emphasis, and it is obviously to the second dimension that our perspective pertains *a priori.*

5

Regarding primordial man, I do not think he either laughed or wept, for his psychism was neither as developed nor therefore as exterior-ized as that of fallen man; primordial man was much closer to the state of *prajnā,* or rather *samādhi,* which means that everything in him was reabsorbed into a certain state of beatific indifferentiation; laughter is only a kind of fallen and vulgar fragment of this beatitude, intensified as a result of outwardness; the physical manifestation of laughter stems from the same source.

What I mean is that there is no primordial laughter, at least not in the sense in which you seem to understand it. It goes without saying of course that to the extent a thing is positive it has a primordial prototype, but this prototype can be markedly different from what is derived from it. Abd al-Qadir al-Jilani says that the Name of *Allāh* dispels all sadness from the heart of man, but he does not say that this Name makes one laugh. I willingly gave up my sadness when God removed it from me. But let no one speak to me of gaiety!

I believe I mentioned to you in my last letter that I have always noticed that vulgar people love above all what makes them laugh, and they flee what is serious; outside their work they seek lighthearted things, abhorring all that is gravity and dignity and all that evokes pain or death. I am surprised I am writing this to you, for it seems to me so obvious. In your article you mentioned several saints who spent the better part of their life laughing and jesting. This is plausible only if their attitude was paradoxical and intentional, as with the *malāmatiyah*; but we are dealing then with an example of asceticism, and this contradicts your interpretation.

I would never think of criticizing spontaneous and unassuming gaiety, provided it is not incompatible with dignity; such gaiety is a question of temperament and thus in itself something neutral. But once gaiety is established as a matter of principle, I do condemn it because it then ceases to be unassuming; it loses its spontaneity and becomes pretentious; it opens the door to stupidity while including a kind of self-sufficiency, which is paralyzing with regard to spirituality even when it is more or less unconscious. Far be it from me to criticize your gaiety as long as it does not harm your path.

6

I am completely against ecumenism as it is envisaged today—with its ineffective "dialogues" and gratuitous and sentimental gestures amounting to nothing. Certainly an understanding between religions is possible and even necessary, though not on the dogmatic plane, but solely on the basis of common ideas and common interests. The common ideas are a transcendent, perfect, all-powerful, merciful Absolute, then a hereafter that is either good or bad depending on our merits or demerits; all the religions, including Buddhism—Buddhist "atheism" is simply a misunderstanding—are in agreement on these points. The common interests are a defense against materialism, atheism, perversion, subversion, and modernism in all its guises. I believe Pius XII once said that the wars between Christians and Muslims were but domestic quarrels compared to the present opposition between the world of the religions and that of militant materialism-atheism; he also said it was a consolation to know that there are millions of men who prostrate themselves five times a day before God.

7

The *philosophia perennis* is founded essentially and intrinsically on the nature of things as perceived by intellectual intuition; only formally and extrinsically is it founded upon a particular revealed Text, and it could never be dependent on it.

It is altogether erroneous to believe that religion in the ordinary sense of the term—including an esoterizing exoterism—is the indispensable condition and sole guarantee of intellectual intuition and of the practical consequences derived from it. The fact that all spirituality extrinsically depends on a tradition in no way signifies that the human Intellect is inoperative outside the framework of a traditional symbolism or sacramental means.

As Meister Eckhart said, "There is something in the soul that is uncreated and uncreatable; if the entire soul were such, it would be uncreated and uncreatable; and this is the Intellect." Similarly, the Islamic formula: "The Sufi is not created."

According to the *Brahma Sūtra*, "Man can acquire true divine Knowledge even without observing the prescribed rites; and indeed in the *Veda* there are many examples of people who neglected to perform such rites or were prevented from doing so and who nonetheless acquired true Knowledge because their attention was perpetually concentrated and focused on the supreme *Brahma*."

In principle man—"made in the image of God"—contains everything within himself; in fact, however, he needs elements of actualization coming from the outside, hence from tradition; this does not mean that a man needs every possible support, but he does need the supports his particular nature requires. Necessity is not the only issue; there is also opportuneness; the useful is not always the indispensable.

According to Guénon, "True esoterism is something quite different from the outward religion, and if it has some connections with it, this is only to the extent it finds in the religious forms a mode of symbolic expression; moreover it matters little whether these forms are those of this religion or that since what is in question is the essential unity of doctrine lying hidden beneath their apparent diversity. This is why the initiates of old, following the established customs of the various countries in which they found themselves, participated in all the outward forms of worship without distinction. . . . Pure metaphysics is neither pagan nor Christian but universal; the mysteries of antiquity were not paganism, but they were superimposed upon it."

It sometimes happens that the pure pneumatic will act in a manner foreign to a given religious perspective and to particular prescriptions, but he never acts in a manner contrary to the nature of things, for he bears the essential, universal, and primordial Law in the depths of his own heart. For this very reason deviation or corruption is impossible in his case, however things may appear from a particular, limited perspective.

8

The errors of the Mahesh Yogi movement are patently obvious. In reality the goal of meditation is not to have access to "limitless energy, heightened efficiency of thought and action, and release from tensions and anxiety [leading] to peace of mind and happiness"! None of these advantages has any spiritual value, for it is not happiness that matters: it is the motive and nature of happiness. The Sadhu says nothing of this, the sole important question, and this is what condemns him.

But there are also extrinsic criteria: the complete lack of intelligence and *barakah*, the propagandistic triviality, the modernist and pseudo-yogic style, the quasi-religious pretension. For instance, the Sadhu preaches in the West; how can he believe that Christ did not bring men everything they need? After all he cannot replace Christianity and the other religions, and yet this is what he pretends to do in declaring that he brings "the *summum bonum* of all that Christ and Krishna, Buddha and Muhammad taught".

Heresies always arise from a terrible lack of any sense of proportion. Add to this the passional and sentimental element and then propaganda, and we have the irreversible infernal circle. I suppose the Sadhu in question is not a very intelligent man but is endowed with some psychic power; he may also be ambitious. None of this is necessarily malicious *a priori*, but it becomes so, and in this sense the Sadhu himself is a victim. False masters are dangerous because they are a mixture of good and evil, and they seduce with the good. I am inclined to believe the Sadhu is largely unconscious of the role the modern situation is making him play.

But this question of knowing what the Sadhu is has no importance, and it is perfectly fruitless to discuss it. This is an appalling case of deviation from a real *barakah*, which stems from an incapacity 1. to discern the nature of the modern world and 2. to resist the temptations resulting from this nature. A typical error is to believe that the rapid expansion of a modern sect—thanks to mechanical means—is comparable to the miraculous expansion of the religions. Everything is "confusion", "belittling", and "falsification".

It must be said that India is a very dangerous terrain for most Westerners; they become imbued there with irremediable prejudices and pretensions. It goes without saying that I prefer the most narrow-minded of Catholics—if he is pious—to these pseudo-Hinduists, arrogant and permanently damaged as they are. They scorn the religious point of view, which they do not understand in the least and which alone could save them. One sometimes hates what one needs the most.

And what can one say about the infinite naiveté of believing that a method of meditation suffices 1. to change man and 2. to change humanity, hence politics as well? What happens in all this to the *Kali Yuga*, and what about the *japa* advocated by the Scriptures? If this "Regeneration Movement" came from Heaven, its first concern would be to defend the religions, to show their validity and unanimity, as Ramakrishna did; it would be to show their absolute necessity, to indict the modern outlook, to explain that this outlook is the culmination of the *Kali Yuga*, and perhaps to teach *japa*, with all the mandatory precautions.

9

In principle the universal authority of the metaphysical and initiatic traditions of Asia, which reflect the nature of things more or less directly, takes precedence—when such an alternative exists—over the generally more "theological" authority of the monotheistic religions; I say "when such an alternative exists" because there are obviously cases where there is no such alternative, in esoterism as in essential symbolism; no one can deny, however, that in Semitic doctrines the formulations and rules are usually determined by considerations of dogmatic, moral, and social opportuneness. But this cannot apply to pure Islam, that is, to the authority of its essential doctrine and fundamental symbolism; the *Shahādah* cannot but mean that "the world is false and *Brahma* is true" and "Thou are That" (*tat tvam asi*) or "I am *Brahma*" (*aham Brahmāsmi*); it is a pure expression of the Supreme Identity and of the unreality of the world; in the same way the other "pillars of Islam" (*arqān al-Dīn*), as well as such fundamental rules as dietary and artistic prohibitions, obviously constitute supports of intellection and realization, which universal metaphysics—or the "Unanimous Tradition"—can illuminate but not abolish.

When universal wisdom states that the Invocation contains and replaces all other rites, this is of decisive authority against those who would make the *sharī'ah* or *sunnah* into a kind of exclusive *karma-yoga*, and it even allows us to draw conclusions by analogy (*qiyās, ijtihād*) that most Shariites would find illicit; or again, if a given Muslim master required that we introduce every *dhikr* with an ablution and two *rak'āt*, the universal and "antiformalist" authority of *japa-yoga* would take precedence over the authority of this master, at least in our case. On the other hand, if a Hindu or Buddhist master advised practicing *japa* before an image or issued an order for such a practice, it goes without saying that it is the authority of Islamic symbolism that would take precedence for us quite apart from any question of universality, for forms are forms, and some of them are essential and thus rejoin the universality of the spirit.

10

These four Sanskrit terms may evoke the four principal dimensions of our Way:

Vedānta: Discernment between the Real and illusory, which implies all subsequent discernments.

Japa: Invocation; essentially, methodic Concentration on the Real.

Dharma: Virtue, the virtues; Conformity to the nature of the Real; beauty of soul, of character.

Tantra: Spiritualization—or Interiorization—of beauty as well as of the natural pleasures, in harmony with the metaphysical transparency of phenomena. All things considered: Nobility of sentiments and experiences, which excludes all excess and is inseparable from sobriety. Or again: sense of the archetypes, return to the essences, to primordiality.

11

What always surprises me with people discussing spirituality is that they are not aware of the essential or else lose sight of it, and in the absence of the one center they get lost in the many-sided periphery. One would like to interrupt them every time with the question, "What is the issue?" and then remind them that what matters first of all is discernment between the world and God, the transitory and the Permanent, the relative and the Absolute, the illusory and the Real, and then union—by means of a quasi-permanent orison—with what is known to be Absolute, hence Real. All the rest is but a question of means or outward covering.

What is essential in this context is the extrinsic as well as intrinsic virtues, such as patience, trust, gratitude, generosity—in short, humility and charity; I mean real humility and charity, not their childish counterfeits. For truth remains sterile in us without the beauties of the soul, and it becomes impossible for us not only to pray from time to time but to pray all the time, and with fruits. What counts in prayer is the fact of praying and that one prays with sincerity, and what makes life finally worth living—what allows one to live with trust and without despair—is the quasi-permanence of a sincere orison. There is also what one might call the sacramental quintessence of prayer: the divine Names, bearers in themselves of a certain saving Presence; the names of Jesus and Mary have this function within Christianity, and the same applies to the Hebrew Names of God, those one is allowed to pronounce; in the final analysis any traditional and liturgical Name of God constitutes a sufficient orison. This of course does not mean that one cannot speak to God as to a man when one feels the need or that canonical prayers—the scriptural ones—do not have a role to play.

In a certain sense the entire message of Christ is in these words: "The kingdom of Heaven is within you." To pray is to remain "within", in "holy inwardness", something presupposing "holy silence". Quintessentially speaking, to live from prayer is to remain blessedly enclosed in the Name of God.

12

The Intelligence, the Will, and the Soul of the human being are capable of objectivity, hence of transcendence; it is because of transcendence—the possibility of knowing God—that the human mind is endowed with objectivity.

Instead of saying "Intelligence, Will, Soul" we could say "to know, to will, to love". To know God is to discern the Absolute and the elements of absoluteness; to will God is to do what brings us near Him; to love God is to find happiness in Him. No man has the right to say he cannot love God, for man always loves something; he always aspires to some happiness; he always makes his choices.

The formulas of consecration and of gratitude—the *Basmalah* and the *Hamdalah*—integrate the contingent objects of our love into our love for the Absolute or the Infinite, which is imperative for us because we are human beings.

To know God is to understand by way of consequence that one must remember Him, that there is no other choice.

To will God is to remember Him in fact, and untiringly, while abstaining from what is opposed to this end.

To love God is to find joy and happiness in this remembrance, not in what separates us from it.

To know things in relation to God, to will them for God, to love them in God.

13

I deplore the fact that a certain number of those who claim to subscribe to an esoteric science believe that human virtues can be neglected or even scorned when in fact they form a part of initiatic qualification and of the way itself, as Sufi treatises tirelessly reiterate; my point of view may strike some people as strange, but it is no more moralistic than that of the *Yoga Shāstras*, for example, which also set a high value on virtue. If it is true that every perfection has primarily a symbolic meaning, this hardly means that perfection itself is superfluous, quite the contrary: the symbol is the necessary support for the reality symbolized, and it is above all a modality of this reality. Every virtue is an eye that sees God.

When I receive a jumble of a letter, for example, full of petty, sterile, impotent, and futile concerns, written hastily and with a worried tone, I do not see in it the reflection of a soul that is a receptacle of the Real Presence; the "structure", "style", or "rhythm" of the soul must correspond to the object of its aspirations, and this object is the divine Reality, free from all infirmity. The Divine is Beauty, Grandeur, Solitude; thus the soul must realize these qualities not by imaginative improvisation, which would be fatal, but in conformity with divine truths; thus "greatness" of soul must not be sought by means of a hollow and sentimental attitude, as the Vivekanandists do, but by hierarchizing the psychic or mental contents and suppressing what opposes the "one thing needful". Abu al-Mawahib al-Shadhili says: "Purify thyself of thy vulgar and contemptible traits and adopt His qualities, worthy of praise and full of glory."

14

Our Character is our personality, and it is what we love in the depth of ourselves; it includes our tendencies, which influence the operation of our Intelligence and Will, though without producing them. Intelligence and Will are also part of our personality, but in themselves they are of an impersonal nature; they are faculties that do indeed belong to us, but it is our Character that is *a priori* our self.

And it is in the Character that the Virtues reside, these being fundamentally Sincerity, Fidelity, Gratitude, and Generosity. Sincerity tends toward the intellectual in the sense that it is inspired by Truth; Fidelity tends toward the existential in the sense that it refers to the Origin and to primordial Perfection. Gratitude is equivalent to Humility and is the consciousness of our dependence on something greater than ourselves; and Generosity is derived from our Liberty: it is Charity that loves to radiate.

By influencing the Intelligence, Sincerity induces it to draw all the conclusions implied in discernment: knowing the world is only an appearance, man must detach himself from it; applying Discernment to the macrocosm, he must also apply it to the microcosm, hence to himself, for self-knowledge is the necessary consequence of knowledge

of the Real as such. Gratitude prompts the Intelligence to an awareness of its dependence and thus cuts short all temptation to luciferian
rationalism; to know is to submit to the Intellect. In a similar manner
Fidelity, by influencing the Will, endows it with the quality of perse-
verance; Generosity for its part gives it a sense of moderation, averting
the temptation to excessive selfishness. Thus the Virtues, though they
are not able to determine the Intelligence and Will with regard to their
capacities, can nonetheless determine their style or operations.

It is obvious that the fundamental Virtues are to varying degrees
lacking in the man who bears the stamp of the Fall, the loss of Paradise—inward as well as outward—though without being entirely lost;
their sufficient presence, however, is the *conditio sine qua non* of the
Way, along with a discriminating and contemplative Intelligence and
an efficient and persevering Will.

In principle the Intelligence does not need the Virtues in order
to draw all the conclusions of which it is capable, but in fact it is far
from being able to do so without constraint; similarly the Will should
without difficulty be inspired by the directives emanating from the
Intelligence, but in fact these directives are not necessarily enough for
it, and it is Virtue that must come to its aid.

Obviously a child is not in full possession of his potential Intelligence or Will, but his personality may nonetheless be endowed with
a thirst for the True, a sense of the Sacred, a love of Beauty, and an
instinct for the Essential, hence for Greatness; and it is this above all
that matters.

15

The argument that the outward ego is not really ourselves is aimed at
individualism, which lends a quasi-absolute value to the fact of being a
given individual, of having certain memories and desires; the argument
helps us break away from this obsession to the extent such detachment is required, for we have the right to be men.

But this spiritual argument cannot dispense with effort toward
perfection, nor for all the more reason can it exonerate the sinner; that
is, it cannot be brought to bear in favor of an imperfection, negligence,
or sin the responsibility for which one would like to shift to something
other than oneself: namely, the empirical ego precisely, hypocritically

charged with "unreality", even though the ego is morally real in the case of the sinner; otherwise the name "sinner" would not be given to one who sins.

When the soul is conscious of being attached to inward or outward phenomena to such a degree that it is drawn away from God, it is necessary to say: this ego, which I cherish and which deceives me, and which is made of images and desires, is not my true being. But when the soul is conscious of an imperfection, a sin, or a vice, one has no right to say: this sin or vice is not myself and hence does not concern me. As long as a man sins by his actions or character, he is identified with his sin. It is only after being purified and with the intention of remaining within the norm that he may tell himself: this sin was not really myself.

Once again, the argument in question operates against individualism, which seduces us and causes us to suffer, and not in favor of an imperfection about which we are complacent. In general a spiritual argument should not be used apart from its concrete intention, for otherwise one may fall into affectation and hypocrisy; the soul should not be told things that it does not understand and that therefore flatter it, so to speak. The individual has a duty to escape evil, but he does not have a duty to be sublime.

There is no Knowledge without objectivity of intelligence; there is no Freedom without objectivity of the will; there is no Nobility without objectivity of the soul. The value of the human person is objectivity, which is at once extinction and reintegration.

16

In *Tasawwuf* one must repeatedly begin a new life in order to maintain grace and not be lost. Man is weak, but God is Strength, and with Him everything is possible, even things that seem impossible. You have often spoken to me of your weakness; if you do not feel you are able to love God, you must at least fear Him. God is merciful, but He is also awesome, and it is impossible to understand His Mercy if one does not understand His Wrath. One must never think oneself too intelligent; our intelligence is nothing in relation to the Absolute. If God has given us the gift of intelligence, it must be combined with a childlike simplicity and purity; God abhors pretension and self-assurance. Thus whatever opinion we may have of ourselves, only one thing is absolutely certain: *lā ilāha illā 'Llāh.* It is also certain—in keeping with this very same supreme certainty—that we must die and appear before God. All the rest is of no importance. Begin a new life this very day; and if you do not want to do it for yourself—although in reality you have no choice—do it for those around you, for you owe them happiness. The only way to be happy is to make those who depend on us happy, to make them happy in God and by Him.

EDITOR'S NOTES

Numbers in bold indicate pages in the text for which the following citations and explanations are provided.

I Thought and Civilization

1

6: *"The wind bloweth where it listeth* [Latin: *spiritus ubi vult spirat*], and thou hearest the sound thereof, but canst not tell whence it cometh, and whither it goeth: so is every one that is born of the Spirit" (John 3:8).

2

15: Auguste *Comte* (1798-1857), a French social theorist and leading proponent of positivism, sought to confine intellectual inquiry to empirically observable facts while eschewing metaphysics and theology.

Arthur *Schopenhauer* (1788-1860) was a German Kantian philosopher who taught that the will is the fundamental reality underlying the world.

3

18: *Dante* Alighieri (1265-1321) was the author of the *Divine Comedy*, one of the summits of world literature (see also editor's notes for "Aesthetics and Symbolism in Art and Nature", Part 1, p. 34; "Contours of the Spirit", Part 1, p. 63, Note 11 and Part 2, p. 78, Note 9; "Knowledge and Love", Part 1, p. 138, Note 9).

II Aesthetics and Symbolism in Art and Nature

1

27: *"One thing needful"*: "One thing is needful: and Mary hath chosen that good part, which shall not be taken from her" (Luke 10:42).

30: The Cathedral of Saint Lazare in *Autun*, the Benedictine abbey of Saint Mary Magdalene in *Vezelay*, and the Cluniac abbey of Saint Peter in *Moissac* are widely celebrated examples of Romanesque architecture and statuary.

33: For *Dante*, see editor's note for "Thought and Civilization", Part 3, p. 18.

34: *La Vita Nuova*, "The New Life", is a poem by Dante in which he celebrated his love for the young woman Beatrice, promising her a poem (*The Divine Comedy*) "such as has been written for no lady before".

Omar ibn al-Farid (c. 1182-1235), author of the *Khamriyah*, and *Omar Khayyam* (1048-1125), author of the *Rubaiyat* ("quatrains"), were Muslim mystics and poets.

The *Song of Songs*, or Song of Solomon, a book of the Hebrew Bible, is an allegorical love poem, traditionally interpreted by Jews and Christians to signify the mystical relationship between God and the soul.

36: *Donatello* (1386-1466), a sculptor, and Benvenuto *Cellini* (1500-71), a goldsmith, painter, and sculptor, were Italian Renaissance artists.

37: The *Sainte Chapelle* is a Gothic chapel in Paris, consecrated in 1248.

Note 6: *Pierre de Montereau*, or Montreuil (c. 1200-67), was the architect of the Sainte Chapelle.

Note 7: *Michelangelo* (1475-1564) painted the ceiling of the Sistine Chapel in the Vatican Palace; *Titian* (c. 1487-1576) is best known for his portraits of royalty and aristocrats; and the work of *Correggio* (c. 1489-1534) includes frescoes on the domes of two churches in Parma, Italy.

2

43: *When Jesus prayed he lifted his eyes toward heaven*: "And when he had taken the five loaves and the two fishes, he looked up to heaven, and blessed, and brake the loaves, and gave them to his disciples to set before them" (Mark 6:41 passim).

Hidden by a cloud: "And when he had spoken these things, while they beheld, he was taken up; and a cloud received him out of their sight" (Acts 1:9).

44: The *Mānava Dharma Shāstra*, or Laws of Manu, is a compendium of traditional Hindu social, ethical, and ceremonial precepts.

Mount *Kailasa*, a Himalayan peak in Tibet, is sacred to Hindus, Buddhists, and Jains.

Note 1: *L'œil du cœur—The Eye of the Heart*—was the second of the author's major works, published in Paris in 1950. In the chapter "Concerning the Posthumous States" he writes: "The point of view peculiar to the religions of Semitic origin is characterized among other things by its tendency to deny all that does not concern man as such: accordingly, it will deny the immortality of the animal soul and, what in a certain respect amounts to the same thing, the transmigration of the soul through nonhuman existences. However, one can speak here of denial only in an altogether outward and quite relative manner, for there are no errors in the Revelations, and what is in question in the present case is rather a very synthetic and simplified conception of the posthumous states, whose totality is reduced to two 'eternal' states, namely, heaven and hell. . . . Any posthumous state that does not correspond to the human state will be assimilated implicitly if not explicitly to the infernal states or the 'limbos', depending on the case" (*The Eye of the Heart: Metaphysics, Cosmology, Spiritual Life* [Bloomington, Indiana: World Wisdom Books, 1997], pp. 47-48).

46: *Pontiac* (c. 1720-69), *Tecumseh* (c. 1765-1813), *Tashunka Witko* (c. 1844-77), and *Tatanka Iyotanka* (c. 1834-90) were famous American Indian chiefs.

III Contours of the Spirit

1

53: "Thine existence is *a fault to which no other fault can be compared*": *hadīth*.

55: *Shankarian* refers to the doctrine of *Shankara* (788-820), the pre-eminent master of *Advaita Vedānta*, whom the author considered the greatest of all Hindu metaphysicians.

56: Note 3 (cont.): *Nagarjuna* (c. 150-250), founder of the *Mādhyamaka* or "middle way" school of Buddhism and widely regarded in the *Mahāyāna* tradition as a "second Buddha", taught that a distinction must be made between conventional truth, according to which the distinctive characteristics of appearances are accepted as real, and supreme or ultimate truth, according to which all things have the same nature of *shūnyatā*, or "emptiness".

57: Note 4: *Ramanujian* refers to the doctrine of Ramanuja (1017-c. 1137), the classic exponent of *Vishishta Advaita*, the Hindu school of "qualified nondualism", in which emphasis is placed on the personal dimension of God.

58: Note 7: "*You have an enemy in your wives and your children*" (*Sūrah* "Mutual Disillusion" [64]:14).

59: *Krishna and the Gopis*: Hindu tradition tells of the youthful dalliance of the *Avatāra* Krishna with the adoring *gopīs* or cowherd girls of Vrindavan.

60: Note 8: For the *Mānava Dharma Shāstra*, see editor's note for "Aesthetics and Symbolism in Art and Nature", Part 2, p. 44.

The *Bhagavad Gītā*, the best known and arguably the most influential of all Hindu sacred texts, consists of a dialogue concerning the different paths to God between the prince Arjuna and his charioteer, the *Avatāra* Krishna.

62: "Unto God belong the East and the West, and *in whatever direction ye may turn*, there is the *Face of God*" (*Sūrah* "The Cow" [2]:115).

Turning for prayer in the direction of the sacred mosque: "Turn thy face in the direction of the sacred mosque: wherever ye are, turn your faces in that direction" (*Sūrah* "The Cow" [2]:144).

The Gospel enjoins a man to "hate" his father and mother. "If any man come to me, and hate not his father, and mother, and wife, and children, and brethren, and sisters, yea, and his own life also, he cannot be my disciple" (Luke 14:26).

Love his neighbor as himself: "Thou shalt love thy neighbor as thyself" (Matt. 22:39 passim).

In Hinduism, the *Veda* is a body of sacred knowledge revealed to ancient Indian seers and transmitted in the *Vedas*, sacred texts composed of hymns, ritual formulas, and metaphysical doctrines regarded as authoritative for both doctrine and practice.

The sands of the desert and the stars of the firmament: "I will multiply thy seed as the stars of the heaven, and as the sand which is upon the sea shore" (Gen. 22:17).

Augustine (354-430), Bishop of the North African city of Hippo, was the greatest of the Western Church Fathers.

63: Note 11: *Meister Eckhart* (c. 1260-1327), a Dominican theologian and mystic, was regarded by the author as the greatest of Christian metaphysicians and esoterists (see also editor's notes for "Knowledge and Love", Part 4, p. 173, Note 2 and p. 175).

The Apostles Peter and John: "Peter therefore went forth, and that other disciple [John], and came to the sepulcher. So they ran both together: and the other disciple did outrun Peter, and came first to the sepulcher" (John 20:3-4).

The *Convivio* or "Banquet" of *Dante* (see editor's note for "Thought and Civilization", Part 3, p. 18), an unfinished series of poems with extensive prose commentary on various philosophical and scientific topics, served in part as a foundation for the *Divine Comedy*.

Moses *Maimonides* (1135-1204), a Jewish rabbi and physician and one of the most important of the medieval philosophers, is best known for his *Guide for the Perplexed*.

The Sefer ha-*Zohar*, that is, "The Book of Splendor", published in Spain c. 1285, is an esoteric commentary on the *Torah* and the most important text in the Jewish mystical tradition.

Basil the Great (c. 330-79), Bishop of Caesarea, was one of the Cappadocian Fathers and the first of the three Holy Hierarchs of the Eastern Orthodox Church (see also editor's note for "Contours of the Spirit", Part 3, p. 84, Note 4).

64: Note 14: *Voltaire* (1694-1778)—the pseudonym of François-Marie Arouet—a deist and the best known of the French "Philosophes", published his *Essai sur les moeurs et l'esprit des nations* ("An Essay on the Manners and Spirit of Nations") in 1756 (see also editor's note for "Knowledge and Love", Part 2, p. 143).

69: Note 19: *Pythagoras* of Samos (c. 569-c. 475) was one of the greatest sages of ancient Greece, teaching a doctrine that was at once philosophical, mathematical, astronomical, and musical.

Thomas Aquinas (c. 1225-74), a giant among the medieval Scholastics and author of the monumental *Summa Theologica*, is considered by the Roman Catholic Church to be the most important Christian theologian in history.

2

73: The *Upanishads*, also referred to as the *Vedānta* since they were tradition-ally placed at the "end" of the *Vedas* (see editor's note for "Contours of the Spirit", Part 1, p. 62) and seen by such authorities as Shankara as a synthesis of Vedic teaching, are Hindu scriptures containing metaphysical, mystical, and esoteric doctrine.

The *Brahma Sūtra*, one of the chief sources of Vedantic wisdom, traditionally attributed to the sage Badarayana (first century B.C.), distills and systematizes the teachings of the *Upanishads* concerning *Brahma*, the Supreme Reality.

The *Tao Te Ching*, traditionally ascribed to the ancient sage Lao-Tzu, is the fundamental sacred text of Taoism.

Note 2: *Clement of Alexandria* (c. 150-c. 215) was head of the famous Cat-echetical School of Alexandria and author of the *Stromata*, a collection of spiritual "miscellanies" (see also editor's note for "Contours of the Spirit", Part 3, p. 85, Note 5).

74: Note 3: *The phenomena of nature are "signs" for those "endowed with understanding"*: "Hast thou not seen how God hath sent down water from the sky and hath caused it to penetrate the earth as watersprings, and after-ward thereby produceth crops of diverse hues; and afterward they wither and thou seest them turn yellow; then He maketh them chaff. Lo! herein verily is a reminder for men endowed with understanding" (*Sūrah* "The Troops" [39]:21 passim).

Note 4: The *Cabala* is the Jewish mystical and esoteric tradition.

Note 5: For *Omar Khayyam*, see editor's note for "Aesthetics and Symbolism in Art and Nature", Part 1, p. 34.

75: Note 5 (cont.): Abu al-Qasim *al-Qushayri* (d. 1074), author of a commentary on the Koran, is best known for his *Risālah*, or "Epistle [to the Sufis]", a manual on the spiritual path.

For *Shankara*, see editor's notes for "Contours of the Spirit", Part 1, p. 55 and Part 2, p. 73.

Chaitanya (1486-1533), a Vaishnavite Hindu spiritual teacher and ecstatic devotee of Krishna, was regarded by his followers as an *Avatāra* of both Krishna and his consort Radha.

Note 6: Muhyi al-Din *Ibn Arabi* (1165-1240), a prolific and profoundly influential Sufi mystic, was the author of numerous works, including *Meccan Revelations* and *Bezels of Wisdom*.

76: Note 7: *Bernard* of Clairvaux (1090-1153) was a Cistercian monk, noted especially for his anagogical homilies on the Song of Songs.

77: *The words of Christ to Nicodemus*: "There was a man of the Pharisees, named Nicodemus, a ruler of the Jews: The same came to Jesus by night, and said unto him, Rabbi, we know that thou art a teacher come from God: for no man can do these miracles that thou doest, except God be with him. Jesus answered and said unto him, Verily, verily, I say unto thee, Except a man be born again, he cannot see the kingdom of God. Nicodemus saith unto him, How can a man be born when he is old? can he enter the second time into his mother's womb, and be born? Jesus answered, Verily, verily, I say unto thee, Except a man be born of water and of the Spirit, he cannot enter into the kingdom of God. That which is born of the flesh is flesh; and that which is born of the Spirit is spirit. Marvel not that I said unto thee, Ye must be born again. The wind bloweth where it listeth, and thou hearest the sound thereof, but canst not tell whence it cometh, and whither it goeth: so is every one that is born of the Spirit. Nicodemus answered and said unto him, How can these things be? Jesus answered and said unto him, Art thou a master of Israel, and knowest not these things? Verily, verily, I say unto thee, We speak that we do know, and testify that we have seen; and ye receive not our witness. If I have told you earthly things, and ye believe not, how shall ye believe, if I tell you of heavenly things?" (John 3:1-12).

The Samaritan woman: "There cometh a woman of Samaria to draw water: Jesus saith unto her, Give me to drink. (For his disciples were gone away unto the city to buy meat.) Then saith the woman of Samaria unto him, How is it that thou, being a Jew, askest drink of me, which am a woman of Samaria? for the Jews have no dealings with the Samaritans. Jesus answered and said unto her, If thou knewest the gift of God, and who it is that saith to thee, Give me to drink; thou wouldest have asked of him, and he would have given thee living water. The woman saith unto him, Sir, thou hast nothing to draw with, and the well is deep: from whence then hast thou that living water? Art thou greater than our father Jacob, which gave us the well, and drank thereof himself, and his children, and his cattle? Jesus answered and said unto her, Whosoever drinketh of this water shall thirst again: But whosoever drinketh of the water that I shall give him shall never thirst; but the water that I shall give him shall be in him a well of water springing up into everlasting life" (John 4:7-14).

The rich young man: "And, behold, one came and said unto him, Good master, what good thing shall I do, that I may have eternal life? And he said unto him, Why callest thou me good? there is none good but one, that is, God: but if thou wilt enter into life, keep the commandments. He saith unto him, Which? Jesus said, Thou shalt do no murder, Thou shalt not commit adultery, Thou shalt not steal, Thou shalt not bear false witness. Honor thy father and thy mother: and, Thou shalt love thy neighbor as thyself. The young man saith unto him, All these things have I kept from my youth up: what lack I yet? Jesus said unto him, If thou wilt be perfect, go and sell that thou hast, and give to the poor, and thou shalt have treasure in heaven: and come and follow me" (Matt. 19:16-21; cf. Mark 10:17-21).

78: "*Render unto Caesar the things that are Caesar's, and unto God the things that are God's*" (Mark 12:17; cf. Matt. 22:21, Luke 20:25).

"*Blessed are the pure in heart:* for they shall see God" (Matt. 5:8).

Note 9: *Dante* Alighieri (see editor's note for "Thought and Civilization", Part 3, p. 18), who in his *Divine Comedy* repeatedly condemned the popes for their involvement in politics, argued in his *De Monarchia*, or "Treatise on Monarchy", that the emperor should be the supreme temporal ruler, as in the time of Augustus.

82: "*They sit in Moses' seat*": "The scribes and Pharisees sit in Moses' seat: All therefore whatsoever they bid you observe, that observe and do; but do not ye after their works: for they say, and do not" (Matt. 23:2-3).

3

83: Note 1: *Moysis doctrina velat quod Christi doctrina revelat* is Latin for "the teaching of Moses conceals what the teaching of Christ reveals".

For *Ibn Arabi*, see editor's note for "Contours of the Spirit", Part 2, p. 75, Note 6.

"My kingdom is not of this world" (John 18:36).

Note 2: *Nicholas Cabasilas* (c. 1320-c. 1390) was a late Byzantine mystical writer whose principal work, a set of seven discourses on *Life in Christ*, explains how spiritual union with Christ may be achieved through the sacraments of Baptism, Chrismation (or Confirmation), and the Eucharist.

Gregory Palamas (c. 1296-1359), a monk of Mount Athos, is best known for his defense of the psychosomatic contemplative techniques employed by the Hesychast Fathers and for his distinction between the divine essence and energies.

In ipso vivimus et movemur et sumus is the Vulgate text of Acts 17:28: "In Him we live, and move, and have our being."

Simeon the New Theologian (949-1022), widely regarded as the greatest of Eastern Christian mystical writers, says in his *Discourses* that tears are both an effect and a deepening of the initiatic mystery of Baptism.

Origen (185-253) was the most prolific and influential of the early Church Fathers, writing many hundreds of books, including *De Oratione*, "On Prayer", and *Contra Celsum*, "Against Celsus", a defense of Christianity against the pagan philosopher Celsus.

Gregory of Nyssa (c. 330-c. 395), a bishop of the early church and an influential mystical and ascetical authority, wrote his famous "Catechetical Orations" or *Great Catechesis* as an aid to those who were responsible for the instruction of catechumens in the basic doctrines of the faith, including the nature of sin and its remedy in the Sacrament of Baptism (see also editor's note for "Knowledge and Love", Part 3, p. 150).

Jean Cardinal *Daniélou* (1905-74) published his study of *Origène* [Origen] in 1948.

84: Note 2 (cont.): *Twenty-Third Psalm*: "The Lord is my shepherd; I shall not want. He maketh me to lie down in green pastures: he leadeth me beside the still waters. He restoreth my soul: he leadeth me in the paths of righteousness for his name's sake. Yea, though I walk through the valley of *the shadow of death*, I will fear no evil: for thou art with me; thy rod and thy *staff* they comfort me. Thou preparest a *table* before me in the presence of mine enemies:

thou anointest my head with *oil;* my *cup runneth over.* Surely goodness and mercy shall follow me all the days of my life: and I will dwell in the house of the Lord for ever."

Platonisme et Théologie Mystique: doctrine spirituelle de saint Grégoire de Nysse [Platonism and Mystical Theology: The Spiritual Doctrine of Saint Gregory of Nyssa] was published in 1944.

"And I will give unto thee the *keys of the kingdom of heaven:* and whatsoever thou shalt bind on earth shall be bound in heaven: and whatsoever thou shalt loose on earth shall be loosed in heaven" (Matt. 16:9).

Note 4: *Basil* the Great (see editor's note for "Contours of the Spirit", Part 1, p. 63, Note 11) wrote his *Treatise on the Holy Spirit* in response to the heretical Pneumatomachi, who denied the Spirit's divinity.

85: Note 5: *Clement of Alexandria* (see editor's note for "Contours of the Spirit", Part 2, p. 73, Note 2) taught that assimilation to God through *gnosis* is the chief aim of the Christian life and the key to human perfection.

Benedict XIV (1675-1758) was Pope of Rome from 1740.

Irenaeus (c. 130-c. 200), a bishop of Lyons and one of the most important of the early Church Fathers, wrote a lengthy treatise commonly referred to as *Against Heresies;* its full title, *The Refutation and Overthrow of All Knowledge Falsely So Called,* underscores the saint's concern to distinguish the heretical claims of sectarian Gnosticism from authentic *gnosis.*

Dionysius the Areopagite, a disciple of the Apostle Paul (Acts 17:34, though dated c. 500 by many scholars) and perhaps the greatest of all Christian masters of apophatic theology, based his teaching on two sources: the divine Scriptures, which are held by all in common, and the "occult tradition of our inspired teachers", into which he had been secretly initiated (*Divine Names,* 4).

Evagrius Ponticus (346-99), who spent much of his life among the Desert Fathers of Egypt, wrote in the introduction to his *Praktikos,* or "Treatise on the Practical Life": "We shall not speak of everything we have seen or heard but only as much as we have been taught by the Fathers to tell to others. . . . So as not to give 'that which is holy unto the dogs' or 'cast pearls before swine' [Matt. 7:6], some of these matters will be kept in concealment and others alluded to only obscurely, and yet in such a way as to keep them quite clear to those who walk in the same Path" (see also editor's note for "Knowledge and Love", Part 1, p. 134, Note 1).

For *Meister Eckhart*, see editor's notes for "Contours of the Spirit", Part 1, p. 63, Note 11; "Knowledge and Love", Part 4, p. 173, Note 2 and p. 175.

Angelus Silesius, that is, the "Silesian Angel", was the pen name of Johannes Scheffler (1624-77), a Roman Catholic priest and mystical poet greatly influenced by the teachings of Meister Eckhart.

87: Note 6: *Zen* is the Japanese pronunciation of *ch'an*, which is the Chinese pronunciation of the Sanskrit *dhyāna*, meaning "meditation".

88: *Teresa of Avila* (1515-82), a Spanish Carmelite nun and mystic, wrote extensively on the stages of the spiritual life and the levels of prayer, as in her most important work, the *Interior Castle*, in which the soul's journey to God is envisioned as a progression from the outer courtyard of a crystal castle to the innermost of its seven mansions or rooms.

89: *Ramakrishna* (1834-86), a devotee of the goddess Kali, was one of the greatest Hindu saints of modern times, notable for his ability to adapt to the needs of many kinds of disciples depending on whether they envisaged God, as he said, "with form" or "without form".

John of the Cross (1542-91), a Spanish priest and mystic and co-founder, with Teresa of Avila, of the reformed or Discalced Carmelites, taught that visions and sensible consolations were sometimes granted by God to beginners in the spiritual life, but that spiritual advancement requires entering, beyond all such experience, into the "dark night of the soul".

"Many are called, but few are chosen" (Matt. 22:14).

Note 9: The *Philokalia* is a collection of ascetical and mystical writings by spiritual masters of the Christian East, compiled by Nikodimos of the Holy Mountain (1748-1809) and Makarios of Corinth (1731-1805).

Hesychasm is the spiritual practice of certain monks of the Christian East whose aim is to attain a state of *hesychia*, or inner stillness, through the practice of the Jesus Prayer or other "prayer of the heart".

For *Chaitanya*, see editor's note for "Contours of the Spirit", Part 2, p. 75, Note 5.

90: *Plotinus* (c. 205-270), founder of the Neoplatonic school of philosophy, endeavored to synthesize the teachings of Plato and Aristotle in his monumental *Enneads*, a collection of discourses compiled by his disciple *Porphyry* (c. 232-c. 305); when Porphyry told his master he should attend a Christian liturgy since angels were said to take part in the worship, Plotinus replied, "It is not for me to go to those beings, but for those beings to come to me."

For *Shankara*, see editor's notes for "Contours of the Spirit", Part 1, p. 55 and Part 2, p. 73.

91: Note 13: *A scriptural foundation for these consolations*: "Blessed be God, even the Father of our Lord Jesus Christ, the Father of mercies, and the God of all comfort; Who comforteth us in all our tribulation, that we may be able to comfort them which are in any trouble, by the comfort wherewith we ourselves are comforted of God. For as the sufferings of Christ abound in us, so our consolation also aboundeth by Christ" (2 Cor. 1:3-5).

Note 14: *Alphonsus Liguori* (1696-1787) was founder of the Congregation of the Most Holy Redeemer, or Redemptorist Order, an influential devotional writer, and a doctor of the Roman Catholic Church.

Note 15: *Sūrah* "Have We Not Enlarged?" [94]:1-3, 5.

Ignatius Loyola (1491-1556), founder and first general of the Society of Jesus, composed a series of *Spiritual Exercises* combining meditation on the events of Christ's life with a prescribed pattern of prayerful reflection and designed to guide the aspirant through the three principal stages of the spiritual life: purification, illumination, and union.

"My yoke is easy, and my burden is light" (Matt. 11:30).

92: Note 18: Elsewhere the author describes the German atheist philosopher Friedrich *Nietzsche* (1844-1900) as "a volcanic genius if ever there was one. . . . There is passionate exteriorization of an inward fire, but in a manner that is both deviated and demented; we have in mind here not the Nietzschian philosophy, which taken literally is without interest, but his poetical work, whose most intense expression is in part his *Zarathustra* [*Thus Spoke Zarathustra: A Book for All and None* (1883-85)]. What this highly uneven book manifests above all is the violent reaction of an *a priori* profound soul against a mediocre and paralyzing cultural environment; Nietzsche's fault was to have only a sense of grandeur in the absence of all intellectual discernment. *Zarathustra* is basically the cry of a grandeur trodden underfoot, whence comes the heartrending authenticity—the grandeur precisely—of certain passages; not all of them, to be sure, and above all not those that express a half-Machiavellian, half-Darwinian philosophy, or minor literary cleverness. Be that as it may, Nietzsche's misfortune, like that of other men of genius, such as Napoleon, was to be born after the Renaissance and not before it, which indicates evidently an aspect of their nature, for there is no such thing as chance" (*To Have a Center* [Bloomington, Indiana: World Wisdom Books, 1990], p. 15).

IV *Vedānta*

1

99: For the *Upanishads*, see editor's note for "Contours of the Spirit", Part 2, p. 73.

For *Shankarian Vedantism*, see editor's note for "Contours of the Spirit", Part 1, p. 55.

Note 1: *Ibn al-Arif* (1088-1141), an Andalusian Sufi master, was best known for his writings on the science of the virtues.

100: Note 2: The chapter *Al-Nūr* [*En-Nūr*] can be found in Part One of the author's book *L'œil du cœur* [*The Eye of the Heart*] (Paris: Dervy-Livres, 1974; see also editor's note for "Knowledge and Love", Part 3, p. 163, Note 16).

103: Note 5: *Ananda K. Coomaraswamy* (1877-1947), for many years curator of Indian art in the Boston Museum of Fine Arts and one of the founding figures of the perennialist school, was the author of numerous books and articles on art, religion, and metaphysics from the point of view of the primordial and universal tradition.

105: Note 7: *René Guénon* (1886-1951), a French metaphysician and prolific scholar of religions, was one of the formative authorities of the traditionalist or perennialist school and a frequent contributor to the journal *Études Traditionnelles* ("Traditional Studies").

107: "*Made in the image of God*": "God created man in His own image, in the image of God created He him; male and female created He them" (Gen. 1:27).

108: *Illā 'Llāh*, an Arabic phrase meaning "but God", is the second half of the first formula of the *Shahādah*; *lā ilāha*, which means "There is no god", is the first half of this formula.

2

109: For *Ramanuja*, see editor's note for "Contours of the Spirit", Part 1, p. 57, Note 4.

For *Shankara*, see editor's notes for "Contours of the Spirit", Part 1, p. 55 and Part 2, p. 73.

For *Nagarjuna*, see editor's note for "Contours of the Spirit", Part 1, p. 56, Note 3.

110: *Plato* (c. 427-c. 347 B.C.), the greatest of the ancient Greek philosophers, taught that the Forms or Ideas of things are more real than their material instantiations. On the subject of "abstraction", see the chapter "Abuse of the Ideas of the Concrete and the Abstract" in the author's *Logic and Transcendence* (London: Perennial Books, 1984).

111: Note 2: According to *Saint Thomas* Aquinas (see editor's note for "Contours of the Spirit", Part 1, p. 69, Note 19), *Ducitur tamen ex sensibilibus intellectus noster in divinam cognitionem ut cognoscat de Deo quia est, et alia hujus modi quae oportet attribui primo Principio*: "Beginning with sensible things our intellect is led to the point of knowing about God that He exists and other such characteristics that must be attributed to the first Principle" (*Summa Contra Gentiles*, Bk. 1, Ch. 3).

112: Note 2 (cont.): *G. Dandoy* published *L'Ontologie du Vedānta:* Essai sur l'acosmisme de l'*Advaita* [The Ontology of the *Vedānta*: An Essay on the Acosmism of *Advaita*] in 1932.

115: "*Why callest thou me good? There is none good but one, that is, God*" (Matt. 19:17, Mark 10:18; cf. Luke 18:19).

For *Ramakrishna*, see editor's note for "Contours of the Spirit", Part 3, p. 89.

116: Note 4: "Jesus saith unto him, I am the way, the truth, and the life: *no man cometh unto the Father, but by me*" (John 14:6).

117: Note 5: *Ramana Maharshi* (1879-1950), widely regarded as the greatest Hindu sage of the twentieth century, experienced the identity of *Ātmā* and *Brahma* while still in his teens, and the fruit of this experience remained with him as a permanent spiritual station throughout his life; his forty verses "On Being", written originally in Tamil with the title *Ulladu Narpadu*, were translated into Sanskrit as *Sad-Vidya*.

3

120: For *Ramakrishna*, see editor's note for "Contours of the Spirit", Part 3, p. 89.

For *Shankaracharya* (Shankara), see editor's notes for "Contours of the Spirit", Part 1, p. 55 and Part 2, p. 73.

121: *Narendra*—or, more fully, Narendranath Datta (1863-1902)—was the pre-monastic name of Vivekananda, a disciple of Ramakrishna and an exponent of Indian social reform.

122: *The divine "Mother"* is the Hindu goddess Kali (see editor's note for "Knowledge and Love", Part 3, p. 150, Note 1).

124: Note 4: *The Gospel of Sri Ramakrishna*, a collection of the master's sayings and deeds compiled by one of his disciples, Mahendranath Gupta ("M"), was first published in 1942.

125: The *Arya Samaj* and the *Brahmo Samaj* are late nineteenth-century Hindu reform movements, characterized by their opposition to the caste system and their promotion of "social justice" and various egalitarian causes.

126: Note 8: *Inspired Talks* were a series of informal addresses given by Vivekananda between 19 June and 6 August 1895; his *Lecture on Vedānta* was delivered 12 November 1897.

Sister Nivedita—Margaret Elizabeth Noble (1867-1911)—was an English social worker, author, and teacher, and a disciple of Vivekananda.

127: Note 10: *Swami Brahmananda*—Rakhal Chandra Ghosh (1863-1922)—was a disciple of Vivekananda and succeeded him as head of the Ramakrishna Mission.

128: Note 11: Mohandas K. *Gandhi* (1869-1948) was well known for spinning the cotton for his clothing on a handloom and for advocating a return to the simplicity of village craftsmanship.

The creator of the "New Turkey" was Kemal Atatürk (1881-1938), the first president of the Republic of Turkey, under whose leadership the country underwent major political, economic, and social changes.

129: For *Ramana Maharshi*, see editor's note for "*Vedānta*", Part 2, p. 117, Note 5.

For the *Upanishads*, see editor's note for "Contours of the Spirit", Part 2, p. 73.

V Knowledge and Love

1

133: *Joan of Arc* (1412-31), the Maid of Orléans, experienced a number of supernatural visitations, which took the form of blazing lights and voices, including those of Saint Michael, Saint Catherine, and Saint Margaret, who revealed her mission to save France.

In the author's original French, the term rendered "evidence" in the phrase *ontological evidence* is *évidence*, which includes the idea of obviousness or self-evidence, while at the same time suggesting corroboration or proof.

Christ's words to the Apostle Thomas: "Jesus saith unto him, Thomas, because thou hast seen me, thou hast believed: blessed are they that have not seen, and yet have believed" (John 20:29).

The Sermon on the Mount (Matt. 5-7) includes the following Beatitude: "Blessed are they that *mourn*: for they shall be *comforted*" (Matt. 5:4).

134: *The faith "that moves mountains"*: "If ye have faith as a grain of mustard seed, ye shall say unto this mountain, Remove hence to yonder place; and it shall remove; and nothing shall be impossible unto you" (Matt. 17:20).

Note 1: *Evagrius Ponticus* (see editor's note for "Contours of the Spirit", Part 3, p. 85, Note 5) stressed the importance of *apatheia*, or "*apathy*"—that is, imperturbable detachment and calm.

Hesychasts—monks of the Eastern Christian tradition whose aim is to attain a state of *hesychia* or inner stillness through the practice of the Jesus Prayer or other "prayer of the heart"—include the sixth-century Palestinian hermits *Barsanuphius* and *John*.

Note 2: *Anselm* (c. 1033-1109), Archbishop of Canterbury and one of the most important of the medieval Scholastics, prefaced his ontological argument for the existence of God with the words: "I do not seek to understand so that I may believe; but I believe so that I may understand", the second phrase being *credo ut intelligam* in Latin.

Note 3: For *Simeon the New Theologian,* see editor's note for "Contours of the Spirit", Part 3, p. 83, Note 2.

"He that believeth on me, as the scripture hath said, *out of his belly shall flow rivers of living water"* (John 7:38).

John Climacus (c. 570-649), a monk and later abbot of Sinai, is best known for his *Ladder of Paradise,* a treatise on the spiritual life in which the thirty steps (chapters) of the "ladder" (*klimax* in Greek) correspond to the age of Christ at his Baptism.

Vladimir Lossky (1903-58) published *Essai sur la théologie mystique de l'Église d'Orient* [The Mystical Theology of the Eastern Church] in 1944.

137: For *Meister Eckhart,* see editor's notes for "Contours of the Spirit", Part 1, p. 63, Note 11; "Knowledge and Love", Part 4, p. 173, Note 2 and p. 175.

"And he that taketh not his cross, and followeth after me, is not worthy of me" (Matt. 10:38).

138: Note 9: *The story of Majnun and Layla,* one of the best known in the Islamic world, tells of a young man nicknamed *majnun,* literally "mad-man", because of his love for a beautiful woman with hair as black as the "night" (*layla*); because their love remained unfulfilled in this world, the story is often interpreted as an allegory of the soul's longing for God.

Dante Alighieri (see editor's notes for "Thought and Civilization", Part 3, p. 18; "Aesthetics and Symbolism in Art and Nature", Part 1, p. 34; "Contours of the Spirit", Part 1, p. 63, Note 11 and Part 2, p. 78, Note 9) made *Beatrice* his spiritual guide in *The Paradiso.*

2

140: Note 1: For Meister *Eckhart,* see editor's notes for "Contours of the Spirit", Part 1, p. 63, Note 11; "Knowledge and Love", Part 4, p. 173, Note 2 and p. 175.

141: Note 2: For *Chaitanya*, see editor's note for "Contours of the Spirit", Part 2, p. 75, Note 5.

For *Ramakrishna*, see editor's note for "Contours of the Spirit", Part 3, p. 89.

For *Omar ibn al-Farid*, see editor's note for "Aesthetics and Symbolism in Art and Nature", Part 1, p. 34.

Jalal al-Din Rumi (1207-73), a Sufi mystic and poet and founder of the Mevlevi order, is well known for his insistence on spiritual love as the proper basis for the seeker's relation to God.

143: *Voltaire* (see editor's note for "Contours of the Spirit", Part 1, p. 64, Note 14) was violently opposed to the Roman Catholic Church and sharply critical of its monastic institutions for their alleged indifference to social problems.

The *Carthusian* Order is a strictly contemplative monastic order known for its austerity and requiring of its members a vow of silence and complete renunciation of the world.

145: "*God alone is good*": "Why callest thou me good? There is none good but one, that is, God" (Matt. 19:17, Mark 10:18; cf. Luke 18:19).

146: *He calls this totality of contemplation "love"*: 1 Corinthians 13.

3

150: *Gregory of Nyssa* (see editor's note for "Contours of the Spirit", Part 3, p. 83, Note 2) taught that the *nous* or Intellect is the fundamental reason for man's intrinsic dignity as the "image of God".

Note 1: *Maximus the Confessor* (580-662), a prolific writer on doctrinal, ascetical, exegetical, and liturgical subjects, is the most authoritative of the "neptic" fathers, spiritual writers of the Christian East for whom intellection, or "intuition", provides direct knowledge of spiritual realities.

For *Meister Eckhart*, see editor's notes for "Contours of the Spirit", Part 1, p. 63, Note 11; "Knowledge and Love", Part 4, p. 173, Note 2 and p. 175.

Kali, worshipped by *Ramakrishna* (see editor's note for "Contours of the Spirit", Part 3, p. 89) as the supreme deity, is the destructive and transformative manifestation of the Hindu goddess Parvati, consort of Shiva.

151: Note 2: For *Ramanuja,* see editor's note for "Contours of the Spirit", Part 1, p. 57, Note 4.

For Shankara, see editor's notes for "Contours of the Spirit", Part 1, p. 55 and Part 2, p. 73.

153: Note 3: *Macarius of Egypt* (c. 300-c. 390), or Macarius the Great, a Desert Father renowned for his sanctity and miracles, founded a community of ascetics that became one of the chief centers of early Egyptian monasticism.

Dorotheus (sixth century), founder and archimandrite of a Palestinian monastery near Gaza, wrote a series of "Instructions" on the ascetical life.

For *Evagrius Ponticus,* see editor's notes for "Contours of the Spirit", Part 3, p. 85, Note 5 and "Knowledge and Love", Part 1, p. 134, Note 1.

For the book by *Vladimir Lossky,* see editor's note for "Knowledge and Love", Part 1, p. 134, Note 3.

154: Note 4: The *Jesus Prayer* is the most common orison of the *Hesychasts* (see editor's notes for "Contours of the Spirit", Part 3, p. 90, Note 9 and "Knowledge and Love", Part 1, p. 184, Note 1) and consists of the words, or some variation, "Lord Jesus Christ, Son of God, have mercy upon us."

157: For *Thomas* Aquinas, see editor's note for "Contours of the Spirit", Part 1, p. 69, Note 19.

158: *"Blessed are they that have not seen, and yet have believed"* (John 20:29).

In God Love is Light: "God is light, and in Him is no darkness at all" (1 John 1:5); *"God is love"* (1 John 4:8).

159: For Muhyi al-Din *Ibn Arabi,* see editor's note for "Contours of the Spirit", Part 2, p. 75, Note 6.

161: *The "peace" Christ gave the Apostles*: "Peace I leave with you, my peace I give unto you: not as the world giveth, give I unto you. Let not your heart be troubled, neither let it be afraid" (John 14:27).

Callistus of Xanthopoulos, later Patriarch of Constantinople, and *Ignatius* of Xanthopoulos (fl. late fourteenth century) were fellow monks on the Holy Mountain of Athos, who together compiled a *Century*—that is, one hundred chapters—of "Directions to Hesychasts".

Palamite teaching is the doctrine of Gregory Palamas (see editor's note for "Contours of the Spirit", Part 3, p. 83, Note 2).

Note 9: *Nikitas Stithatos*, an eleventh-century monk, three of whose "centuries" are preserved in the *Philokalia* (see editor's note for "Contours of the Spirit", Part 3, p. 89, Note 9) entered the monastery of Studios at Constantinople c. 1020 and may have become abbot in his old age, sometime between 1076-92.

Note 10: The *Alexandrians* included Clement (see editor's notes for "Contours of the Spirit", Part 2, p. 73, Note 2 and Part 3, p. 85, Note 5) and Origen (see editor's note for "Contours of the Spirit", Part 3, p. 83, Note 2), whose Catechetical School in Alexandria was marked by strong Platonic tendencies and a preference for mystical and allegorical interpretations of Scripture.

"*Holy silence*" is a translation of the Greek *hesychia*, whence the term Hesychasm (see editor's note for "Contours of the Spirit", Part 3, p. 89, Note 9).

162: Note 11: For *Angelus Silesius*, see editor's note for "Contours of the Spirit", Part 3, p. 85, Note 5.

The *Curé d'Ars* was Jean-Baptiste Marie Vianney (1786-1859), a parish priest and much sought-after confessor from the French village of Ars, who was widely known for his gift of reading souls.

The tears of Saint Mary Magdalene at the Savior's feet: "A woman in the city, which was a sinner, when she knew that Jesus sat at meat in the Pharisee's house, brought an alabaster box of ointment, and stood at his feet behind him weeping, and began to wash his feet with tears, and did wipe them with the hairs of her head, and kissed his feet, and anointed them with the ointment" (Luke 7:37-38).

163: *The ante-Nicene Fathers* were spiritual authorities of the early Church who lived and wrote prior to the Council of Nicaea, the first of the Ecumenical Councils, which was convened in 325.

Note 16: *The hymn of praise to charity in the First Epistle to the Corinthians*: 1 Corinthians 13.

L'œil du cœur (see editor's note for "*Vedānta*", Part 1, p. 100, Note 2), pp. 105-6; English edition: *The Eye of the Heart: Metaphysics, Cosmology, Spiritual Life* (Bloomington, Indiana: World Wisdom Books, 1997), p. 127.

166: Note 19: Mansur *al-Hallaj* (858-922), the first Sufi martyr, was dismembered and crucified for his mystical pronouncement, "I am the Truth".

167: Note 20: "*The kingdom of God is within you*" (Luke 17:21).

168: *Saint Louis* IX (1214-70) was King of France from 1226 and one of the leading Crusaders.

Note 21: For *Chaitanya*, see editor's note for "Contours of the Spirit", Part 2, p. 75, Note 5.

For *Origen*, see editor's note for "Contours of the Spirit", Part 3, p. 83, Note 2.

Prays without ceasing: "Pray without ceasing" (1 Thess. 5:17).

169: Regarding *love of the neighbor* and the implications of that love for the *individual* and the *collectivity*, whether *qualitative* or *quantitative*, the author writes elsewhere: "Love of God is higher than love for man; in a distantly analogous way, love for the collectivity takes precedence over love for the individual. The collective interest comes before individual interest if both interests are of the same order, or if the parties concerned are qualitatively equivalent; this means that the collectivity must be of the same quality as the individual either by the fact of its totality or by reason of a specific quality, a caste for example; in no case does the purely quantitative collectivity come before the qualitative individual. . . . Society comes before the individual, if need be, as the norm comes before the exception, not as quantity crushes quality—which implies, precisely, that society should be organized with a view to man's spiritual welfare" (*Stations of Wisdom* [Bloomington, Indiana: World Wisdom Books, 1995], pp. 105-8).

Note 22: For *Augustine*, see editor's note for "Contours of the Spirit", Part 1, p. 62.

"*With all our heart*": "Thou shalt love the Lord thy God with all thy heart" (Matt. 22:37, Mark 12:30, Luke 10:27).

Richard of Saint Victor (d. 1173) was prior of the Abbey of Saint Victor in Paris.

4

170: "*God doeth what He will*" (*Sūrah* "The Family of Imran" [3]:40 passim).

171: "*Made in His image*": "God created man in His own image, in the image of God created He him; male and female created He them" (Gen. 1:27).

"And the *Word* was *made flesh*" (John 1:14).

172: "*God alone is good*": "Why callest thou me good? There is none good but one, that is, God" (Matt. 19:17, Mark 10:18; cf. Luke 18:19).

Note 2: *Basil* the Great (see editor's notes for "Contours of the Spirit", Part 1, p. 63, Note 11 and Part 3, p. 84, Note 4) and *Cyril of Alexandria* (d. 444), Patriarch of that city, were key figures in promoting the classical Patristic teaching that the purpose of the Incarnation is the deification of man.

173: For *Macarius of Egypt*, see editor's note for "Knowledge and Love", Part 3, p. 153, Note 3.

Note 2 (cont.): According to *Meister Eckhart* (see editor's notes for "Contours of the Spirit", Part 1, p. 63, Note 11; "Knowledge and Love", Part 4, p. 173, Note 2 and p. 175), all food is Holy Communion for those who are pure in heart.

For *Angelus Silesius*, see editor's note for "Contours of the Spirit", Part 3, p. 85, Note 5.

Note 3: *The Sufi Hasan al-Shadhili* (1196-1258) was the founder of the Shadhiliyya Sufi *tarīqah*, an initiatic lineage from which are derived a number of other Sufi orders, including the Alawiyya and the Darqawiyya.

174: *Vishnuites,* or Vaishnavites, are members of a Hindu theistic sect who worship the God Vishnu as the supreme Deity.

Note 4: *The Shaykh Ahmad al-Alawi* (1869-1934), a famous Algerian Sufi *shaykh,* was the author's spiritual master.

175: For *Shankara,* see editor's note for "Contours of the Spirit", Part 1, p. 55 and Part 2, p. 73.

For *Ibn Arabi,* see editor's note for "Contours of the Spirit", Part 2, p. 75, Note 6.

The teaching of Meister *Eckhart* that *aliquid est in anima quod est increatum et increabile . . . et hoc est Intellectus*—"there is something in the soul that is uncreated and uncreatable . . . and this is the Intellect"—was among the articles for which he was charged with heresy, and which he himself subsequently retracted "insofar as they could generate in the minds of the faithful a heretical opinion" (The Bull *In agro dominico* [1329]).

176: Note 6: Abu Hamid Muhammad *al-Ghazzali* (1058-1111), an Islamic jurist and theologian, entered upon the Sufi path in search of a direct confirmation of God, which he described in his *Munqidh min al-Dalal,* "Deliverance from Error".

Hallajian refers to Mansur al-Hallaj (see editor's note for "Knowledge and Love", Part 3, p. 166, Note 19), who in a moment of mystical ecstasy declared, *Anā'l-Haqq,* "I am the Truth", Truth being one of the Names of God.

VI The Spiritual Virtues

1

184: "But when thou doest alms, *let not thy left hand know what thy right hand doeth*" (Matt. 6:3).

189: "Though I speak with the tongues of men and of angels, and have not charity, I am become as *sounding brass,* or a tinkling cymbal" (1 Cor. 13:1).

192: "*Beauty is the splendor of the true*" is an axiom the author attributes to Plato (see editor's note for "*Vedānta*", Part 2, p. 110).

"Wisdom after the flesh": "In simplicity and godly sincerity, not with fleshly wisdom, but by the grace of God, we have had our conversation in the world" (2 Cor. 1:12).

"Hardened heart": "He hath blinded their eyes, and hardened their heart; that they should not see with their eyes, nor understand with their heart, and be converted, and I should heal them" (John 12:40; cf. Exod. 7:13, Deut. 2:30, 2 Chron. 36:13, Isa. 63:17 passim).

193: "Behold, I send you forth as sheep in the midst of wolves: *be ye therefore wise as serpents*, and harmless as doves" (Matt. 10:16).

194: In his *Rubaiyat* ("quatrains"), *Omar Khayyam* (see editor's note for "Aesthetics and Symbolism in Art and Nature", Part 1, p. 84) concealed a mystical apprehension of God under the veil of seeming skepticism and hedonism.

2

198: For the axiom *"Beauty is the splendor of the true"*, see editor's note for "The Spiritual Virtues", Part 1, p. 192.

For *Ibn al-Arif*, see editor's note for *"Vedānta"*, Part 1, p. 99, Note 1.

"God alone is good": "Why callest thou me good? There is none good but one, that is, God" (Matt. 19:17, Mark 10:18; cf. Luke 18:19).

199: Note 1: For the *Philokalia*, see editor's note for "Contours of the Spirit", Part 3, p. 89, Note 9.

200: *"The soul is all that it knows"* is the doctrine of Aristotle (384-322 B.C.), for whom "the thinking part of the soul, while impassible, must be capable of receiving the form of an object; that is, it must be potentially identical in character with its object without being the object" (*On the Soul*, 3.4).

3

201: *"Made in the image of God"*: "And God said, Let us make man in our image, after our likeness" (Gen. 1:27).

202: For *Ramakrishna*, see editor's note for "Contours of the Spirit", Part 3, p. 89.

Note 1: *Bernadette* of Lourdes (1844-79), to whom the Blessed Virgin miraculously appeared several times, suffered much from persistent ecclesiastical questioning and publicity.

Teresa of the Child Jesus (1873-97)—also known as Thérèse of Lisieux—gained admission to the Carmelite convent at Lisieux when she was fifteen years old in spite of the opposition of its superior, who objected to a religious profession at so young an age.

203: Note 2: *Russian heretics* such as the Khlysti or Khlysts (from the word *khlestat*, meaning "to lash or whip"), a sect which emerged in the seventeenth century and with which Rasputin (c. 1871-1916) was reputedly associated, combined self-flagellation and sexual license in their efforts to cultivate humility.

205: Note 3: *Dante* Alighieri (see editor's notes for "Thought and Civilization", Part 3, p. 18; "Aesthetics and Symbolism in Art and Nature", Part 1, p. 34; "Contours of the Spirit", Part 1, p. 63, Note 11 and Part 2, p. 78, Note 9; "Knowledge and Love", Part 1, p. 138, Note 9) places himself among the greatest poets of history, including Homer, Horace, Ovid, Lucan, and his master *Virgil* (70-19 B.C.), as he journeys through Limbo in *The Inferno*, Canto IV:88-102.

207: "For whosoever exalteth himself shall be abased; and *he that humbleth himself shall be exalted*" (Luke 14:11; cf. Luke 18:14).

Note 4: For *Ibn Arabi*, see editor's note for "Contours of the Spirit", Part 2, p. 75, Note 6.

208: "But when thou doest alms, *let not thy left hand know what thy right hand doeth*" (Matt. 6:3).

The "talents" of the parable: "The kingdom of heaven is as a man traveling into a far country, who called his own servants, and delivered unto them his goods. And unto one he gave five *talents*, to another two, and to another one; to every man according to his several ability; and straightway took his journey" (Matt. 25:14-15).

"*God alone is good*": "Why callest thou me good? There is none good but one, that is, God" (Matt. 19:17, Mark 10:18; cf. Luke 18:19).

209: For *Augustine*, see editor's note for "Contours of the Spirit", Part 1, p. 62.

Anicius Manlius Severinus *Boethius* (c. 480-c. 524), canonized under the name of Saint Severinus for his martyrdom, was a Christian philosopher, statesman, and master of the seven liberal arts.

Note 5: For *Joan of Arc*, see editor's note for "Knowledge and Love", Part 1, p. 133.

Note 6: *Cabalists* are Jewish mystics and esoterists; the *Baal Shem* (Hebrew for "master of the Name") is the title given to someone who possesses a secret knowledge of the Name of God, notably to the founder of the eighteenth-century Hasidic current of Cabalism, Israel ben Eliezer (1700-60).

211: Note 7: *Diadochos of Photike* (c. 400-c. 486), whose works include a century of texts *On Spiritual Knowledge and Discrimination,* is one of the most important of the Orthodox Fathers anthologized in the *Philokalia* (see editor's note for "Contours of the Spirit", Part 3, p. 89, Note 9).

212: *Basilian spirituality* is based upon the monastic *Rule* of Basil the Great (see editor's notes for "Contours of the Spirit", Part 1, p. 63, Note 11 and Part 3, p. 84, Note 4; "Knowledge and Love", Part 4, p. 172, Note 2).

For *Bernard* of Clairvaux, see editor's note for "Contours of the Spirit", Part 2, p. 76, Note 7.

213: For *Meister Eckhart,* see editor's notes for "Contours of the Spirit", Part 1, p. 63, Note 11; "Knowledge and Love", Part 4, p. 173, Note 2 and p. 175.

Catherine of Siena (1347-80), a Roman Catholic visionary, ascetic, and mystical spouse of Christ, was the author of a *Dialogue,* or *Treatise on Divine Providence,* which consists of a series of conversations between God and the human soul.

Note 8: For *Shankaracharya* (Shankara), see editor's note for "Contours of the Spirit", Part 1, p. 55 and Part 2, p. 73.

For *Chaitanya,* see editor's note for "Contours of the Spirit", Part 2, p. 75, Note 5.

214: For *Teresa of Avila*, see editor's note for "Contours of the Spirit", Part 3, p. 88.

For *Ignatius Loyola*, see editor's note for "Contours of the Spirit", Part 3, p. 91, Note 15.

Note 11: For Abu al-Qasim *al-Qushayri*, see editor's note for "Contours of the Spirit", Part 2, p. 75, Note 5.

Note 12: Muhammad ibn Ali *al-Tirmidhi* (d. c. 932), surnamed *al-Hakim*, "the philosopher", was the first Sufi authority to connect the degrees of spiritual knowledge with a hierarchy of sanctity, headed by the *qutb*, the spiritual "pole" or "pivot" for a given age.

Note 13: For Abu Hamid Muhammad *al-Ghazzali*, see editor's note for "Knowledge and Love", Part 4, p. 176, Note 6.

4

215: The *motionless mover*, or Unmoved Mover, is Aristotle's (see editor's note for "The Spiritual Virtues", Part 2, p. 200) classic expression for the divine Principle, as in the *Metaphysics*, 1072b.

Note 1: *Francis of Sales* (1567-1622), whose most important spiritual writings include an *Introduction to the Devout Life* and a *Treatise on the Love of God*, was a leading figure in the Counter-Reformation and the founder of the Visitation Order.

For the *Curé d'Ars*, see editor's note for "Knowledge and Love", Part 3, p. 162, Note 11.

5

217: For Moses *Maimonides*, see editor's note for "Contours of the Spirit", Part 1, p. 63, Note 11.

"Therefore to him that knoweth to do good, and doeth it not, to him it is sin" (James 4:17).

218: *Benedict* of Nursia (c. 480-c. 550), known as the "patriarch of Western monasticism", composed a short *Rule* for his monks, in which he laid special emphasis on the virtues of humility and self-abnegation.

For *Bernard* of Clairvaux, see editor's note for "Contours of the Spirit", Part 2, p. 76, Note 7.

6

223: Note 1: For *John of the Cross*, see editor's note for "Contours of the Spirit", Part 3, p. 89.

224: *Before sacrificing, says the Gospel, man must be reconciled with his brother.* "If thou bring thy gift to the altar, and there rememberest that thy brother hath aught against thee; leave there thy gift before the altar, and go thy way; first be reconciled to thy brother, and then come and offer thy gift" (Matt. 5:23-24).

226: "*One thing* is *needful*" (Luke 10:42).

Appendix

231: Selection 1: Letter of 5 October 1977.

232: Mircea *Eliade* (1907-86), a Romanian historian and philosopher of religion, was especially noted for his work on archaic cultures and shamanic traditions.

Selection 2: "The Book of Keys", No. 1196, "Colors".

233: Selection 3: Letter of January 1971.

Selection 4: Letter of 27-28 July 1984.

For René *Guénon*, see editor's note for "*Vedānta*", Part 1, p. 105, Note 7.

234: "*God became man that man might become God*": The essential teaching expressed by this *Patristic formula* is common to many Church Fathers, including Irenaeus (see editor's note for "Contours of the Spirit", Part 3, p. 85, Note 5), according to whom "the Son of God became the Son of man so that man, by entering into communion with the Word and thus receiving divine sonship, might become a son of God" (*Against Heresies*, 3:19); and Athanasius (c. 296-373), who wrote, "The Son of God became man in order that we might become God" (*On the Incarnation*, 54:3).

For *al-Hallaj*, see editor's notes for "Knowledge and Love", Part 3, p. 166, Note 19 and Part 4, p. 176, Note 6.

Aliquid est in anima quod est increatum et increabile: "There is something in the soul that is uncreated and uncreatable" (see editor's note for "Knowledge and Love", Part 4, p. 175).

"*Made in the image of God*": "God created man in His own image, in the image of God created He him; male and female created He them" (Gen. 1:27).

For *Meister Eckhart*, see editor's note for "Knowledge and Love", Part 4, p. 173, Note 2.

235: Selection 5: Letter of 1 May 1940.

Abd al-Qadir al-Jilani (1077-1166) was a gifted preacher and teacher and the founder of the Qadiriyya Sufi order.

236: Selection 6: Letter of 22 February 1976.

Pius XII (1876-1958) was Pope of Rome from 1939.

Selection 7: "The Book of Keys", No. 1075, "Not To Be Lost from Sight".

237: "*There is something in the soul that is uncreated and uncreatable*": see editor's note above for p. 234.

For the *Brahma Sūtra*, see editor's note for "Contours of the Spirit", Part 2, p. 73.

238: Selection 8: Letter of 15 March 1961.

Mahesh Prasad Varma *Yogi* (b. 1917) founded the "Spiritual *Regeneration Movement*" in 1957, with a view to the "spiritual regeneration of the world"; in 1958 he began referring to all of his organizations as the Transcendental Meditation movement; the author here quotes in English from a promotional pamphlet for the earlier organization.

239: For *Ramakrishna*, see editor's note for "Contours of the Spirit", Part 3, p. 89.

Selection 9: Letter of 28 January 1956.

"*The world is false; Brahma is true; the soul is not other than Brahma*": this summation of *Advaita Vedānta* is traditionally ascribed to Shankara (see editor's notes for "Contours of the Spirit", Part 1, p. 55 and Part 2, p. 73).

"An invisible and subtle essence is the Spirit that pervades the whole universe. That is Reality. That is Truth. *Thou art That*" (*Chāndogya Upanishad*, 6.14.3).

"The Self was indeed *Brahma* in the beginning. It knew only that '*I am Brahma*'. Therefore It became all. And whoever among the gods knew It also became That; and the same with sages and men. . . . And to this day whoever in like manner knows '*I am Brahma*' becomes all this universe. Even the gods cannot prevail against him, for he becomes their Self" (*Brihadāranyaka Upanishad*, 1.4.10).

240: Selection 10: "The Book of Keys", No. 1042, "*Vedānta, Japa, Dharma, Tantra*".

241: Selection 11: Letter of 7 July 1969.

"*The kingdom of heaven is within you*": "The kingdom of God is within you" (Luke 17:21).

242: Selection 12: "The Book of Keys", No. 477, "To Know, To Will, To Love".

Selection 13: Letter of 11 September 1945.

243: *Vivekanandists* are followers of Vivekananda (see editor's note for "*Vedānta*", Part 3, p. 121.

Abu al-Mawahib al-Shadhili (1417-77), the author among other works of the *Qawānīn Hikam al-Ishrāq* (translated as *Illumination in Islamic Mysticism*), was a noted proponent of the teachings of Ibn Arabi (see editor's note for "Contours of the Spirit", Part 2, p. 75, Note 6).

Selection 14: "The Book of Keys", No. 1046, "Virtue, a Requisite of the Truth and the Way".

244: Selection 15: "The Book of Keys", No. 689, "Against the Abuse of an Argument".

245: Selection 16: Letter of February 1968.

GLOSSARY OF FOREIGN TERMS AND PHRASES

Ab extra (Latin): "from outside"; proceeding from something extrinsic or external.

Actus purus (Latin): "pure act"; in medieval Scholastic philosophy, the distinguishing characteristic of God.

Advaita (Sanskrit): "nondualist" interpretation of the *Vedānta*; Hindu doctrine according to which the seeming multiplicity of things is the product of ignorance, the only true reality being *Brahma*, the One, the Absolute, the Infinite, which is the unchanging ground of appearance.

Aham Brahmāsmi (Sanskrit): "I am *Brahma*."

Ahankāra or *Ahamkāra* (Sanskrit): literally, "I-maker"; in Indian philosophy, the ego or ego principle; the ontological root of the individual being.

Anā'l-Haqq (Arabic): "I am the Truth."

Ānanda (Sanskrit): "bliss, beatitude, joy"; one of the three essential aspects of *Apara-Brahma*, together with *Sat*, "being", and *Chit*, "consciousness".

Apara-Brahma (Sanskrit): the "non-supreme" or penultimate *Brahma*, also called *Brahma saguna*; in the author's teaching, the "relative Absolute".

Ashram (Sanskrit): in Hinduism, a center for meditation and religious study, often located near the hermitage of a saint or sage, whether living or dead.

Ātmā or *Ātman* (Sanskrit): the real or true "Self", underlying the ego and its manifestations; in the perspective of *Advaita Vedānta*, identical with *Brahma*.

Avatāra (Sanskrit): the earthly "descent", incarnation, or manifestation of God, especially of Vishnu in the Hindu tradition.

Barakah (Arabic): "blessing", grace; in Islam, a spiritual influence or energy emanating originally from God, but often attached to sacred objects and spiritual persons.

Basmalah (Arabic): traditional Muslim formula of blessing, found at the beginning of all but one of the *sūrahs* of the Koran, consisting of the words *Bismi 'Llāhi 'r-Rahmāni 'r-Rahīm*, "In the Name of God, the Clement (*Rahmān*), the Merciful (*Rahīm*)".

Bhakta (Sanskrit): a follower of the spiritual path of *bhakti*; a person whose relationship with God is based primarily on adoration and love.

Bhakti, bhakti-mārga (Sanskrit): the spiritual "path" (*mārga*) of "love" (*bhakti*) and devotion; see *jnāna* and *karma*.

Brahma or *Brahman* (Sanskrit): the Supreme Reality, the Absolute.

Chit (Sanskrit): "consciousness"; one of the three essential aspects of *Apara-Brahma*, together with *Sat*, "being", and *Ānanda*, "bliss, beatitude, joy".

Corruptio optimi pessima (Latin): "the corruption of the best is the worst".

Creatio ex nihilo (Latin): "creation out of nothing"; the doctrine that God Himself is the sufficient cause of the universe, needing nothing else; often set in contrast to emanationist cosmogonies.

Dharma (Sanskrit): in Hinduism, the underlying "law" or "order" of the cosmos as expressed in sacred rites and in actions appropriate to various social relationships and human vocations; in Buddhism, the practice and realization of Truth.

Dhikr (Arabic): "remembrance" of God, based upon the repeated invocation of His Name; central to Sufi practice, where the remembrance is often supported by the single word *Allāh*.

Ex nihilo (Latin): "out of nothing".

Fanā' (Arabic): "extinction, annihilation, evanescence"; in Sufism, the spiritual station or degree of realization in which all individual attributes and limitations are extinguished in union with God; see *Nirvāna*.

Fiat lux (Latin): "Let there be light" (Gen. 1:3).

Gnosis (Greek): "knowledge"; spiritual insight, principial comprehension, divine wisdom.

Guru (Sanskrit): literally, "weighty", grave, venerable; in Hinduism, a spiritual master; one who gives initiation and instruction in the spiritual path and in whom is embodied the supreme goal of realization or perfection.

Hadīth (Arabic, plural *ahādīth*): "saying, narrative"; an account of the words or deeds of the Prophet Muhammad, transmitted through a traditional chain of known intermediaries.

Hamdalah (Arabic): traditional Muslim formula of praise, a common form consisting of the words *al-hamdu lillāh*, "Praise to God".

Haqīqah (Arabic): "truth, reality"; in Sufism, esoteric or metaphysical knowledge of the supremely Real; also the essential reality of a thing.

Ijtihād (Arabic): literally, "exertion"; in Islamic law, an independent judgment concerning a legal or theological question, arrived at by those possessing the necessary qualifications through a reinterpretation of the Koran or *Sunnah*.

In actu (Latin): "in act, action".

Īshvara (Sanskrit): literally, "possessing power", hence sovereign; God understood as a personal being, as Creator and Lord; manifest in the *Trimūrti* as *Brahmā*, *Vishnu*, and *Shiva*.

Japa-Yoga (Sanskrit): method of "union" or "unification" (*yoga*) based upon the "repetition" (*japa*) of a *mantra* or sacred formula, often containing one of the Names of God.

Jīvan-mukta (Sanskrit): one who is "liberated" while still in this "life"; a person who has attained a state of spiritual perfection or self-realization before death; in contrast to *videha-mukta*, one who is liberated at the moment of death.

Jivātmā or *jivātman* (Sanskrit): literally, "the living self"; in Hindu tradition, the personal or individual soul associated with the physical body, as distinct from *Ātmā*.

Jnāna or *jnāna-mārga* (Sanskrit): the spiritual "path" (*mārga*) of "knowledge" (*jnāna*) and intellection; see *bhakti* and *karma*.

Jnānin (Sanskrit): a follower of the path of *jnāna*; a person whose relationship with God is based primarily on sapiential knowledge or *gnosis*.

Jōdo (Japanese): "pure land"; the untainted, transcendent realm created by the Buddha Amida (Amitabha in Sanskrit), into which his devotees aspire to be born in their next life.

Jōdo-Shinshū (Japanese): "true pure land school"; a sect of Japanese Pure Land Buddhism founded by Shinran, based on faith in the power of the Buddha Amida and characterized by use of the *nembutsu*.

Kali Yuga (Sanskrit): in Hinduism, the fourth and final *yuga* in a given cycle of time, corresponding to the Iron Age of Western tradition and culminating in a *pralaya* or the *mahāpralaya*; the present age of mankind, distinguished by its increasing disorder, violence, and forgetfulness of God.

Karma, karma-mārga, karma-yoga (Sanskrit): the spiritual "path" (*mārga*) or method of "union" (*yoga*) based upon right "action, work" (*karma*); see *bhakti* and *jnāna*.

Khalīfah (Arabic, plural *khulafā*): literally, "successor"; a representative or vicar, often used in reference to the successors of the Prophet Muhammad; in Sufism, every man is in principle a *khalīfah* of God.

Lā ilāha illā 'Llāh (Arabic): "There is no god but God"; see *Shahādah*.

Logos (Greek): "word, reason"; in Christian theology, the divine, uncreated Word of God (cf. John 1:1); the transcendent Principle of creation and revelation.

Mahāpralaya (Sanskrit): in Hinduism, the "great" or final "dissolving" of the universe at the end of a *kalpa*, or "day in the life of *Brahmā*", understood as lasting one thousand *yuga*s.

Mahāyāna (Sanskrit): "great vehicle"; the form of Buddhism, including such traditions as Zen and *Jōdo-Shinshū*, which regards itself as the fullest or most adequate expression of the Buddha's teaching; distinguished by the idea that *Nirvāna* is not other than *samsāra* truly seen as it is.

Malāmatiyah (Arabic): literally, "the blameworthy"; a Sufi sect that accentuated self-reproach and endeavored to conceal virtue behind a façade of ignoble action.

Mantra (Sanskrit): "instrument of thought"; a word or phrase of divine origin, often including a Name of God, repeated by those initiated into its proper use as a means of salvation or liberation; see *japa-yoga*.

Materia prima (Latin): "first or prime matter"; in Platonic cosmology, the undifferentiated and primordial substance that serves as a "receptacle" for the shaping force of divine forms or ideas; universal potentiality.

Mater misericordiae (Latin): "Mother of mercy"; traditional Catholic epithet of the Blessed Virgin.

Māyā (Sanskrit): "artifice, illusion"; in *Advaita Vedānta*, the beguiling concealment of *Brahma* in the form or under the appearance of a lower reality.

Moksha (Sanskrit): "release" or "liberation" from *samsāra*; according to Hindu teaching, the most important of the aims of life, attained by following one of the principal *mārga*s or spiritual paths; see *bhakti, jnāna*, and *karma*.

Mukta (Sanskrit): one who has attained *moksha* or "liberation"; see *jīvan-mukta*.

Nembutsu (Japanese): "remembrance or mindfulness of the Buddha", based upon the repeated invocation of his Name; same as *buddhānusmriti* in Sanskrit and *nien-fo* in Chinese.

Nirvāna (Sanskrit): "blowing out, extinction"; in Indian traditions, especially Buddhism, the supremely blissful state of liberation resulting from the extinction of the fires of passion, egoism, and attachment; see *fanā'*.

Niyama (Sanskrit): "discipline", whether on the bodily or psychic level; in Hinduism, the second step in the eightfold path of the *yogin*, consisting in the practice of cleanliness, contentment, austerity, recitation of sacred scriptures, and devotion to God; see *yama*.

Nyāya (Sanskrit): argument, inference; dialectic as a means to spiritual liberation; one of the six orthodox *darshana*s, or perspectives, of classical Hinduism.

Para-Brahma (Sanskrit): the "supreme" or ultimate *Brahma*, also called *Brahma nirguna*; the Absolute as such.

Paramahamsa (Sanskrit): literally, "highest flyer" or "supreme swan"; in Hinduism, a title given to certain great saints and renunciates, who have attained the supreme state of *moksha*.

Parousia (Greek): literally, "presence", "arrival"; in Christian doctrine, the Second Coming of Christ.

Philosophia Perennis (Latin): "Perennial Philosophy".

Pontifex Maximus (Latin): "supreme pontiff"; a phrase claiming for the Bishop of Rome (Pope) the right of universal jurisdiction over the entire Church both East and West.

Prajnā (Sanskrit): "wisdom, intelligence, understanding"; in Hinduism, the self-awareness of *Ātmā*; knowledge of things as they truly are.

Prakriti (Sanskrit): literally, "making first" (see *materia prima*); the fundamental, "feminine" substance or material cause of all things; see *Purusha*.

Pralaya (Sanskrit): "dissolution"; Hindu teaching that all appearance is subject to a periodic process of destruction and recreation; see *mahāpralaya*.

Purusha (Sanskrit): literally, "man"; the informing or shaping principle of creation; the "masculine" demiurge or fashioner of the universe; see *Prakriti*.

Qiyās (Arabic): literally, "measure, analogy"; analogical reasoning in Islamic logic and law; a method for applying the teachings of the Koran and *Sunnah* to issues and circumstances not explicitly dealt with in the traditional sources.

Al-Rahmānu tanaffasa (Arabic): "the breath of the Compassionate (God)".

Rajas (Sanskrit): in Hinduism, one of the three *gunas*, or qualities, of *Prakriti*, of which all things are woven; the quality of expansiveness, manifest in the material world as force or movement and in the soul as ambition, initiative, and restlessness.

Rak'ah (Arabic, plural *rak'āt*): literally, "bowing"; in Islamic prayer, one complete set of movements and postures comprising an upright stance, bowing at the waist, two prostrations, and sitting on the heels.

Samādhi (Sanskrit): "putting together, union"; in Hindu *yoga*, a state of supreme concentration in which consciousness is entirely absorbed in the object of meditation.

Samsāra (Sanskrit): literally, "wandering"; in Hinduism and Buddhism, transmigration or the cycle of birth, death, and rebirth; also the world of apparent flux and change.

Sānkhya or *sāmkhya* (Sanskrit): literally, "enumeration, calculation"; Hindu cosmological teaching in which nature is understood to result from the union of *Purusha* and *Prakriti*; one of the six orthodox *darshanas*, or perspectives, of classical Hinduism.

Sanātana Dharma (Sanskrit): "eternal law"; in Hinduism, the universal or absolute law or truth underlying specific and relative laws and truths.

Sat (Sanskrit): "being"; one of the three essential aspects of *Apara-Brahma*, together with *Chit*, "consciousness", and *Ānanda*, "bliss, beatitude, joy".

Sattva (Sanskrit): in Hinduism, one of the three *gunas*, or qualities, of *Prakriti*, of which all things are woven; the quality of luminosity, manifest in the material world as buoyancy or lightness and in the soul as intelligence and virtue.

Shahādah (Arabic): the fundamental "profession" or "testimony" of faith in Islam, consisting of the words *Lā ilāha illā 'Llāh, Muhammadan rasūlu 'Llāh*: "There is no god but God; Muhammad is the messenger of God."

Shakti (Sanskrit): creative "power", expressed in Hinduism in the form of divine femininity.

Sharī'ah (Arabic): "path"; in Islam, the proper mode and norm of life, the path or way willed and marked out by God for man's return to Him; Muslim law or exoterism.

Shraddhā (Sanskrit): literally, "application of faith"; in Hinduism, an offering to the sages, the gods, or the ancestors; the trustful obedience of the Hindu *bhakta*.

Summum bonum (Latin): "supreme good".

Sunnah (Arabic): "custom, way of acting"; in Islam, the norm established by the Prophet Muhammad, including his actions and sayings (see *hadīth*) and serving as a precedent and standard for the behavior of Muslims.

Sūrah (Arabic): one of the one hundred fourteen divisions, or chapters, of the Koran.

Talmud (Hebrew): "learning, study"; in Judaism, a body of writings and traditional commentaries based on the oral law given to Moses on Sinai; the foundation of Jewish civil and religious law, second in authority only to the *Torah*.

Tamas (Sanskrit): in Hinduism, one of the three *gunas*, or qualities, of *Prakriti*, of which all things are woven; the quality of darkness or heaviness, manifest in the material world as inertia or rigidity and in the soul as sloth, stupidity, and vice.

Tantra (Sanskrit): literally, "warp on a loom"; in Hindu tradition, any of several methods of interiorizing and transforming sensual enjoyment for the sake of a spiritual end.

Tasawwuf (Arabic): a term of disputed etymology, though perhaps from *sūf* for "wool", after the garment worn by many early Sufis; traditional Muslim word for Sufism.

Torah (Hebrew): "instruction, teaching"; in Judaism, the law of God, as revealed to Moses on Sinai and embodied in the Pentateuch (Genesis, Exodus, Leviticus, Numbers, Deuteronomy).

Trimūrti (Sanskrit): literally, "having three forms"; in Hindu tradition, a triadic expression of the Divine, especially in the form of *Brahmā*, the creator, *Vishnu*, the preserver, and *Shiva*, the transformer.

Upanishad (Sanskrit): literally, "to sit close by"; hence, any esoteric doctrine requiring direct transmission from master to disciple; in Hinduism, the genre of sacred texts that end or complete the Vedas; see *Vedānta*.

Upāya (Sanskrit): "means, expedient, method"; in Buddhist tradition, the adaptation of spiritual teaching to a form suited to the level of one's audience.

Vacare Deo (Latin): literally, "to be empty for God"; to be at leisure for or available to God; in the Christian monastic and contemplative tradition, to set aside time from work for meditation and prayer.

Vaisheshika (Sanskrit): literally, "referring to the distinctions"; Hindu philosophy of nature, including an analysis of the various categories and objects of sensory experience; one of the six orthodox *darshanas*, or perspectives, of classical Hinduism.

Vedānta (Sanskrit): "end or culmination of the Vedas"; one of the major schools of traditional Hindu philosophy, based in part on the *Upanishads*, esoteric treatises found at the conclusion of the Vedic scriptures; see *advaita*.

Vox populi vox Dei (Latin): "the voice of the people is the voice of God".

Yama (Sanskrit): "restraint", whether on the bodily or psychic level; in Hinduism, the first step in the eightfold path of the *yogin*, which consists in resisting all inclinations toward violence, lying, stealing, sexual activity, and greed; see *niyama*.

Yoga (Sanskrit): literally, "yoking, union"; in Indian traditions, any meditative and ascetic technique designed to bring the soul and body into a state of concentration; one of the six orthodox *darshana*s, or perspectives, of classical Hinduism.

Yogin (Sanskrit): one who is "yoked or joined"; a practitioner of *yoga*.

Yuga (Sanskrit): an "age" in Hinduism, one of the four periods into which a cycle of time is divided.

For a glossary of all key foreign words used in books published by World Wisdom, including metaphysical terms in English, consult: www.DictionaryofSpiritualTerms.org.
This on-line Dictionary of Spiritual Terms provides extensive definitions, examples, and related terms in other languages.

INDEX

Abraham, 57, 62
Absolute, 3, 18, 36, 57, 71, 78, 107, 111, 111n, 115, 135, 170, 178, 183, 203, 236, 241-42, 245
actus purus, 112n
Adam, 52-54, 57-58, 216-17, 221
Advaita Vedānta. See *Vedānta*
aesthetics, 21, 23-26, 141n, 247, 250, 252, 263-64, 270-71
African rhythms, 18
aham Brahmāsmi, 234, 239
ahankāra, 115
ahl al-Kitāb, 60n
al-Alawi, Ahmad, 174n, 269
Alexandrian perspective, 166
Alexandrians, 161n, 266
All-possibility, 106-107, 113
Alphonsus Liguori, 91n
American Indians, 38, 45-46, 231-32
anā'l-Haqq, 176n, 234, 269
Ānanda, 102
angelotheism, 69
Angelus Silesius, 85n, 162n, 173n, 257, 266, 268
Anniyah, 101n
Anselm, 134n
anthropomorphism, 51, 92, 94
anuvāda, 62
Apara-Brahma, 107
apavāda, 62
Apocalypse, 66n
al-'Āqil, 101n
Aristotelianism, 74
arqān al-Dīn, 239
art, 9-10, 15, 21, 23, 26-33, 35-38, 85, 87n, 101, 103, 103n, 105, 141, 225, 254, 259

Arya Samaj, 125, 261
atheism, 10, 236
Ātmā, 57, 100-103, 105-107, 110, 115, 231, 260. *See also* Self
Augustine, 62, 169n, 209
Autun, 30, 248
Avatāra, Avatāras, 3, 24n, 66, 75n, 102, 105n, 114, 118, 123, 250, 253
avidyā, 102-103, 105, 114, 220

bālya, 201
Baptism, 83n, 84n, 134n, 255, 263
Baroque, 36
Barsanuphius, 134n, 262
Basil, 63n, 84n, 172n, 268
Basilian spirituality, 212, 272
Basmalah, 242
bast, 91
Beatrice, 138n, 248, 263
beauty, 23, 24, 24n, 25, 27-29, 33, 35, 38, 47, 52, 86, 129, 138, 138n, 140, 140n, 141, 141n, 152, 159, 166n, 168, 172n, 192, 198, 203, 227, 233, 240, 243-44, 269-70
Being, 42, 80n, 81n, 101, 102, 106-107, 111n-112n, 159, 163n, 173n, 177, 186, 200, 216, 221-22, 260
Benares, 44
Benedict, 218
Bernadette, 202n
Bernard, 76n, 212-13, 218
Beyond-Being, 81n, 110n, 177
Bhagavad Gītā, 60n, 250
bhakta, bhaktas, 65, 75n, 91n, 120,

BIOGRAPHICAL NOTES

Frithjof Schuon

Born in Basle, Switzerland in 1907, Frithjof Schuon was the twentieth century's preeminent spokesman for the perennialist school of comparative religious thought.

The leitmotif of Schuon's work was foreshadowed in an encounter during his youth with a marabout who had accompanied some members of his Senegalese village to Basle for the purpose of demonstrating their African culture. When Schuon talked with him, the venerable old man drew a circle with radii on the ground and explained: "God is the center; all paths lead to Him." Until his later years Schuon traveled widely, from India and the Middle East to America, experiencing traditional cultures and establishing lifelong friendships with Hindu, Buddhist, Christian, Muslim, and American Indian spiritual leaders.

A philosopher in the tradition of Plato, Shankara, and Eckhart, Schuon was a gifted artist and poet as well as the author of over twenty books on religion, metaphysics, sacred art, and the spiritual path. Describing his first book, *The Transcendent Unity of Religions*, T. S. Eliot wrote, "I have met with no more impressive work in the comparative study of Oriental and Occidental religion", and world-renowned religion scholar Huston Smith said of Schuon, "The man is a living wonder; intellectually apropos religion, equally in depth and breadth, the paragon of our time". Schuon's books have been translated into over a dozen languages and are respected by academic and religious authorities alike.

More than a scholar and writer, Schuon was a spiritual guide for seekers from a wide variety of religions and backgrounds throughout the world. He died in 1998.

James S. Cutsinger (Ph.D., Harvard) is Professor of Theology and Religious Thought at the University of South Carolina.

A widely recognized writer on the *sophia perennis* and the perennialist school, Professor Cutsinger is also an authority on the theology and spirituality of the Christian East. His publications include *Advice to the Serious Seeker: Meditations on the Teaching of Frithjof Schuon*, *Not of This World: A Treasury of Christian Mysticism*, *Paths to the Heart: Sufism and the Christian East*, *The Fullness of God: Frithjof Schuon on Christianity*, and *Prayer Fashions Man: Frithjof Schuon on the Spiritual Life*.